Illuminating Faith

Illuminating Faith: An Invitation to Theology

Francesca Aran Murphy
Balázs M. Mezei
Kenneth Oakes

Bloomsbury Academic
An imprint of Bloomsbury Publishing Plc

B L O O M S B U R Y
LONDON · NEW DELHI · NEW YORK · SYDNEY

Bloomsbury T&T Clark

An imprint of Bloomsbury Publishing Plc

50 Bedford Square
London
WC1B 3DP
UK

1385 Broadway
New York
NY 10018
USA

www.bloomsbury.com

BLOOMSBURY and the Diana logo are trademarks of Bloomsbury Publishing Plc

First published 2015

© Francesca Aran Murphy, Balázs M. Mezei and Kenneth Oakes, 2015

Francesca Aran Murphy, Balázs M. Mezei and Kenneth Oakes have asserted
their right under the Copyright, Designs and Patents Act, 1988, to be
identified as Authors of this work.

British Library Cataloguing-in-Publication Data
A catalogue record for this book is available from the British Library.

ISBN: HB: 978-0-567-65604-9
PB: 978-0-567-65605-6
ePDF: 978-0-567-65607-0
ePub: 978-0-567-65606-3

Library of Congress Cataloging-in-Publication Data
A catalogue record for this book is available from the Library of Congress.

Series: Illuminating Modernity

Typeset by Integra Software Services Pvt. Ltd
Printed and bound in India

ILLUMINATING MODERNITY

Illuminating Modernity is dedicated to the renewal of faith in a world that is both godless and idolatrous. This renewal takes the legacy of faith seriously and explores the tradition in the hope that the means of its contemporary development are to be found within it. This approach takes the historical crisis of faith seriously and makes sincere efforts to receive the strength necessary for a renewal. We call our way *the Franciscan option*. And yet, one of the greatest resources upon which we hope to build is Thomism, especially those hidden treasures of modern Thomistic thought to be found in Continental and phenomenological philosophy and theology.

The Franciscan option takes the history of faith seriously both in its continuity and in its change. It takes seriously the tragic experiences of the history of faith since the Wars of Religion and especially in late modernity. But it also takes seriously the rich heritage of faith. As Michael Polanyi argued, faith has become the fundamental act of human persons. Faith involves the whole of the person in his or her absolute openness to the Absolute. As Hegel saw, the logic of history is prefigured in the story of the Gospels, and the great and transforming experience of humanity has remained the experience of resurrection in the aftermath of a dramatic death.

The series editors are boundlessly grateful to Anna Turton, whose support for this series made a hope into a reality. We also owe a huge debt of gratitude to Notre Dame's Nanovic Institute for European Studies for giving us crucial financial and moral support at the outset of our project. Many thanks to Anthony Monta and A. James McAdams for caring about the 'Hidden Treasures'.

TO OUR MOMS, IN LOVE AND GRATITUDE

Diana Leslie (1926–2012)
Klara Mezei (1931–)
Melanie Oakes (1955–)

CONTENTS

Introduction: Faith Rules

It could be the beginning of a joke: three Christians went into a bar, a Protestant, a Catholic and a Hungarian. This book is written by three different people, indeed, a Protestant and a Catholic theologian, and a philosopher from Budapest. It is a textbook in three voices. It is a textbook in theology. Why would a textbook in theology be about the different understandings of faith held over the centuries? Because 'faith' is the unique and central notion in every kind of Christian theology. It rules every kind of Christianity, whether it is Protestant, Orthodox or Catholic, liberal or conservative, dogmatic or hazy, cognitive or devotional, ritualist or Pentecostal. Faith is the defining notion in Christian theology. But many different kinds of Christians define faith in their own ways. How is that going to work?

Bronze Age warriors called the rods which preserved the shape of their shields *kanones*. In Homer's day, a *kanon* was the only thing that held it all together when the chips were down and the spears flying.[1] The Greek word *kanon* came to mean a rule or measure, and sometimes thus a standard or model example.

Philo (c. 50 BC–50 AD) was a Jewish philosopher who lived in cosmopolitan Alexandria and who tried to explain the Hebrew Scriptures to Greek thinkers by reading them allegorically. He spoke of 'the *kanon* for allegorizing Scripture', meaning the rules governing interpretation of the Scriptures. For Philo a *kanon of faith* was not so much a list of things to be believed. It was not a 'canon' in the modern sense of a list of texts, telling us what's in and what's out. It was a means or measure of interpretation. A *kanon of faith* was a way of looking at things, like the Scripture.

From very early times, Christian thinkers like Clement of Alexandria (150–215) spoke of a '*kanon* of faith', that is a *rule* of faith. His near contemporary Tertullian (160–225) wrote that,

> It is the rule of faith...that we now profess what we henceforth defend; that rule by which it is believed that there is only one God...Creator of the world, who brought forth everything from nothing through his Word, which was sent out before everything; and that this Word, called his Son, appeared in various visions in the name of God to the patriarchs, was heard always in the prophets, and finally was brought down by the Spirit and the power of God the Father into the Virgin Mary, made flesh in her womb and was born from her as Jesus Christ. Thereafter, he claimed a new law and a new promise of the kingdom of heaven, performed great deeds, was nailed to the cross, rose again on the third day, was taken up to heaven and sat on the right hand of the Father, and sent in his place the power of the Holy Spirit who guides believers and he will come again in glory to summon saints into eternal life and to the enjoyment of celestial promises, and

---

[1] The *kanones* of Nestor's fabled shield, for instance, are most likely rods which give and maintain the shield's structure. See the mention of the 'rods' in Homer's *Odyssey*, bk. 8, 194–5.

to condemn the impious to perpetual fire, both parties being raised from the dead and having their flesh restored. This rule is from Christ.[2]

For Tertullian, the 'Kanon of Faith' is a summary statement of how Christians believe in the Triune God and of why they do so ('This rule is from Christ'). Christians do not believe in the Triune God because they have some great analogies for God, but because Jesus Christ taught them to do so. In a sense the early Christian 'Rule of Faith' is from Christ, and in another sense it *is* Christ. For, like Philo, when the early Church spoke about the 'rule of faith', they meant rules for interpreting Scripture. These rules were invariably Christological: Scripture was interpreted with reference to Christ. The Christian 'list of books which belong to Scripture' was not their 'kanon', or rule of faith. Rather, their way of interpreting Scripture was their rule. So the 'rule of faith' was a kind of perspective on Scripture. It was a way of looking at Scripture and God's history with humanity as Christ would have them see it.

If Christians are 'ruled by faith', are they 'fideists'? We have heard John Webster, the great Barthian-Thomist scholar, call himself a fideist. But apart from a few genius individuals, very few people self-identify as 'fideists'. It is normally a term of reprobation. Today, Stanley Hauerwas is often accused of 'fideism', because he thinks Christianity is its own perspective and way of living in the world. Several twentieth-century popes registered disapproval of fideism: John Paul II did so gently in *Fides et ratio* (1998), while Pius X thundered against 'fideism' in the 1907 *Pascendi*. Today, people casually use the term to refer to diverse figures such as the Scotsman David Hume and Tertullian, the second-century Father of the Church. But the term was only invented in the mid-nineteenth century, and it is anachronistic to use it outside of this context. It becomes a catch-all term which does not mean very much. 'Faith' has had many different accents and emphases, and likewise 'fideism' probably means different things to different people, depending on what they mean by 'faith' in the first place.[3] All Christians are 'fideists' or 'faith-ists' in different ways, depending on how they are 'ruled by faith'.

Early Christians like Tertullian and Clement said that the 'Rule of Faith' was received at baptism. That is probably true today, even for those whose initiation into baptism is very different from the rituals and catechesis of the first five centuries. For Christians understand 'faith' to be not just a body of knowledge or dogma, and not even just a perspective, but a *saving gift from God*. The three very different Christians who wrote this book, and any number of other Christians, could agree that faith somehow 'saves' us, and that faith is not of our own making but comes to us from God. This is the heart of Christianity, and so we think that learning about faith is the best way into theology itself, for theology is faith thinking, the reflection of any and every baptised believer of God and everything that relates to God (well, everything).

---

[2]Tertullian, *De praescriptione haereticorum*, as cited in Jason E. Vickers, *Invocation and Assent: The Making and Remaking of Trinitarian Theology* (Grand Rapids, Mich.: Eerdmans, 2008), pp. 5–6.
[3]Thomas D. Carroll, 'The Traditions of Fideism', *Religious Studies* 44:1 (2008), pp. 1–22.

1
Faith in the Bible

A unique notion

The notion of faith is unique to the Judeo-Christian tradition. Although versions of this notion exist in several cultural and religious forms outside this tradition, the epoch-making development took place in the culture originating in the Bible. This determined the character of the Christian era, and has been instrumental in shaping the sources of spiritual practice even today. Other words often translated as 'faith' into English have an original meaning different from our notion of faith. For instance, the word 'islam' is sometimes translated as 'faith', though its actual meaning is 'voluntary submission to God'. This meaning is not very far from the idea of obedience as understood in Christianity. Yet the latter notion of faith is a complex and dynamically evolving idea which 'voluntary submission' does not quite capture entirely. Faith has synthesized many influences over the centuries and created a rich culture of spiritual, theological and philosophical reflection.[1]

The Old Testament

In the Old Testament, expressions associated with our understanding of faith are related to the notion of firmness. The Hebrew root *'mn* is used in various forms in the Old Testament and it refers to firm places, posts, positions and stability, and when used of human beings it signifies confidence, trust, loyalty and faithfulness (Gen. 15.6 and Hab. 2.4).[2] The two most important nouns derived from the verb 'to trust' (*'aman*) are *'emunâ* and *'emet*, the first referring to firmness or stability, the second to truthfulness and faithfulness. Both can be understood as being divine or human: the God of Abraham, Isaac and Jacob shows firmness and faithfulness to His chosen people, thus His people are expected to remain firm and faithful to her Chooser. Human firmness and faithfulness are based on reverential fear: 'The fear of the Lord' is paradoxically inseparable from trust in Him. On the divine side, instead of fear, we find jealousy: God is 'jealous', He does not tolerate any rival and thus demands fear and trust (Exod. 20.5).

---

[1]Avery Dulles, *The Assurance of Things Hoped For: A Theology of Christian Faith* (Oxford: Oxford University Press, 1994), ch. 1.

[2] *'mn* refers to the root composed of three Hebrew letters *aleph*, *mem* and *nun* (as in *amen*). In the Unicode Block (Spacing Modifier Letters), *aleph* is written with the sign U+02BE – ʾ – to express what is called a 'modifier letter right half ring'.

After the Babylonian conquest in 587 AD, the Jewish people went into exile. In response to their despair, the prophets deepened the word 'trust' to involve the entire life of the community. The most important sign of this deepening is the wordplay in Isa. 7.9: 'If ye will not believe, surely ye shall not be established'. (Also translated as 'If you do not believe, you will not understand'.) In this verse, 'to believe' and 'to be established' are expressed by two different forms of 'aman. The meaning of this verse is that if you do not have a deep trust in the Lord, when facing your enemies around the city, your life will not be saved. Thus faith as firmness and salvation as the act of the Lord in the worldly sense are linked; and on a deeper level, faith and salvation in the theological sense are connected. Faith in this ancient sense is realized in a situation of utmost peril.

In the age of the prophets, the importance of the individual, the 'person', slowly comes to the fore. The believer is more and more the individual representing the community. His faith is less based on fear and more on hope and love, such as in Isa. 28.16, 40.31 or 43.10. This development is reflected in the wisdom literature, such as the Book of Job. Job not only believes 'in' the Lord but believes his own blamelessness. His faith develops from fear to hope and from 'hearsay' to 'seeing' (Job 42.5). In Psalms, the 'lovingkindness' (*hesed*) of the Lord is stressed as a feature of His 'truth', 'faithfulness', 'strength', the right answer to which is equally faithfulness, testimony and praise. The intimate relationship between the soul and God is now most important. Faith is about the personal closeness of the psalmist to God: 'The Lord is my rock, and my fortress, and my deliverer; my God, my strength, in whom I will trust' (Ps. 18.2). The Lord becomes 'my God' (*eli*), a God not only of the community but of the psalmist himself.

One of the most important Old Testament verses about faith is Hab. 2.4b: 'the just shall live by his faith'. 'Faith' in the original Hebrew text is 'emunâ (firmness, trust, faithfulness). From the context, it is evident what the prophet wants to tell us: when facing a dreadful enemy, the just (*tzaddik*) has no other way of surviving than to trust the Lord and His promise of life. 'Faith' here is keeping in mind this promise in the face of death and destruction; if the just survives the crisis, it is because of his faithfulness to the Lord's promises. In this sense, the just live by trust, faithfulness. This verse is referred to in Rom. 1.17 and Gal. 3.11, where we find the Greek word *pistis*, faith, in a more general sense than is conveyed by the Hebrew 'emunâ. In this context *pistis* means believing. For Christian authors from Augustine to the Protestant Reformers, the verse possessed a central role in emphasizing the priority of faith in justification.

Before the composition of the New Testament texts, important changes occurred to the ancient notion of faith in the Hellenistic Judaism found in big city centres, such as Alexandria. The Greek translation of the Hebrew Bible (the Septuagint, or LXX) and the composition of various extra- and non-canonical writings (such as Ecclesiastes, the Wisdom of Solomon etc.) introduced the notion of biblical faith into Greek thought. The Septuagint translated all words with the root 'mn into Greek words with the root *pist*- (*pistis, pisteuein*: faith, to believe), thereby offering an overall interpretation of *pistis* in a culture which had previously connected this word mainly to Plato's theory of perception.

The Hellenistic Jewish philosopher Philo worked in Alexandria too. Without his interpretation of the Old Testament faith as a *virtue* – a virtue characteristic of heroes like Abraham – the birth of the New Testament notions of faith would be unimaginable. Philo connected the ancient Jewish notion of faith as faithfulness and firmness to Platonic and Stoic conceptions of faith as a power of conversion from unbelief to the trust in God. In view of some New Testament texts, such as the Letter to the Hebrews, Philo's identification of faith with virtue is especially important. By faith, understood as a virtue, the central figures of the Old Testament attached themselves to the One God and rejected non-philosophical polytheism. In Philo, the bearer of faith is no longer the community but the individual aspiring to live a philosophical life in the framework of a Hellenized Judaism.

The New Testament

In the New Testament, the notion of faith continues earlier developments with the consequence that instead of a cohesive meaning of 'faith' we find a variety of meanings and interpretations sometimes divergent from one another. The reason for this variety is the unique combination of influences on New Testament authors: Old Testament literature, Alexandrine culture, the role of the Qumran sect (where the ancient notion of the faithfulness of God and the community have an apocalyptic setting) and, at some points, the presence of popular, mainly Stoic philosophy. In the background, we see the impact of the belief-language of the mystery-cults as well (1Tim. 3.9).

There are about *fifteen different meanings* of the noun 'faith' (*pistis*) and the verb 'to believe' (*pisteuein*) in the New Testament. These meanings converge to some extent, but this does not mean a seamless unity. We can say, rather, that a scrupulous investigation of these meanings reveals even more differences, resulting in the picture of the New Testament as a melting pot of various notions of faith. The meanings can be discriminated either by their object (God, Jesus, the Gospel: Mk. 11.22, Jn. 14.1; Jn. 4.21, Rom. 3.22; Mk. 1.15), by the kind of act they involve (faithfulness, trust, hope, realization: Heb. 11.1; Mk. 13.21, Mt. 6.30, Phil. 2.19, Phlm.1.5; 2 Cor. 10.15; Jn. 20.31), or again by their results (works, conversion, resurrection, eternal life: Jas. 2.14; Heb. 10.22; 1. Cor. 15.14; 1 Tim. 6.12). There is a notion of faith as virtue (Gal. 5.22, 1 Tim. 1.5), and we have the peculiar expression of 'the faith of Christ', *pistis Christou* (Rom. 3.22, Gal. 2.16, Eph. 3.12, Phil. 3.9). The 'faith of Christ' may refer grammatically either to faith *in* Christ or the faith Christ had, and while the biblical expressions are certainly about the former, we can speak of the problem of the faith Christ had. Most importantly, Jesus' amen-sayings ('Verily [*amen*], I say to you...', which occur about eighty times in the Gospels) can be seen as expressions of a specific kind of faith, a kind of fundamental firmness as the expression of divine self-consciousness. In the Revelation of John, Jesus is referred to as a personified Amen: 'These things saith the Amen, the faithful and true witness, the beginning of the creation of God' (Rev. 3.14). One has to add a further kind of faith in the New Testament, the so-called *pisteuein eis* ('to believe on...') expressions, a novelty of New Testament Greek, especially the Gospel of John, and an obvious Hebraism with no parallel in the classical Greek language (Jn. 1.12 etc.) 'To believe on' expresses strong emotional, volitional and intellectual dynamism.

Historically, the amen-sayings may have been the origin of all the other varieties of the notion of faith in the New Testament. Jesus' self-affirmation as the Son of God was the expression of his fundamental faith or firmness, an attitude rooted in the central Old Testament meaning of faith. This faith is reflected in the sayings about the essence of faith as firmness in the miracle-stories of the Gospels where a miraculous event is often depicted as a result of faith. The sayings about little or great faith have a similar meaning: with little faith, we cannot achieve anything; with great faith almost everything is possible (Mt. 8.26: 'Why are ye fearful, O ye of little faith?'; Mt. 8.10: 'I have not found so great faith, no, not in Israel'.) The other meanings of faith may be interpreted as derivative of these fundamental features, such as faith as 'coming to believe in' or to 'convert to' God, Christ, the Gospel, the resurrection and so on. Faith as faithfulness, as in the Letter to the Hebrews, stands the closest to the notion of 'emunâ in the Old Testament. The famous definition of faith in Heb. 11.1 ('Now faith is the substance of things hoped for, the evidence [argument] of things not seen') generated endless meditations during the subsequent centuries about the exact meaning of 'substance' and 'argument/evidence' and their relationship, until scholarship realized that we are dealing here with a parallelism, characteristic of Hebrew rhetoric, so that the two words have the same referent, namely 'reality'.

The most important difference of all the New Testament expressions of faith from the Old Testament is that faith is the act of the believer personally believing in the physical presence of God in Jesus; the emphasis is not on the faith of the community hoping for a future fulfilment, but on the faith of the individual related to an already realized fulfilment. Already the amen-sayings of Jesus reflect this new emphasis. Acts 2.44 ('And all that believed were together') refers to the believers' community and not to the community as believing; and even when Paul speaks in terms of 'we' ('we have believed in Jesus Christ', Gal. 2.16), he means the community *of* individual believers. The strongest witness of the new Christian community of individual believers is the author of the Letter to the Hebrews. In his understanding, the community of the Old and the New Testaments forms one body in which the followers of the old covenant exemplify those of the new covenant with Christ. Just as the head of the old covenant was Moses, the head of the new one is Christ; Christ is the eternal high priest of the community of the believers (Heb. 7.26), in which the individual's responsibility before God is unavoidable ('with whom we have to do', Heb. 4.13). The individual piety is recommended ('Let us hold fast the profession of the faith without wavering; for he is faithful that promised', Heb. 10.23). Within such a context, we may say that the New Testament's novelty is the encouragement of individual faith with a strong personal dimension. This is concretized by the contents of the faith in Christ, in God or in the Gospel. The recurring expression of 'by faith' in the Letter to the Hebrews is obviously about faith as an act, just as Paul's famous 'justified by faith apart from works' proposition (Rom. 3.28; translated by Luther as *sola fide*) does not mean that many expressions referring to faith in the letters of Paul are not about the contents of faith, such as 'the word of faith' (Rom. 10.8).

If we want to find a simple definition of faith in the New Testament, then we can refer to faith based on *concrete fulfilment*. In the Old Testament, the psalmist desires the presence of the Lord and he prays for it; in the New Testament, this presence is already realized in Jesus Christ. This is the case even if the definition of faith in the Letter to the Hebrews applies a slightly different emphasis. The fulfiller of faith is the Holy Spirit, as we see it in the person of Stephen, 'a man full of faith and of the Holy Ghost'. It is the fulfilled character of faith which gives its solidity, strength, power; it is the concrete vision of faith that leads to martyrdom (Acts 7.56). This fulfilled faith is enriched by all the other meanings, which made possible the development of this notion during the subsequent centuries of theological, spiritual and philosophical interpretations.

Study questions

1. Why is the notion of faith unique to Christianity?
2. What are the basic meanings of faith in the Old Testament?
3. What is the original meaning of Hab. 2.4?
4. What are the basic meanings of faith in the New Testament?
5. What are the 'amen-sayings'?

Further reading

Benedict XVI (Joseph Ratzinger), *Jesus of Nazareth: From the Baptism in the Jordan to the Transfiguration* (London: Doubleday, 2007).
Pope Benedict XVI (Joseph Ratzinger), *Jesus of Nazareth: Holy Week: From the Entrance into Jerusalem to the Resurrection* (San Francisco: Ignatius, 2011).
Brown, Raymond E., *Responses to 101 Questions on the Bible* (New York: Paulist, 1990).
McKenzie, Steven L., *How to Read the Bible* (Oxford: Oxford University Press, 2005).

2

Personal Faith: St. Augustine

Synthesis

The place of St. Augustine (354–430) in the history of faith is central. On the one hand, he synthesizes the most important developments of the notion of faith of the post-Biblical and early Patristic period; on the other hand, as the first great Latin Christian author, he opens the way to more significant intellectual and spiritual developments in Western Christianity. His spirituality became exemplary for half a millennium after his death and inspired new waves of theological reflection in the Franciscan tradition, the Protestant Reformation and both Catholic and Protestant spirituality. Finally, his genius shone forth with renewed vigour in the twentieth century, when both theology and philosophy searched for new ways of understanding the role of faith in the context of modernity.

Two kinds of faith

The three most important developments of the Patristic age ending with Augustine in the West are the surfacing of the mystical interpretation of faith, the important appearance of the Latin vocabulary in the history of faith and Augustine's renewed notion of faith. The mystical interpretation of faith comes to the fore in Clement of Alexandria (150–215), who speaks of 'two kinds of faith', one resulting in knowledge, the other in opinion. As to the first kind, Clement offers a number of approaches: logically, faith is that by which we accept the highest axiom in a universal demonstration, the axiom which cannot be known but whose supposition leads to knowledge. In this sense, faith is the mind's highest action. He also mentions some images taken from the Gospels, such as the parable of the mustard seed, as indicative of the power of faith. Finally, Clement offers a cosmo-theological schema of faith, according to which the faithful ascend through all the regions of the universe – the mundane, the planetary and the sphere of the fixed stars – until they reach 'the perfect number which is above the nine' and thus receive 'knowledge of God'.[1]

Clement does not say too much about the second kind of faith: he attributes merely a mundane function to it in accordance with Plato's notion of belief (*pistis*) as a probable opinion. While Clement is not detailed in his arguments, it is clear that he emphasizes the function of faith as the basis of mystical knowledge. He suggests that

---

[1] Clement of Alexandria, *Stromata 1–3*, trans. John Ferguson (Washington, D.C.: Catholic University of American Press, 1991), pp. II, X–XI.

'faith is power in order to salvation and strength to eternal life'.[2] When the Gospels speak of faith, they refer to this mystical gift to human beings, a gift without a natural analogy. The analogy which Clement uses is clearly the Hebrew meaning of faith as 'firmness' or 'steadfastness'. Clement defines faith as 'the faculty of uniformity and perpetuity' which is capable of conceiving the ultimate and unmovable God.[3]

The development of Latin theology was defined by a unique linguistic situation. In Greek, both 'faith' and 'to believe' come from the same root *pist-*. In Latin, faith as a noun comes from *fides* and the verb from the root *cred-* (as in *credo*.) This made many of the Latin authors perceive two kinds of faith and thus helped them to define the terms more accurately than the Greek writers did. For the Latin authors, the articulate individuality of the act of faith became even more emphatic; and in the same way, the propositional content of faith received an equally definite treatment. For Tertullian, faith is such that it conflicts with our everyday views. Contrary to legend, Tertullian never pronounced the sentence *credo quia absurdum est*, 'I believe for it is an absurdity'. What he actually said was, 'The Son of God was crucified: I am not ashamed – because it is shameful. The Son of God died: it is immediately credible – because it is silly. He was buried, and rose again: it is certain – because it is impossible'.[4]

Augustine's witness

The most important thing Augustine gave to the notion of faith is the witness of his own personal faith. Relying on the then traditional literary genre of a dialogue – a form used for philosophical and spiritual purposes by Platonic authors – Augustine personalized this form to an extent which had never occurred before his *Confessions* (397). In his early pieces, such as the *Soliloquia* (386–387), the author converses with a personified Reason, which he understands as the world-governing mind. In this dialogue the main emphasis is on intellectual problems, especially the knowledge of God and the soul. Even this early Augustine emphasizes the importance of faith: 'If it is by faith that those find Thee, who take refuge with Thee, then grant faith: if by virtue, virtue: if by knowledge, knowledge. Augment in me faith, hope, and charity. O goodness of Thine, singular and most to be admired!'[5]

Nevertheless, faith is still considered intellectually here and one has to turn to mature texts, such as the *Confessions* or *The City of God* (413–426) to find the more characteristically Augustinian notion of faith. In these texts, Augustine's personal attitude to the expression of his faith in God astonishes readers even today. The very form of 'confessions', a lively, intimate and personal dialogue with God, displays Augustine's novelty.[6] In Augustine's personal faith, a new phase in the history of

---

[2]Clement, *Stromata*, II, XII.
[3]Clement, *Stromata*, II, XI.
[4]Tertullian, *Treatise on the Incarnation*, ed. and trans. Ernest Evans (London: SPCK, 1956), p. 19.
[5]Augustine, 'Two Books of Soliloquies', in Philip Schaff (ed.), *Nicene and Post-Nicene Fathers*, trans. C. C. Starbuck; First Series, vol. VII (New York: Cosimo, 2007), pp. 537–560 (I, 5, p. 539).
[6]Brian Stock, *Augustine's Inner Dialogue: The Philosophical Soliloquy in Late Antiquity* (Cambridge: Cambridge University Press, 2010), ch. 1.

faith comes to the fore, which could not have been produced by the esoteric and formalistic Greek writers of the previous centuries. In some Latin authors, most importantly in Tertullian, we see a similarly affective nature expressed in a personally 'confessional' form. However, Augustine's deep erudition and logically structured mind secured him a perspective in which his 'confessional' style kept a right balance between mysticism and rationality.

The Bible

Augustine relied on various sources, but what mattered most to him was the Bible. He studied and used patristic sources, yet he never closely followed Alexandrian theology. Popular Platonism and Stoicism, as the philosophy of life of educated Romans, were influential in the works of Augustine too, but they cannot explain his creative genius. Augustine's reading of the Bible is omnipresent in everything he wrote. We can even say that Augustine read the Bible in whatever topic he discusses and cannot discuss any topic without latently reading the Bible. He finds the Bible in his own life, in the events of history, in the surrounding nature and even in the sky; for him the sky itself is the Scripture ('figuratively', as he writes), and the inner meaning of the Bible is expressed in all our endeavours. Since both the Bible and reality itself is the production of the Word of God ('which does not have syllables'), it is no wonder that they refer mutually to each other. Principally, it is the Bible that contains the clue to understanding reality, since Holy Scripture is directly dictated by the Holy Spirit, while human and physical nature are corrupted by original sin and personal vices. Unlike the patristic authors, Augustine considered the Bible open to its readers if they let themselves be led by God's love in reading and interpreting. Augustine distanced himself from the rather esoteric approach of the Alexandrians, especially Clement and Origen, who considered the inner core of the Bible a mystery open only to initiates.[7]

Instrumental faith and personal faith

Augustine's notion of faith can be divided into two main groups. In the first group, we find interpretations of faith consistent with earlier conceptions; nevertheless, even these conceptions offer at some points characteristic novelties. In the second group, we find his own unique and momentous notion of faith, which could be said to have created a new epoch in the history of faith. The conceptions which belong to the first group are arranged around the central point of faith *instrumental* to knowledge. *Instrumental faith* is often seen by Augustine as permeating the whole range of mental activities, inasmuch as there are various kinds of credible things: those always believed but never understood; those understood as soon as believed; and those things first believed and afterwards understood. History and the temporal

---

[7]See Erich Przywara, *An Augustine Synthesis* (New York: Sheed & Ward, 1936), ch. 2.

things of humanity belong to the first group; mathematical and logical axioms and rules belong to the second group; and 'things divine' belong to the third group. It is interesting to see how Augustine subsumes various mental activities under the rubric of 'faith', for he seems to think that faith equally has a probability character (first group), an axiomatic nature (second group) and a theological feature (third group). Naturally, these cases deal with different mental activities, but for Augustine it is more important to emphasize that 'believing' permeates and naturally present in the human mind.[8]

Instrumental faith has a morally purifying function. Augustine refers to Acts 15.9 ('purifying their hearts by faith') in order to emphasize the role of faith in preparing higher states of mystical consciousness, knowledge and vision. Purity of heart is the precondition of the knowledge of God, 'faith is understanding's step and understanding is faith's reward'.[9] 'Seek not to understand that you may believe, but believe that you may understand'.[10] 'Believe that you may understand' is the key expression Augustine unremittingly emphasizes, thereby making faith the instrument of knowledge of God.

On the other hand, instrumental faith is underpinned by authority and reason. This seems to be circular, since Augustine often declares faith to be the beginning of knowledge. However, faith is motivated by love, authority and everyday reason alike; faith purifies the heart and opens the 'eyes of reason', which leads us to a higher order of faith. This later opens the way to the knowledge of the mysteries of God, a knowledge supernatural and ineffable at the same time. 'For there are some things which we do not believe unless we understand them, and there are other things which we do not understand unless we believe them'.[11] In this mutual relationship, faith is often depicted as intellectual, as 'an assent to the truth of what is said'.[12] Yet Augustine never really sees faith as purely intellectual. His central expressions, such as 'assent' or 'will', always involve 'the heart', 'love' and the 'interior eyes'. These expressions help us to determine the other kind of faith in Augustine which we may term faith 'sui generis' or personal faith.

With respect to personal faith, an important reference for Augustine is the verse from Isaiah: 'If ye will not believe, surely ye shall not be established' (7.9).[13] Characteristically, Augustine – following the Greek and Latin translations of his time – understands this verse as 'Unless you believe, you shall not understand'. In his interpretation, this faith is not merely initial or instrumental. Faith here is a faith of absolute magnitude which permeates the whole range of human activities and goes even deeper into the 'heart'; it grasps the core of personhood. Augustine's unparalleled novelty is his clearly formulated notion of the necessity of a personal faith. Certainly, many of his formulas reflect the traditional aspects of instrumental faith, but at crucial points the new dimension of sui generis faith comes to the fore.

---

[8]See Przywara, *An Augustine Synthesis*, p. 105.
[9]Przywara, *An Augustine Synthesis*, p. 84.
[10]Przywara, *An Augustine Synthesis*, p. 95.
[11]Przywara, *An Augustine Synthesis*, p. 99.
[12]Przywara, *An Augustine Synthesis*, p. 91.
[13]See ch. 1 on Faith in the Bible.

In spite of the eloquent and often lecturing style of the professional rhetorician, Augustine seems to be hesitating about the very nature of faith. Even in the circle of instrumental faith, he does not clearly distinguish between rational, emotional, purifying and mystical faith. He does, however, have to distinguish the personal kind of faith from all other kinds.

The eyes of faith

When he uses the expression 'the eyes of faith',[14] Augustine applies one of his favourite ideas to the problem of faith. He likes to underline the importance of the 'inner person', the spiritual and contemplative nature of the soul, and he also enjoys applying terms of external perception to spiritual or 'inner' perception.[15] In such expressions, Augustine follows neo-Platonic patterns, but he adds his characteristically personal emphasis. It may not be sufficient to call his understanding of faith 'affective', because there is much more at stake in Augustine than mere affectivity: it is about a new and emphatic notion of faith. The 'eyes of faith' or 'eyes of the heart' refer to the most personal dimension of the believer. It is a new and deep perception of individual human personhood that determines Augustine's notion of faith.

One example that illuminates this point is his famous distinction between faith as an act that believes (*fides qua creditur*) and faith as a content to be believed (*fides quae creditur*). In making this distinction, Augustine follows the traditional distinctions between kind and individual or form and matter. However, he ingeniously perceives that, in matters of faith, it is not only the *regula fidei*, the rule of faith or the general contents, which really count. He certainly emphasizes that faith in Christ is the most important thing, but he observes that *the way* a human person believes, his act of faith, is fundamental. It is the believer who is called by Christ to salvation and the believer's answer – always under the influence of God's grace – is decisive. It is personal faith – elicited by God – that informs the soul so that she becomes prepared to receive salvation.

Augustine expresses this point in a beautiful way when he compares the individual act of faith to the individual countenance (*facies*) of a human person. We can speak of a 'human face' in general, just as we can speak of certain dogmatic contents of faith. However, a 'human face in general' is actually meaningless. What we see is always the concrete face of a concrete human person, a face ultimately unique and non-interchangeable with any other human face. Similarly, the act of faith must be ultimately personal and non-interchangeable. Essentially, faith is a personal matter; the 'eyes of faith' are my eyes and my seeing; they are 'deeply seated within me', as my personal matter. In this way, perhaps the distinction between *fides qua*, the faith by which we believe, and *fides quae*, the faith which we believe, hides this

---

[14]Augustine, *The City of God*, trans Henry Bettenson (New York: Penguin Books, 1984), pp. XIV, 9, 563.
[15]As in his often-cited sentence: *Noli foras ire, in te ipsum redi, in interiore homine habitat veritas.* 'Do not go outside, return to within yourself; truth dwells in the inner man'. Augustine, *De vera religione*, 39, 72.

epoch-making insight into the personal nature of faith. Our face expresses our faith, at least in the sense that our faith, just as our face, must be ultimately personal.[16]

Study questions

1. What is the highest end of faith for Clement of Alexandria?
2. What is characteristic of St. Augustine's synthesis of earlier notions of faith in the Bible and patristic literature?
3. What is instrumental and personal faith for St. Augustine?
4. What are 'the eyes of faith'?
5. Why is a human countenance so decisive in Augustine's understanding of faith?

Further reading

Augustine, *Confessions* (Louisville: John Knox Press, 1955).
Dulles, Avery, *The Assurance of Things Hoped For: A Theology of Christian Faith* (Oxford: Oxford University Press, 1994).
Levering, Matthew, *The Theology of Augustine: An Introductory Guide to His Most Important Works* (Grand Rapids, Mich.: Baker Academic, 2013).
Stump, Eleonor and Kretzmann, Norman (eds), *The Cambridge Companion to Augustine* (Cambridge: Cambridge University Press, 2001).

---

[16]See Augustine, 'On the Holy Trinity', in Philip Schaff (ed.), *Nicene and Post-Nicene Fathers*, trans. Arthur West Haddan; First Series, vol. III (Grand Rapids, Mich.: Christian Classics Ethereal Library, 1956), pp. 6–475 (XIII, 2, p. 346) especially this:

> But that which is believed is a different thing from the faith by which it is believed. For the former is in things which are said either to be, or to have been or to be about to be; but the latter is in the mind of the believer, and is visible to him only whose it is; although not indeed itself but a faith like it, is also in others. For it is not one in number, but in kind; yet on account of the likeness, and the absence of all difference, we rather call it one than many. For when, too, we see two men exceedingly alike, we wonder, and say that both have one countenance.

3

Ecclesial Faith

Personal or collective?

Every believer makes his or her own journey of faith. This journey is a personal adventure in which each pilgrim experiences his or her own certainties and confusions, joys and hopes, grief and anxieties. The pilgrimage has a common destination, but every person climbs the slopes and descends the mountains on their own. And yet it does not make sense, within Christianity, to say that 'every one is on their own pilgrimage'.

Some theologians assert that 'the Church is an essential prerequisite without which I cannot believe'.[1] Such an affirmation of the centrality of the Church to Christian faith seems to run against the personal character of faith which every believer experiences. Faith is a life's adventure with God, as uniquely personal a thing as a lifelong marriage of two lovers. We seem to experience the highs and lows of our beliefs in God and about God within ourselves, not as a collective group like the Church. How could the subject of the act of faith be 'we', the Church, not 'I', the individual believer? How could it be that the person who confesses faith in the Creeds is not any one particular speaker, but the Church as a whole? Who could be churchy enough to want an 'ecclesial faith'? Wouldn't they have to march along in lockstep with everyone else?

Baptism

We cannot take the Church out of Christian faith without forfeiting the 'given' character of faith. The Church gives us faith as a gift from God. Before it is a list of propositions to be believed, faith is an action which God performs on us at the moment of baptism. Baptism turns a pagan into a Christian believer, by enacting in him or her the death and resurrection of Christ. Baptism ignites faith in a human soul by giving it a share in both the death and the new life of Christ. It is because a believer shares in the resurrected life of Christ that he or she can later see with the eyes of faith. Whether it happens in a river or a basilica, a roadside chapel or a cathedral, baptism is an action of God performed by the hands of the Church's ministers. Baptism 'is not … something secondary to the act of faith but its ecclesial dimension'.[2] Today's theologians emphasize that the earliest Creeds were

---

[1]Joseph Ratzinger, *Principles of Catholic Theology: Building Stones for a Fundamental Theology*, trans. Sister Mary Frances McCarthy, S.N.D. (San Francisco: Ignatius Press, 1987), p. 35.
[2]Ratzinger, *Principles*, p. 112.

'interrogatory' creeds, used when the bishop asked a baptismal candidate, 'Do you believe in the Father?' 'Do you believe in the Son?' 'Do you believe in the Holy Spirit?' The early Church bishops' questioning of the baptismal candidates reminds us that 'Credal Faith' does not mean primarily a list of propositions we believe, but a deeply personal confession of conversion of heart.

Church as witness

Ever since the first Easter in 33 AD, the body of Christian believers witnesses to the bodily resurrection of the Messiah. Christian faith is ecclesial because it is as a corporate body that it witnesses to the resurrection of Christ. Every individual believer may have a (weak or strong) conviction that Christ has defeated death: and that is just what they have, a conviction, or a belief or an opinion. This belief is incommunicable: it may shape a person's life, but it cannot be transferred or shared. The Church as a whole, however, is a testimony to the resurrection. That is not because there is safety in numbers or because a very large number of convictions is more convincing and persuasive than just one. The Church does not 'evidence' the resurrection of Christ in and of itself. That many people believe that Christ 'rose again on the third day' is not evidence *of* the resurrection of Christ. The Church and its subjective belief did not roll away the stone, and the believing Church is not evidence *of* the resurrection. But the Church is evidence *to* the resurrection of Christ from the dead: that is, it witnesses to it, attesting it. The Church is a sign.

In 1870 the First Vatican Council stated that 'the church herself by reason of her astonishing propagation, her outstanding holiness and her inexhaustible fertility in every kind of goodness, by her catholic unity and her unconquerable stability, is a kind of great and perpetual motive of credibility and an irrefutable witness of her own divine mission'.[3]

The Church is a 'motive of credibility', a sign that Christianity is believable. The Second Vatican Council asserted that

> this Sacred Synod gathered together in the Holy Spirit eagerly desires … to bring the light of Christ to all men, a light brightly visible on the countenance of the Church … the Church is in Christ like a sacrament or as a sign and instrument both of a very closely knit union with God and of the unity of the whole human race.[4]

Lumen Gentium says that the Church is a 'sacrament' or 'sign' of humanity's union with God: that is, it attests to the intimate bond between God and humanity, just as a wedding marks the love of a man and a woman and bonds them together.

---

[3]Decrees of the First Vatican Council (1870), *Dei Filius*, 3.12.
[4]Documents of Vatican II (1962–1965), *Lumen gentium* 1.1.

Church and the Gospels

To speak of the Church as a permanent testimony to the life, death and resurrection of Christ is to say that the Church is like a walking version of the New Testament. Richard Bauckham has claimed that the Gospels are history as 'testimony'. He thinks the Gospels are compiled out of dozens of testimonies of individual eyewitnesses. If, as Bauckham says, 'the Gospels … embody the testimony of eyewitnesses',[5] then the Gospels and the Church are inseparable as means to faith in the resurrection of Christ and the Triune God.

An eyewitness *testifies*, or gives *testimony*. As Bauckham notes, one can observe

> two inseparable aspects of testimony: on the one hand, its quasi-empirical aspect, the testimony of the senses, the report of the eyewitnesses to the facts, and, on the other hand, the interiority of testimony, the engagement of the witness with what he or she attests. The faithful witness … is not merely accurate but faithful to the meaning of what is attested … in the most … significant cases this is where bearing witness becomes a costly commitment of life, and the Greek *martus* … takes in Christian Greek usage the sense that its English derivative, 'martyr' has in English.[6]

Testimony has the connotation of a report based on direct observation, but also the connotation of personal commitment: it is a direct observation which a person swears by or vouches for. In the long run, an ecclesial faith based on eyewitness accounts is more *personal* than a private faith which traces its origins to the storytelling of Christian groups and local churches.

The stories in the Gospels are more weird and fantastical than anything in Tolkien: the hero walks on water, turns water into wine, makes the blind see and raises the dead Lazarus to life. He is crucified and rises from the dead. The *only* kind of history writing which is adapted to this material is testimony. The best way to make sense of a piece of purportedly historical writing in which the hero is born of a virgin, makes the blind see and exorcises devils, is crucified and rises from the dead is to say that these escapades got into the narrative because the author took them on someone's – or many people's – claim to have witnessed the events.

The claim that the sources of the Gospels are eyewitness accounts is subtly different from the tradition which posits an Apostle behind each of the Gospels. A venerable tradition claimed that Matthew the tax collector is the author of Matthew's Gospel and Luke and Acts can call on the Apostle Paul for backup. The claim made here is wider and more populist: we are thinking of a cast of a few dozen, each a named personality who makes a tangential appearance in the Gospels. Perhaps the Gospels come back to multiple eyewitness accounts from named figures, such as Cleopas or Jairus. Perhaps the authors of the Gospels were

---

[5]Richard Bauckham, *Jesus and the Eyewitnesses: The Gospels as Eyewitness Testimony* (Grand Rapids, Mich.: Eerdmans, 2006), p. 6.
[6]Bauckham, *Jesus and the Eyewitnesses*, p. 505.

artful practitioners of 'oral history', drawing on the testimonies of dozens of named individuals to compose their 'Lives' of Jesus.[7]

In the second century, when the Gnostics produced imitation 'Gospels', Christians like Bishop Irenaeus of Lyons called the Gnostics bluff on their claim to secret 'insider' information about Jesus. He traced his contemporary church back to the Apostles, and the Apostles he called eyewitnesses par excellence. The elite intellectual cadre of the second- and third-century Gnostics was countered with an assertion to insider knowledge which outmatched theirs in selectiveness. Faith in the Church includes faith in the Apostles and their successors. It also takes its view of Christ from the constellation of individual witnesses who have walk-on parts in the Gospels.

The Church mediates between the factual evidence (the living, dying and resurrected Christ himself whom the Apostles touched with their hands and saw with their eyes) and the faith of every individual believer. It mediates the evidence *to* the believer, through its unbroken chain of witnesses. At the base of the Church are those who touched with their hands and saw with their eyes: they were present at that fish barbecue breakfast with the risen Christ described in John 21. Cardinal Cajetan wrote

> It is necessary for mankind…that some persons receive such a revelation from God concerning the things to be believed, that they possess a self-evident certainty…Otherwise, the Church would not possess in herself any certainty about what ought to be believed – that is to say, if she did not have within herself any witnesses.[8]

The Church is the channel to believers of the evidence about Christ. But the Church simultaneously mediates Christ's *believability* to us. The Church is the means through which believers can envisage Jesus as crucified-and-resurrected and as God-and-man. The Gospels often record that the disciples were confused when the events occurred, but 'remembered' after the resurrection and figured it out. The events made sense after the resurrection. In the memory of the Church, Christ's *persona* takes shape and becomes believable as that of the God-man. The figure of Christ never makes sense without the believing alchemy of the Church's memory. Hence, it is in the Church that we find a balance between reason and evidence, on the one hand, and faith, on the other. The Church as living memory of God's history with humanity strikes the balance between evidential reason and faith. It is because the 'seat of all faith is, then, the *memoria Ecclesiae*, the memory of the Church, the Church as memory' that Christian faith is ecclesial.[9]

Christian faith is ecclesial because the Holy Spirit guides the Church. Sometimes that happens through staid affairs like Ecumenical Councils, and other times in rowdy charismatic jamborees. Pentecost was a bit of both. It was after the descent of the Holy Spirit at Pentecost that the twelve were able to grasp exactly whose disciples they were. Once Jesus was gone from their sight, and the Word had fallen

---

[7]Bauckham, *Jesus and the Eyewitnesses*, pp. 8–10.
[8]Cardinal Cajetan, cited in Hans Urs von Balthasar, *The Glory of the Lord: A Theological Aesthetics*, vol. 1, *Seeing the Form*, trans. Erasmo Leiva-Merikakis (Edinburgh: T&T Clark, 1982, 1989), p. 308.
[9]Ratzinger, *Principles*, p. 23.

silent, they were able to see and to hear him for the first time. Jesus says, in John's Gospel, 'it is good for you that I go' (Jn. 16.7): good because his absence enables the Holy Spirit to make him present. By the faith-creating work of the Holy Spirit, the form and figure of Christ is made to 'become visible in the body of the Church', so that 'the person who truly lives through Christ's Holy Spirit' sees Christ ('the world will see me no more, but you will see me, because I live and you also live', Jn. 14.19).[10]

The Holy Spirit

The Holy Spirit is love, and the Spirit creates in us the means by which to see Christ, turning Christ into a visible form within the Church and the Church's first teachings, the epistles of Paul and the Gospels. As the bond of love between Father and Son, the Holy Spirit bonds us with Christ: it is within the charity of the Spirit that our faith exists and lives.

The Spirit is the 'medium' by means of which we apprehend Christ for who he is. The incarnate Son is the 'what' of faith, the content, and the Spirit is the 'by which' of faith, its means or channel. In the act of faith, God is made known by God, Jesus Christ by the Holy Spirit. The material object, the person of Christ, is spotlighted by the Holy Spirit. The Holy Spirit is the formal medium shaping our sight. The Holy Spirit is that 'by which' faith is brought about.

In common speech, 'taking it on faith' means operating on trust in someone else rather than on evidence we've seen or understood for ourselves. Christian faith believes through the witness of the Holy Spirit. The form of Christ as the Son of the Father has to be believed to be seen. By the illuminating testimony of the Holy Spirit, the Christian believer is able to see the form of Christ as the eternal Son of God the Father. This form and this relationship is exhibited in flesh and blood, but the 'seeing' is not simply empirical seeing. Some of the witness on which faith relies is internal and some of it is external: faith relies on both interior and exterior witnesses. In both the case of interior and of exterior testimony, the witness is not to the fact that the believer believes, but to the object of the believer's faith, Jesus Christ. Both the interior and the exterior testimony alike refer to Christ in the relation to his Father, that bond or relationship being the Holy Spirit. Interior and exterior testimony reinforce one another: unless something within us witnessed to the truth and beauty of the form of Christ, no external evidence could convince us. But there is external evidence: what is seen is flesh and blood and though the *content* of the external evidence is miraculous, the evidence for it is not weak or negligible.

If 'The Church is the … immediate space in which' Christ's 'form shines',[11] this is because the Church of the eyewitnesses is where he is really present. The form of Christ shaped the experience of those who first and originally saw with their eyes and touched with their hands. These eyewitnesses become 'archetypal witnesses of

---

[10]von Balthasar, *Glory of Lord* I, p. 319.
[11]von Balthasar, *Glory of Lord* I, pp. 421, 307.

Christian faith' to all believers who come after them.[12] Mystics are those who seem to dip into the 'archetypal experiences of the Prophets and the Apostles'. Because of their foundational character for the Church, there is a 'vital relationship' between the 'experience of faith' in our day and those of the ones who first touched and saw.[13]

Study questions

1. Does the ecclesial character of faith contradict or obstruct the personal character of faith?
2. Is faith a matter of believing propositions about God or is it something God does to us?
3. How does God's being a *Trinity* of persons affect our definition of what faith is?
4. Were there any believers in Jesus Christ before Pentecost?
5. Do 'I believe' in the Creed or do 'We believe' in the Creed? Some versions of the Creeds begin 'I believe' and others begin 'We believe'. Which is better? Why?

Further reading

Bauckham, Richard, *Jesus: A Very Short Introduction* (Oxford: Oxford University Press, 2011).

---

[12]von Balthasar, *Glory of Lord* I, p. 301.
[13]von Balthasar, *Glory of Lord* I, p. 421.

4

The Limits of Reason 1:
The Council of Orange

Religion and philosophy

The border between religion and philosophy is often blurry. The philosopher Socrates claimed to be addressed by an inner daemon and to do its bidding. Socrates' inner 'daemon' is both the voice of his conscience and an internal inspiration. Socrates' philosophical mission came from a Delphic oracle, which told him to 'know thyself'. There are lots of poetry and made-up stories about the gods in Plato, as if he were trying to invent a new religion. So the earliest Western philosophy sometimes invades what we might think is the territory of religion. In the East, Confucius speaks about the directions of 'Heaven' in a way that shows he believed he received divine revelation.

On the other side, some religions present themselves almost as if they were philosophies. For instance, Buddhism claims it is not a religion, because it is not dependent upon any revelation. Buddhism claims it is grounded on assertions which can be tested out in everyday life without recourse to revelation. You do not have to have faith to believe it; you simply need logic and the daily practice of Buddhism to be convinced of its rightness. Even some religions which claim to be based on a supernatural revelation, like Islam, simultaneously claim that one can be convinced of the truth of this religion by the evidence and by rational argument. Within Islam, 'faith' means absolute submission to the will of God. It does not refer to dependence on God's own actions to be able to know the saving truth about God.

So, throughout the world, philosophy crosses over into religion, and religions commonly present themselves as 'true philosophies', albeit philosophies backed up by a divine revelation. It may be that religions are just philosophy 'as a way of life'. Most philosophies begin and end as religions of some sort, and most religions are 'life philosophies' which sometimes add that they are backed up by divine revelation.

Christianity claims it is unbelievable without God to help

If that is true, then Christianity is not a philosophy or a religion! For it is the only teaching about God which claims to be *unknowable* and totally unbelievable unless God works on the thinker, and brings about his or her conviction of the truth of this teaching. Christianity formally anathematizes the idea that it could be believed on the basis of argument, rational conviction or experience. From quite early on, Christian dogma said it is a *heresy* to claim that one can prove the salvific truth of Christianity to someone on purely rational or experiential grounds. Christianity ruled out the notion that it is simply a true philosophy (it cannot be demonstrated through reason alone) or a true religion (one cannot be convinced of its value solely by practice or experience). Christianity dogmatically defines faith as a gift of God, and it holds that its own teachings cannot be believed without this gift.

St. Paul strongly and repeatedly affirmed that he did not believe in the truth of God's work in Jesus Christ on his own volition, on his own willpower, or because his own reasoning taught him to do so. He spoke of himself as a splintered self, who could not do or think as he wished to do, and whose actual deeds and thoughts ran counter to what he wished he could do. Paul wrote 'midrash' or interpretations of the Genesis story about the serpent, Eve, Adam and a certain tempting but forbidden fruit. Paul's midrash of Gen. 3 turned that story into a 'fall' story, in which the human race, represented by Adam, is banished from Eden forever as a result of breaking God's command not to eat the fruit of the Tree of the Knowledge of Good and Evil.

Paul underwent the terrifying experience of liberation by Christ. His visions of the resurrected Christ taught him to believe that Christ alone had defeated death and the devil. This led him to a conviction that, on the one hand, the human race before Christ had been enslaved to sin, death and the devil, and, on the other hand, that only through participation in Christ's victory over death and sin could human beings be freed from the powers of darkness. Paul's interpretation of Gen. 3 turned it into a story about 'original sin' and 'original death': Paul believed himself and all human beings to be 'fallen' because of his charismatic experience of the risen Christ. Christ's victory was so dazzling that it exposed the depths of human blindness and simultaneously revealed that the darkness into which humanity had fallen had been breached.

Paul's teaching that Christ had brought light into creaturely darkness and overcome the demonic powers was central to the Christians in the catacombs. This is attested by the dozens of ancient paintings of Jonah leaping out of the whale, which symbolically represent Christ's defeat of death. But Paul's teaching that we cannot achieve anything without Christ was not especially emphasized in the catacombs. It is true that baptism was always represented in the early Church as an 'illumination' and that Christ was pictured as a healer and a bringer of light or enlightenment. Early Christianity presented itself as the 'true philosophy', the best and most religious way of life on offer.

Augustine versus Pelagius

It was Augustine who revived the Pauline teaching that only by the grace of Christ can human beings overcome their fallen ignorance of God and become God's friends. Augustine claimed that he could only do as God asks when God gave him the grace to do so: he could only keep God's commandments 'under orders' from the grace of the Holy Spirit. Back to St. Paul!

But what did Paul mean? There was a flaming row about this between Augustine and the British monk Pelagius. Pelagius thought that being 'fallen in Adam' was simply a matter of bad precedents and social conditioning. Augustine interpreted Paul's understanding of Gen. 3 more stringently, to mean that human beings are so fragmented and wounded by sin that they cannot be healed and restored to right living without the grace of the Holy Spirit. The debates between Pelagius and Augustine led to dogmatic teachings about the reach of 'original sin'. Pelagianism was condemned at a council in Carthage in 418. The ecumenical council of Ephesus, where Mary was proclaimed *Theotokos*, or 'God-bearer', reiterated the Augustinian rejection of Pelagianism.

In *The City of God*, Augustine claimed that while the religious philosophies of his time (like Neo-Platonism) enabled their practitioners to master the fear of death, only Christianity can make us happy, because it empowers us to overcome death itself. Augustine thought that 'the Platonists' had come close to grasping that God is Triune. The limits he placed on reason do not set particular boundaries on how *much* we can know about God by our natural reasoning powers. The question is not whether we can know God exists, or is Triune, or became Incarnate, but whether we can have 'saving knowledge' of God. Paul says that we get no profit from visions of God if we do not have charity (1 Cor. 13). The Council of Orange of 529 will say that nothing we can know about God can be 'saving' unless we know it by faith. It does not say that everything philosophy or natural religion knows about God is untrue, but that nothing we know by these means saves us from death.

The Council of Orange (529)

Orange is in Southern France, or 'Gaul' as it was called back in the day. At the Council of Orange, Caesarius of Arles and a dozen or so other bishops rejected the semi-Pelagian notion that belief in Christianity is a matter of the right use of freewill. The Council of Orange is not an ecumenical council, like Nicaea, Ephesus or Trent, but it was hugely influential, both on pre-Reformation Christians of all stamps and for post-Reformation Catholics and Protestants.

The second Canon of Orange rejects the Pelagian notion that Adam's sin only corrupted Adam himself 'and not his descendants also'; this canon affirms that Adam's sin corrupts both the body and the soul of all humanity. Sin leads to the death of the body and to the death of the soul and spirit of each human being.

The Fifth Canon of Orange states that faith is 'unnatural': it does not come to us by our natural powers, by reasoning or by our own volition. It is a pure gift from God. The Fifth Canon runs:

> If anyone says that not only the increase of faith but also its beginning and the very desire for faith ... belongs to us by nature and not by a gift of grace, that is by the inspiration of the Holy Spirit amending our will and turning it from unbelief to faith and from godlessness to godliness, it is proof that he is opposed to the teaching of the Apostles, for blessed Paul says, 'And I am sure that he who began a good work in you will bring it to completion at the day of Jesus Christ'

(Phil. 1.6) ... 'For by grace you have been saved through faith; and this is not your own doing, it is the gift of God'. (Eph. 2.8)

The Fifth Canon states that those who do not receive the sacraments (the means of grace) must not be called believers: belief is empowered by grace, which comes through the sacraments. Orange effectively denies that Christianity is a philosophy, a way of life or a religion. No religion considers itself to be 'a faith' in the way that this Council says that Christianity is.

The Sixth Canon of Orange claims that, in and of themselves, learning, studying or even prayer cannot liberate us or lead us towards salvation. Once again invoking the authority of Paul (1 Cor. 4.7 and 1 Cor. 15.10), the Sixth Canon denies that 'God has mercy upon us when, apart from his grace, we believe, will, desire, strive, labor, pray, watch, study, seek, ask, or knock, but d[o] not confess that it is by the infusion and inspiration of the Holy Spirit within us that we have the faith, the will, or the strength to do these things as we ought'.

The Council of Orange does not deny that we can have any knowledge of God without grace. It denies, as mediaeval Christianity and both Catholicism and Protestantism will later do, that we can have *saving* knowledge of God. We can know that God exists, but we cannot know what we must do in order to be saved without God's gift of faith. We are entirely dependent on outside help, it claims, to escape from our own blindness, the power of death and the demonic powers. This makes it a core teaching of Christianity that one must call for help and receive help in order to reach God as one's saviour. Christianity teaches that faith is divine help in seeing and knowing the truth about God as liberator. Canon Seven of the Council of Orange states,

> If anyone affirms that we can form any right opinion or make any right choice which relates to the salvation of eternal life ... or that we can be saved, that is, assent to the preaching of the gospel through our natural powers without the illumination and inspiration of the Holy Spirit, who makes all men gladly assent to and believe in the truth, he is led astray by a heretical spirit, and does not understand the voice of God who says in the Gospel, 'For apart from me you can do nothing' (Jn. 15.5) and the word of the Apostle, 'Not that we are competent of ourselves to claim anything as coming from us; our competence is from God'. (2 Cor. 3.5)

Rejection of dual predestination (to hell and to heaven)

The Council of Orange is said to have repelled 'semi-Pelagianism' with 'semi-Augustinianism'. The council's concluding words reject extreme Augustinianism, such as the teaching that 'any are foreordained to evil by the power of God'. It denies that human beings are God's puppets, fated to good or evil, noting that 'after grace has been received through baptism, all baptized persons have the ability and responsibility ... to perform with the aid and cooperation of Christ what is of essential importance with regard to the salvation of their soul' (Conclusion). Life is not, according to the Council of Orange, like a Coen Brothers movie.

Setting limits to reason

With the widespread acceptance of Orange's teaching as Christian dogma, it was off-limits to claim that we can give credence to the Christian 'salvation story' by thinking it through for ourselves. Orange does not deny that there is truth in philosophy or in non-Christian religion. It does deny that Christianity can be equated with such philosophies or religions. It claims in effect (though not in those words) that Christianity is uniquely a matter of 'faith' as a gift of God. Many religions claim to be based on a divine revelation. Even philosophers (like Socrates) have claimed some kind of inspiration or have created 'sacred mythologies' (as Plato did). Christianity claims that its own divine revelation is not transparent or self-illuminating; it is only by the power of God that God's Word can be heard and seen by us. Christianity claims that there is no 'assent' to the divine teaching without grace, and that this grace is faith.

Orange's dogmas set limits to what Christians can believe regarding what human reason is able to know about the saving God. In the future, as a consequence of these dogmas, rationalists from Abelard to Voltaire would be stigmatized by Christians not only as having an unreasonable confidence in the powers of reason but as *Pelagian*, that is, as people who reject Paul's midrash of Gen. 3, Adam and Eve, the serpent and the forbidden fruit of the Tree of the Knowledge of Good and Evil.

Study questions

1. Look at the Decrees of the Council of Trent online and work out how they use the Council of Orange.
2. View the Reformation Confessions online and explain how the Council of Orange influenced them.
3. What is the difference between knowledge of God and saving knowledge of God?
4. If we cannot have saving knowledge of God without supernatural faith, can we know by natural reason that God is three persons in one being?
5. Is Christianity a religion or philosophy of life?
6. Is it meaningful to talk about the five great 'world faiths' or 'world religions' (Hinduism, Judaism, Christianity, Islam and Buddhism)?
7. What limits would *you* set on reason in terms of what we can know about Ultimate Truth?

Further reading

Augustine, Saint, *Concerning the City of God against the Pagans*, trans. Henry Bettenson (London: Penguin, 1972), pp. X–XI.

5

Thomas Aquinas: Systematic Faith

How theology becomes 'Scholastic'

The Fathers of the Church were copious writers and preachers but not systematic ones. In the eleventh century, Anselm of Canterbury (1033–1109) led the development of theology towards 'scholasticism'. Scholasticism is theology taught in schools, by 'school-men', as distinct from theology taught by monks in monasteries. The Scholastics produced teachable, systematized theological texts to be used in schools. Logic was important to them. Anselm was one of the first to put logic at the pedagogical service of theology. In his *Cur Deus homo* ('Why God became human'), Anselm sought to show, without relying upon Scriptural authority and purely on logical grounds, that it made sense for God to become human. One reason for relying on logic rather than revealed doctrine is that one could not preach to (or against) Muslims out of Scripture and Tradition. The use of logic enabled theologians to build their treatises like Lego castles, with one conclusion snapping into another. While the structure of patristic theology is rhetorical or homiletic, the structure of scholastic theology is logical.

Half a century later, Peter Abelard (1079–1142), one of the first great Scholastics, gained notoriety by appearing to some to *subject* the truths of faith to those of logic. Abelard also composed the *Sic et non* ('Yes and No'), which laid apparently contradictory conclusions of the Fathers alongside one another.

Peter Lombard (1096–1164) then wrote a four volume *Book of Sentences* (I, Trinity; II, Creation; III, Christ; IV, Sacraments). Lombard's *Book of Sentences* supplies an encyclopaedic anthology of the main conclusions of the Fathers. The *Sentences* show where the Fathers agree and disagree. Commenting on these *Sentences*, and wringing convergence out of apparent divergence, was the mainstay of theological education for the next 500 years, down to and including Luther and Calvin. Lombard's compendium of apparently antithetical patristic conclusions is the beginning of what moderns call 'systematic theology'. Commentators on the *Sentences* drew on logic to synthesize apparently diverse conclusions: this is the origin of systematic theology. For the Authorities must not be seen to disagree. It would be disrespectful.

The thirteenth century is thus the age of the *Summas*, vast theological constructions which are often compared to the Gothic cathedrals, both in size, in elegance and in the determination to represent everything in heaven and on earth. Thomas Aquinas (1225–1275) wrote an enormous *Summa theologica*, which advances systematically through every theological topic from the nature of theology, to the Triune God and his attributes, Creation, the angels, human nature with its virtues and vices, the Incarnation and the seven sacraments of the Church. The shorter but no less systematic *Summa contra gentiles* was perhaps intended

as a manual for missionaries in the Islamic world. When he takes detours off the
main road to God, Thomas composed multiple long and short treatises, detailing
a few of his *Summa* topic for close inspection. Such are the *De Malo* (on evil) and
the *Disputed Questions on Truth*. Thomas dictated dozens of commentaries on
Scripture and on the works of Aristotle, his favourite philosopher.

Sacra doctrina

For Thomas, it is *sacra doctrina*, that is, Scripture and its interpretation by the Church,
which is the highest science. The word of God, not the word of men like himself, is
the original 'science of God', of which Thomas speaks. *Sacra doctrina* covers all of
Scripture and the ecumenical Councils of the Church. Thomas regards the Fathers
of the Church, like Augustine and Athanasius, as high authorities, although not on a
par with sacred doctrine. For him, *sacra doctrina* is a 'knowledge', a *scientia* because
it substantially consists in God's sharing of his self-knowledge with human beings.
God's self-understanding is thoroughly scientific, and, in *sacra doctrina*, he shares it
with humanity.

God shared his mind with us because we cannot be saved unless he does so.
Thomas thought we could not be fulfilled as human beings without intimate
friendship with and knowledge of God. Thomas writes that 'the soul is by nature
capable of or open to grace; for as Augustine says, "by the very fact that it is made
to the image of God, it is capable of or open to God by grace"'.[1] We cannot receive
the vision of God for which our human nature naturally longs unless we *know* God.
We do not have the means of acquiring the knowledge we need to liberate our desire
for friendship with God. So God told us what he knows about himself, sharing his
mind with us, and this 'inside story' is the basis of all 'scientific' theology. Thomas
begins his *Summa theologica* with this affirmation:

> It was necessary for man's salvation that there should be a knowledge revealed
> by God besides philosophical science built up by human reason. Firstly, indeed,
> because man is directed to God, as to an end that surpasses the grasp of his
> reason ... But the end must first be known by men who are to direct their thoughts
> and actions to the end. Hence it was necessary for the salvation of man that
> certain truths which exceed human reason should be made known to him by
> divine revelation ... Whereas man's whole salvation, which is in God, depends
> upon the knowledge of this truth. Therefore, in order that the salvation of men
> might be brought about more fitly and more surely, it was necessary that they
> should be taught divine truths by divine revelation. It was therefore necessary that
> besides philosophical science built up by reason, there should be a sacred science
> learned through revelation.[2]

Theology is the study of God based on *sacra doctrina* or divine revelation. It is the
study of God undertaken in the light of faith.

---

[1] Thomas Aquinas, *Summa theologica* I–II, q. 113, a. 10, citing Augustine, *De Trinitate*, XIV.8.
[2] Aquinas, *Summa theologica* I, q. 1, a. 1.

The need for faith

Sacred doctrine gives us access to scientific knowledge of God. But here's the rub: only sacred doctrine as received in faith opens the door to God's interiority. Hence what comes out of God as his self-'knowledge' enters us as *faith*. Although *sacra doctrina* is a science, a 'knowledge', it leaves us knowing God by faith, not with a body of solid information about God which we can inspect and bank upon outside of the act of faith. Theology as a science does not happen without faith.

According to St. Thomas, we cannot simultaneously *know* God and have faith in God. More precisely, we cannot simultaneously know and believe in *the same aspect* of God. For instance, we can know by reason that God *exists* and believe by faith that God is triune at one and the same time, but we cannot believe and *know* that God is Triune: since knowledge and faith rule one another out, and we know some things and simply believe others about God, 'faith and science are not about the same object', that is, not about the same 'aspect' of God.[3] Thomas does not think we will have faith in heaven, and he thinks that Jesus Christ did not have faith in God the Father, since he *knew* God by direct sight at all times.

Thomas values the 'knowledge' of God which flows from faith higher than the understanding of God which we acquire by using our own minds. Thomas discriminates in favour of 'faith knowledge', arguing that,

> Between knowledge through science and knowledge through faith there is this difference: science shines only on the mind, showing that God is the cause of everything, that he is one and wise, and so forth. Faith enlightens the mind and also warms the affections, telling us not merely that God is first cause but also that he is savior, redeemer, loving, made flesh for us. Hence the phrase 'maketh manifest the savior of his knowledge'.[4]

Thomas tackles the question of what 'theology' would be like without divine self-communication in the first article of the first question of the *Summa theologica*. He claims that, were we to rely for our theology upon philosophers and intellectuals, such as his beloved Aristotle, 'the truth about God such as reason could discover, would only be known by a few, and that after a long time, and with the admixture of many errors'.[5] So even those matters concerning God which could, in theory, come 'naturally' to the philosophers were shared by God with the prophets, just to make sure that they did not make a fine mess of our prospects for salvation. Thomas understudies Aristotle's script for *Metaphysics*, *Ethics* and even *Physics* like a devout disciple. He makes copious use of the most detailed aspects of Aristotle's conception of nature and metaphysics. But when Thomas performs theology for himself, the reader hears the voice of the Dominican saint, not the Attic philosopher. This is because, for Thomas, what is *axiomatic* is revealed Scripture and Tradition. Aristotle's philosophy, as *known* by Thomas to be intellectually sound, must subserve

---

[3] Aquinas, *Summa theologica* I–II, q. 1, a. 5.
[4] Thomas Aquinas, *Commentary on II Corinthians*, ii, lect. 3, citing 2 Cor. 2.14.
[5] Aquinas, *Summa theologica* I, q. 1, a. 5.

sacra doctrina, as believed in faith by Thomas to illuminate the heart of God. The matter of Thomas' intellectual vision is drawn from Aristotelian metaphysics, but it is ensouled and shaped throughout by revealed doctrine, because the 'unscientific knowledge' of faith is, for Thomas, saving truth.

Formal object and material object of faith

We can distinguish within the act of faith *what we believe* and *by what means* we believe it. What we believe is the *content* of faith. Thomas calls *what we believe* the material object of faith. That would be, for instance, the propositions in Scripture and revealed Tradition. The *means* of believing is *how* we achieve belief. Thomas calls the *means* of believing the 'medium of demonstration'; this is the formal object of faith, that is, God. Within a philosophical treatise, the *matter* is the conclusions drawn, and the *formal* or shaping element is the proofs to these conclusions. So the *formal* object of faith (God) is what 'proves', or leads the mind to see, the validity of the material content (such as the propositions of *sacra doctrina*). For one of his examples, Thomas explains that 'in the science of geometry the content known is the conclusions; the formal objective of the science's assent to them is the medium of demonstration through which the conclusions are known'.[6] The reason for assenting to *sacra doctrina* is that God, 'the first Truth' (the highest Truth), is behind it. The formal object of the believer's intention is the first Truth, God illuminating our minds. The light shed by the first Truth enables the believer to see the total content of *sacra doctrina*, the material object of faith.

Thomas was more interested in the formal object of faith (God) than in the human phenomenology of faith: his *Summas* bear on realities far more than they bear on our apprehension of these things. So far as the inner workings of the act of faith are concerned, Thomas offers a threefold distinction: *believing in God* (intending the material object of faith), *believing God* (intending the formal object of faith) and *believing unto God* (the act of faith as stimulated by the will). Thomas states that the act of *believing in God* (*credere Deum*) is that in which the mind is related to the material object of faith: we 'believe in God' when we recite the Nicene Creed or hear the gospel and assent to it. The act of *believing God* (*credere Deo*) 'serves as the medium of assent to the material object'; it is 'because of the first truth' that we assent to the content of sacred doctrine. The act of *believing unto God* (*credere in Deum*) is that in which we *voluntarily* aim at God as the goal of our act of faith.[7]

Theology as a science

According to Aristotle, a science is a body of knowledge which has been reasoned out from self-evident first principles. Taking up this definition of a science, St. Thomas

---

[6]Aquinas, *Summa theologica* II–II, q. 1, a. 1.
[7]Aquinas, *Summa theologica* II–II, q. 2, a. 2.

defines theology as a science based on the first principles revealed by God. Here his distinction between the material and formal object of faith is important. Patristic Christian theology was *about* the Bible. With the rise of Scholasticism, people had begun to ask, what makes theology a science? Thomas was able to answer that, materially, it is *about* the Bible, or the biblical revelation is the *content* of theology, but *formally*, theology is *from the Bible*. Formally (in terms of what forms it), theology works *from the light of God's self-revelation*. Operating *by the light of faith*, out of the light God sheds on himself, theology is able to use reason to think about the biblical revelation (its material) in a scientific way. Theology is a *secondary* science, because it is not based on its own first principles, but on someone else's, namely God's. This is not a bad way to be secondary.

Thomas Aquinas' theology is a *systematic* portrayal of God, creation and Incarnation seen in the light of faith. Thomas is able to *systematize* his depiction of the objects of faith because in his mind two things converge: the light of faith and the light of natural reason. His confidence that faith can axiomatically synthesize the material contents of faith combined with his confidence that reason can logically analyze those same materials. Faith gave him the big picture, the synthetic axioms, and reason gave him the means to piece it together in a logical formation.

Study questions

1. Is it possible to put theology, or the things we know by faith, into a complete 'system'?
2. Did Jesus Christ have faith?
3. Does God cause us to know everything we know in the same way? Do we know natural objects naturally and independently of God and supernatural objects only with God's help?
4. Explain in your own words what Thomas means by the material and formal object of faith.
5. Can we know and believe something at the same time?

Further reading

Aquinas, Thomas, *Summa Theologica* II–II, qq. 1–10 on Faith.
Marenbon, John, *Medieval Philosophy: An Historical and Philosophical Introduction* (London: Routledge, 2006).
Gilson, Étienne, *The Spirit of Medieval Philosophy* (South Bend: University of Notre Dame Press, 1991).
———, *The Christian Philosophy of Saint Thomas Aquinas* (San Francisco: Ignatius Press, 1994).

6
Faith, Hope and Love: The Supernatural Virtues

Finally beloved, whatever is true, what is honorable, whatever is just,
whatever is pure, whatever is pleasing, whatever is commendable,
if there is any excellence and if there is anything worthy of praise,
think about these things. (Philippians 4.8)

And now faith, hope, and love abide, these three; and the greatest
of these is love. (1 Corinthians 13.13)

The Greek word for 'excellence' that Paul uses in Philippians 4.8 is *aretē*, which in the Latin translation of the Vulgate becomes *virtus*. *Aretē*, sometimes translated as 'excellence', sometimes as 'virtue', has a long and privileged place within ancient Greek thought, just as *virtus*, or 'virtue', does in ancient Roman thought. Providing a list of the different virtues, examples of them in the stories of gods and heroes and the ways one can achieve them was an important and common practice in ancient philosophers and thinkers (sometimes called 'aretology'). While these thinkers offered a profusion of different virtues, the four most important ones were prudence or wisdom, justice, temperance or self-control and courage or fortitude. These four are called the 'cardinal virtues' (from the Latin *cardo*, which means 'hinge') because all the other virtues depend on these.

Not only do Paul and other New Testament authors appeal to *aretē* (1 Pet. 2–9; 2 Pet. 2.5), but they also offer lists of various excellences and vices, examples that should be followed and guidelines for the household (all of which are known as *paraenesis*). While the New Testament and the Greek and Roman moral philosophers may agree on some rather simple matters, such as the importance of courage, temperance, patience and modesty, they certainly seem to disagree rather strongly on others. Who is the person, for instance, to whom we should look and appeal to for moral guidance and exhortation? Paul's crucified Jewish Messiah seems starkly different from Aristotle's cultured and balanced 'magnificent man'. Faith, hope and love, the centre of the Christian life for Paul, will not be found on the lists of virtues given by Plato, Aristotle or Cicero. Paul also notes that 'the greatest of these is love'. We are thus left with two questions: how does Aristotle's account of *aretē* square with Paul's version of *aretē*, and what is the relationship between faith, hope and love?

Virtue

For Aristotle, moral virtues are an active disposition, an expectant readiness to take the middle road between two extremes in any given situation. The virtues allow one to maintain an equilibrium between the poles of deficiency and excess, both of which are vices. They are related to different types of pleasure and pain. For instance, when faced with physical pleasures, temperance allows one to avoid indulging too much (the excess) and never enjoying any of the finer things in life (the deficiency). In the face of fear and danger, the virtue of courage enables one to avoid cowardice (acting from an excess of fear) as well as rashness (acting from a deficiency of fear).

More broadly speaking, excellences and virtues perfect or complete what they are a virtue of. They develop certain kinds of natural abilities and allow something to perform its intended function well. Physical virtues train and tone the body's natural capabilities. Intellectual virtues perfect the mind, bringing out the full range of its abilities. Moral virtues perfect one's 'appetites' or feelings such that one can act well regardless of the situation and the affections it might elicit. The virtues aid in living a good life by developing and perfecting the different aspects of a person. The overall goal of the virtues is that they allow one to live the good life, which for Aristotle means a 'happy' or 'flourishing' life.

Just as with most things, one learns the virtues by practice, by consistently doing virtuous deeds: 'Anything that we have to learn to do we learn by the actual doing of it: people become builders by building and instrumentalists by playing instruments. Similarly we become just by performing just acts, temperate by performing temperate ones, brave by performing brave ones'.[1] By continuing to act in virtuous ways, by avoiding giving in to too much pleasure or pain, or too little pleasure and pain, one develops these habits and dispositions to act the same way in the future. You are what you do. What you normally do and how you act day in and day out tells you what kind of person you are. Virtues are thus a matter of one's overall character and the whole course of one's actions in life.

Supernatural virtue

Aristotle's account of ethics, virtue and the good life had a tremendous impact upon ancient Greek, Roman and Christian thought. Yet the thirteenth century saw a marked increase in theologians who dealt with, and at times incorporated, Aristotle's thought into Christian theology. Largely responsible for the positive view regarding the use of Aristotle's works for theology were the English Franciscan Alexander of Hales (c. 1185–1245) and the German Dominican Albert the Great (c. 1206–1280). Nevertheless, it was actually Albert the Great's prize student, Thomas Aquinas, who offered us the most creative and influential engagement with Aristotle.

At first glance the supernatural virtues of faith, hope and love seem quite different from the natural virtues proposed by Aristotle. First, they are not the mean or middle

---

[1]Aristotle, *Nicomachean Ethics*, ed. and trans. Roger Crisp (Cambridge: Cambridge University Press, 2000), pp. 1103a33–1103b3.

between two extremes. For Aristotle, having too much courage means not having courage at all, for one has become rash or foolhardy. Having too much temperance means that one ceases to enjoy in moderation everything life has to offer. Such is not the case with the supernatural virtues. One cannot have 'too much' faith, hope or love. With these three, the more one has the better! The supernatural virtues are thus not means between extremes, but have opposites instead: unbelief, despair and hatred of God. Second, the supernatural virtues are not gained by practice or repetition. They are directly 'infused' or given to people by the Holy Spirit. They are a gift of grace. For instance, when speaking of the supernatural virtue of faith, Thomas maintains that

> Two things are requisite for faith. First, that the things which are of faith should be proposed to man…The second thing requisite for faith is the assent of the believer to the things which are proposed to him…as regards the first of these, faith must needs be from God. Because those things which are of faith surpass human reason…As regards the second, viz. man's assent to the things which are of faith, we may observe a twofold cause, one of external inducement, such as seeing a miracle, or being persuaded by someone to embrace the faith: neither of which is a sufficient cause, since of those who see the same miracle, or who hear the same sermon, some believe, and some do not. Hence we must assert another internal cause, which moves man inwardly to assent to matters of faith. The Pelagians held that this cause was…man's free-will: and consequently they said that the beginning of faith is from ourselves…But this is false, for, since man, by assenting to matters of faith, is raised above his nature, this must needs accrue to him from some supernatural principle moving him inwardly; and this is God. Therefore faith, as regards the assent which is the chief act of faith, is from God moving man inwardly by grace.[2]

If faith, hope and love differ so much from the natural virtues, why call them 'virtues' at all? Although they differ from the natural virtues, the supernatural virtues are still analogous to them. First, just as with Aristotle's account of virtues as dispositions or readiness, the supernatural virtues also are the 'principle' or 'source' of good actions. Second, while the natural virtues direct one towards earthly happiness, the supernatural virtues direct one towards eternal happiness. Third, as the natural virtues perfect and complete one's faculties and abilities, so do the supernatural virtues. Faith perfects the intellect by directing it to the true. Hope perfects the will by directing it to the divine goodness. Love also perfects the will by directing all of one's actions to God.

The supernatural virtues not only perfect a faculty, or an aspect of human nature, but they also perfect each other. More specifically, love is the supernatural virtue which perfects both faith and hope.[3] In the words of Gal. 5.6, neither circumcision nor uncircumcision matters, but only faith expressing itself through love. Genuine faith, the type of faith worthy of the name, is faith formed by love (*fides caritate*

---

[2]Thomas Aquinas, *Summa theologica* II, q. 6, a. 1.
[3]Thomas Aquinas, *Summa theologica* II–II, q. 23, a. 6.

formata). Without the 'form' of love, of being expressed in acts of love, faith is dead, lifeless and 'formless' (*fides informis*). Such is the kind of faith criticized in Jas. 2.17. Love, then, perfects and completes faith. Hope is also formed or perfected by love. Love for others leads one away from hoping only for oneself. Love for others means that one will also hope for others.[4] In the 'order of perfection', then, love is the greatest of these three. Love completes and perfects faith and hope.[5] However, in the 'order of generation', or their logical sequential order, faith precedes hope, which precedes love. The person knows God (faith), knows that God is good (hope) and wishes to be united with God (love).

Reformation views

Using virtue language to discuss faith, hope and love has not been without its critics. One of the most ferocious and influential of these critics was the German reformer Martin Luther (1483–1546). As a university student and later as a member of the Augustinian Hermits, Luther was educated in the liberal arts, in Aristotle's logic and metaphysics, the works of Augustine and medieval mystics and the thought of William of Ockham (1287–1347) as interpreted by his disciple Gabriel Biel (c. 1425–1495). It is unclear how much the young Luther read directly from Thomas Aquinas, but Luther did know contemporary Thomists and was probably familiar with the criticisms of Thomism offered by the followers of Ockham and fellow Augustinians. Luther even lectured on Aristotle's *Nicomachean Ethics* in 1508–1509 at the University of Wittenberg (the notes have unfortunately not been preserved).

From the same time period as his Ninety-Five Theses on indulgences, Luther also penned his 1517 'Disputation against Scholastic Theology'. There are many different polemic targets in the provocative ninety-seven theses Luther set out to be debated. While Augustine is the main hero of this work and Pelagius the main villain, Luther can also offer stinging criticisms of Aristotle, Aristotle's account of the moral life and the use of Aristotle's moral philosophy in the theology of justification and sanctification as put forward by various scholastics. Luther does not mince words: 'Briefly, the whole Aristotle is to theology as darkness is to light'.[6] Or again, 'Virtually the entire *Ethics* of Aristotle is the worst enemy of grace'.[7] The crux of Luther's disagreement with Aristotle and his account of virtue can be found in thesis 40: 'we do not become righteous by doing righteous deeds but, having been made righteousness, we do righteous deeds'.[8] It is not by repeating certain actions that one becomes righteous and pleasing to God, but one becomes righteous and pleasing to God solely by the free gift of God's grace. The existence of sin and grace means that Aristotle's teaching on acts and a person's character must be reversed. Given that the

---

[4]Thomas Aquinas, *Summa theologica* II–II, q. 17, a. 8.
[5]Thomas Aquinas, *Summa theologica* II–I, q. 62, a. 4.
[6]Martin Luther, 'Disputation against Scholastic Theology', in Timothy F. Lull (ed.), *Martin Luther's Basic Theological Writings* (Minneapolis: Fortress Press, 1989), pp. 13–20 (16).
[7]Luther, 'Disputation against Scholastic Theology', p. 16.
[8]Luther, 'Disputation against Scholastic Theology', p. 16.

church sided with Augustine and not Pelagius, Luther thinks it should be clear that it is 'Catholic doctrine' itself which contradicts Aristotle's teachings on happiness and virtue.

Luther's view is that faith is the reorientation and turning inside out of the whole person. The gospel is preached in external words which transform and remake the 'inner' person. It is this new agent who then goes about doing good works. It is, then, not enough to say that faith perfects one faculty or power within the person. Faith does deeper than that. In Luther's view, there is not one and the same person who has faith or who might not have faith. Here the one in control is the agent, the subject who does the works. Maybe this subject has faith, maybe not, but the subject in charge is the same. It is not the person who produces faith or the act of faith. It is faith which makes the person: *fides facit personam*.[9]

The mismatch between the life of virtue and the life of faith, hope and love is that faith, hope and love are a kind of 'suffering'. Luther notes this contrast when he says, 'other virtues may be perfected by *doing*; but faith, hope, and love, only by *suffering*; by suffering, I say; that is, by being passive under the divine operation'.[10] Being 'passive' in English usually means lazily and quietly accepting anything. In this context, however, being passive means receiving divine grace as *passio*, as passion, a fierce disturbance of the subject. Faith, hope and love are *passiones*, things that are received and suffered rather than *virtutes*, things that allow certain acts to be done.

If Luther is highly suspicious of speaking about faith, hope and love as virtues, the equally influential Reformer John Calvin (1509–1564) was concerned about the relationship between faith and love in Roman Catholic accounts of justification. In response Calvin argues that, at least in this life, faith enjoys a relative priority within the triad of faith, hope and love. In his *Institutes of the Christian Religion* (final Latin edition 1559), Calvin agrees that 'if we regard excellence, love of God should rightly take first place'.[11] Love alone will remain in the end, while faith and hope are passing realties that one needs in life but not in the hereafter. That being said, however, Calvin thinks that in this life faith, as the 'instrument' by which we receive the divine mercy and forgiveness, has logical priority over love and hope, and yet is never without them.

One of the definitions of faith Calvin offers us is 'knowledge of the divine benevolence towards us and a sure persuasion of its truth'.[12] When filled with the knowledge of God's mercy, goodness and love in Christ, one becomes 'wholly kindled to love God'.[13] It is faith, or knowledge of the divine beneficence, which first engenders love of God as a joyful and grateful response. Faith is also the 'the foundation upon which hope rests' and yet hope in turn 'nourishes and sustains

---

[9]Martin Luther, 'Die Zirkulardisputation *de veste nuptiale*', in Weimar Ausgabe (ed.) *Luthers Werke*, vol. 39/1 (Weimar: Hermann Böhlaus Nachfolger, 1926), pp. 264–333 (283).
[10]Martin Luther, *Commentary on the First Twenty-Two Psalms*, trans. Henry Cole, vol. 1 (London: Simpkin and Marshall, 1826), p. 258.
[11]John Calvin, *Institutes of the Christian Religion*, ed. John T. McNeill, trans. Ford Lewis Battles, vol. 1 (Louisville: Westminster John Knox Press, 1960), III.xviii.8, p. 829.
[12]Calvin, *Institutes*, III.ii.12, p. 556.
[13]Calvin, *Institutes*, III.ii.42, p. 589.

faith'.[14] Within this time of waiting, it is hope in God and his promises of eternal life which strengthens, refreshes, sustains and invigorates faith.

Similar sentiments can be found in Calvin's commentary on 1 Corinthians (1546).[15] In some aspects, love is superior to faith. Faith and hope can mean that one desires advantages for oneself, but love extends its benefits to others. Likewise, love will remain in the hereafter, while faith and hope will pass away. In many other aspects, however, faith is superior to love. For instance, faith is the cause, while love is the effect. In 1 Jn. 5.4, faith is called 'the victory that conquers the world'. Finally, it is by faith that we become adopted children of God, inherit eternal life and have Christ dwell within us (Eph. 3.17).

Study questions

1. How helpful is Aristotle's account of virtue for discussing faith, hope and love?
2. What sounds similar and what sounds different between Aquinas' and Luther's view of faith, hope and love as supernatural virtues and as things suffered?
3. What sounds similar and what sounds different between Aquinas' and Calvin's view of the relationship between faith, hope and love?

Further reading

Aristotle, *Nicomachean Ethics*, 1103a14–1103b26 (book 2, ch.1).

Aquinas, Thomas, *Summa theologica*, II–I, q. 62, aa. 1–4.

Calvin, John, *Institutes of the Christian Religion*, ed. John T. McNeill; trans. Ford Lewis Battles; vol. 1. (Louisville: Westminster John Knox Press, 1960), III. ii, 41–43, pp. 588–592.

Luther, Martin, 'Disputation against Scholastic Theology', in Timothy F. Lull (ed.), *Martin Luther's Basic Theological Writings* (Minneapolis: Fortress Press, 1989), pp. 13–20.

---

[14]Calvin, *Institutes*, III.ii.42, p. 590.

[15]John Calvin, *The First Epistle of Paul the Apostle to the Corinthians*, trans. John W. Fraser (Grand Rapids, Mich.: Eerdmans, 1960), pp. 282–283.

7

Faith and the Freedom to Serve: Martin Luther

The good news

A village was once plagued for years and years by a terrible dragon. Worn down by the tyranny of the vicious beast, the villagers were fearful of going outside and distrusted each other. Their homes became prisons with themselves as guards. One day a hero came and after a mighty battle defeated the villainous dragon. Those who had witnessed this event came to the village and proclaimed, 'The dragon has been slain! You're free!' The villagers shook off the dust and spite from their bones and joyfully left their houses, celebrating together the fall of the wicked tyrant.

An old and dying man had amassed a vast fortune. Having no children of his own, the wealthy man arranged his will such that all his earthly belongings should be given to his nephew, an unpleasant man who lived far away and thought little of his uncle, or anyone else.

Martin Luther uses two similar examples to express that the gospel is 'good news' (*euangelion*) and an inheritance which comes to those who have done nothing to merit it. Upon hearing that David slew Goliath, the women in the villages came out and danced in the streets (1 Sam. 18.6). Jesus Christ, Luther explains, is a true David who rescued those in captivity to sin, afflicted with death and overpowered by the devil, giving them in turn righteousness, life and peace with their God.[1] Likewise, Luther points out that another name for the gospel is 'testament', as in one's Last Will and Testament. In this case, the emphasis is placed upon Christ promising us everything he has and sealing this promise with his death. The only difference between a testament and a promise, Luther notes, is that a testament involves the death of the giver.[2]

The gospel is good news, a testament, a promise about who Jesus Christ is and what he has done for us. The gospel announces to us and assures us that our sins are forgiven, that the great dragon is defeated and that death itself has been swallowed up. As with any promise or good news, the most one can do is trust and believe in the one who has promised these things; everything else has already been done.[3] Faith,

---

[1]Martin Luther, 'Preface to the New Testament', in Timothy F. Lull (ed.), *Martin Luther's Basic Theological Writings* (Minneapolis: Fortress Press, 1989), pp. 112–117 (113).

[2]Martin Luther, 'Babylonian Captivity of the Church', *Martin Luther's Basic Theological Writings*, pp. 267–313 (294).

[3]Luther, 'Babylonian Captivity', p. 298.

then, means trusting that God is and will be faithful in his promises (Heb. 10.23).[4] It means being confident not in ourselves, but in the one who has spoken these promises. It would be strange to focus the action in the above stories not on the benefactors but instead on the reactions of the recipients: '*I* was the one who walked outside of my house when I heard the news about the dragon!' or '*I* was the one who boldly said "yes" to all that money!'[5] But is receiving a promise or being given an inheritance an act which we could call our own?

Faith comes from hearing (Rom. 10.7), just as promises are spoken in words and wills are read aloud. These are not words or speech acts that we say to ourselves or invent in the quiet of our own hearts. These are noisy, physical and external words (*verbum externum*) that are spoken to us. Luther calls the sacraments 'visible signs', a kind of visible word inasmuch as the water, bread and cup take part in God's promises to us.[6] Luther defines the preaching of Word and the sacraments as 'external acts', and the presence and working of the Holy Spirit inside the Christian as an 'internal act'. So much emphasis is placed upon the embodied, physical reality of these words and promises that Luther can argue that '[t]he inward experience follows and is effected by the outward. God has determined to give the inward to no one except through the outward'.[7] The promises of the gospel are spoken aloud and performed, and they concern me. They call me to trust and believe not myself, not even my own faith and belief, but to have confidence and gratitude in the one who promises.

A Christian has everything because Jesus Christ has promised and bequeathed everything. Having all, what is there left for the Christian to do? Luther's answer in his 1520 treatise 'The Freedom of a Christian' is that the Christian's life should be guided by this one thought alone: 'that he may serve and benefit others in all that he does, considering nothing except the need and advantage of his neighbor'.[8]

Free and bound

In 1 Cor. 9.19 the apostle Paul writes, 'For although I am free with respect to all, I have made myself a slave to all, so that I might win more of them.' This jarring combination of being free yet bound to one another is also found in Rom. 13.8: 'Owe no one anything, except to love one another.' The first half of the verse declares my freedom from debt and obligation to others and hints that I might finally be free of the interference and presence of others; the second half requires me to surrender what is dearest and most personal: my love. Luther thinks that Paul sees this pattern

---

[4]Luther, 'Babylonian Captivity', p. 298.

[5]Luther, 'Babylonian Captivity', p. 303.

[6]That a sacrament needs such a 'visible sign' was even part of Luther's argument that only baptism and the Lord's Supper are sacraments properly understood.

[7]Martin Luther, 'Against the Heavenly Prophets in the Matter of Images and the Sacraments', in Conrad Bergendoff (ed.), trans. Berhard Erling and Conrad Bergendoff, *Luther Works*, vol. 40 (Philadelphia: Muhlenberg Press, 1958), pp. 79–223 (146).

[8]Martin Luther, 'Freedom of a Christian', *Martin Luther's Basic Theological Writings*, pp. 585–629 (617).

of being free and yet bound in Jesus Christ. Paul begins a hymn with the following words: 'Let the same mind be in you that was in Christ Jesus.' Christ 'was in the form of God' and yet 'emptied himself, taking the form of slave' (Phil. 2.6–7). As one who has been liberated and given everything, a Christian must do likewise.

The Christian freedom that faith brings about is freedom to serve and love others. Luther calls the freedom of a Christian the 'freedom of love'.[9] So tightly bound together are faith in God and love of neighbour that Luther can say that 'faith is the agent, love is the act',[10] and that 'it is impossible, indeed, to separate works from faith, just as it is impossible to separate light from fire'.[11] 'O, when it comes to faith what a living, creative, active, powerful thing it is.'[12] This love and service of the other does not justify us before God or entail that we have merited God's love.[13] It comes from unshakeable confidence in the sufficiency of God's grace to us and in the presence and outworking of the Holy Spirit.

In giving us the freedom to serve and love, Christ frees us from ourselves. Luther borrows a line from Augustine to describe sin as being curved in upon oneself (*incurvatus in se*). This being curved in upon myself takes a myriad of forms, from thinking myself as the centre of the universe, to trusting in myself and my own abilities rather than on God, to seeking my profit and advantage before that of others. It can even take root in my most selfless acts of service or worship inasmuch as I think they may purge my sins, make me better than my worldly neighbours or give me reason to boast. The call of faith to Christian freedom is a call away from all forms of self-concern, pride and anxiety, even the religious ones.[14]

Luther ups the ante by remarking that a Christian does not live in herself, but lives in Christ through faith and in the neighbour through love. What does it mean to live 'in' Christ or 'in' the other as opposed to living 'in' myself? It is not simply that I have been made freed and so then decide in my freedom to trust in God and to serve and love my neighbour. Locked within myself, I am free as I am 'in' the other, with them, loving them, suffering with them and serving them. It is in my trust in God and in love that I am free, free from sin, from working for myself, from considering myself the centre of all.

Christian freedom, then, is not the lack of any restraints or limits upon my will and desires. It is not the ability to do whatever I please without regard for anyone else. (In fact, this common definition of freedom seems suspiciously close to being curved in upon ourselves!) Instead Christian freedom has a certain kind of form, a direction and a goal. For Luther the shape of Christian freedom to serve and love is given in the Ten Commandments, which he says is 'the greatest treasure God has

---

[9]Luther, 'Freedom of a Christian', p. 621.

[10]Martin Luther, *Luthers Werke* (Weimar Ausgabe, vol. 17/II; Weimar: Hermann Böhlaus Nachfolger, 1927), p. 98, quoted in Bernd Wannenwetsch, 'Luther's Moral Theology', in Donald H. McKim (ed.), *The Cambridge Companion to Martin Luther* (Cambridge: Cambridge University Press, 2003), pp. 120–135 (128).

[11]Martin Luther, 'Preface to the Epistle of St. Paul to the Romans', in John Dillenberger (ed.), *Martin Luther: Selections from His Writings* (New York: Anchor Books, 1962), pp. 19–34 (24).

[12]Luther, 'Preface to the Epistle to the Romans', p. 24.

[13]'Our faith in Christ does not free us from works but from false opinions concerning works, that is, from the foolish presumption that justification is acquired by works.' Luther, 'Freedom of a Christian', p. 625.

[14]Luther, 'Freedom of a Christian', p. 622.

given us'.[15] Luther regards the Ten Commandments as a practical, everyday guide to living with and serving one another, one which flows out of and returns to faith and confidence that God is God (the First Commandment).

Faith and reason

Luther was an outspoken scourge of reason, infamously labelling reason the 'devil's whore' and 'Aristotle's evil brew', and even speaking about 'sacrificing reason': one must 'sacrifice reason in the morning and glorify God in the evening'.[16] Nonetheless, Luther also praises reason, the sciences and the practical arts as 'a divine blessing', 'an indispensable guide to life and learning', with reason in particular being 'the most important and the highest rank among all things and, in comparison with other things in this life, the best and something divine'.[17] Even the Fall was not able to erase the good gift which God gave to humanity in the form of reason.

Luther adopts the medieval distinction between 'temporal matters' and 'spiritual matters', or 'matters below' and 'matters above'. In everyday matters, our reason operates just fine. For Luther, 'reason' is usually a matter of thinking about practical matters, the things we do, or experiential matters, the things we have felt, seen and experienced. Luther can praise human ingenuity in the arts and sciences and human craftsmanship in building roads, houses and boats, and in planting and raising food. Luther can even say, 'In all these things exercise your mind to the best of your ability!'[18] Reason can even know the 'natural law', which for Luther means the Ten Commandments that God gave to Moses. Luther jokes that Moses 'came too late' inasmuch as nature itself teaches us what the Ten Commandments ask of us to do.[19] Most people (even princes!) can know what is right and wrong in everyday matters simply by following their reason. Whether they do the right thing or not does not cancel out the fact that reason accomplishes beneficial and creative things.

In spiritual matters, however, Luther is much less confident about reason's ability. He thinks, for instance, that people can look around at history, nature, human society and even their own lives, and reasonably conclude that there is no God, or that God must hate us, or that God will judge us according to what we do, or that God exists in his own splendid glory far away from the sufferings of his creatures.[20] Even the

---

[15]Martin Luther, 'Large Catechism', in Robert Kolb and Timothy J. Wengert (ed.), trans. Charles Arand et al., *The Book of Concord: The Confessions of the Evangelical Lutheran Church* (Minneapolis: Fortress Press, 2000), pp. 377–480 (431).

[16]Martin Luther, 'Commentary on Galatians', in John Dillenberger (ed.), *Martin Luther: Selections from his Writings* (New York: Anchor Books, 1962), pp. 99–165 (131).

[17]Martin Luther, 'Disputation on Humanity', in Lewis W. Spitz (ed.), *Luther's Works*, vol. 34 (Philadelphia: Muhlenberg Press, 1960), pp. 135–144 (137).

[18]Martin Luther, *A Compend of Luther's Theology*, ed. Hugh Thompson Kerr (Philadelphia: Westminster Press, 1943), p. 3.

[19]Martin Luther, 'Against the Sabbatarians: Letter to a Good Friend', in F. Sherman (ed.), trans. Martin H. Bertram, *Luther's Works*, vol. 47 (Philadelphia: Fortress Press, 1971), pp. 59–98 (89).

[20]Martin Luther, 'Bondage of the Will', in John Dillenberger (ed.), *Martin Luther: Selections from his Writings* (New York: Anchor Books, 1962), pp. 166–203 (201).

line about 'sacrificing reason' in the morning is about the danger of reason pointing out your sins and leading you to conclude that Jesus Christ is angry with you. The consolation Luther gives to reason is that it cannot know what God is, but can know 'what God is not'. The primary issue, for Luther, is not whether God exists, but whether or not this God is the God of Jesus Christ, who is merciful, slow to anger, quick to forgive and who loved us before we loved God in return. For Luther, it is better to cling to the promises of the gospel than to a reason which might remind you that in life you can never get something for nothing, so work harder to please God and earn what God might deign to give you.[21] Luther's worry is that looking around at our everyday experiences, reason might try to tell you that God acts just like humans do, in terms of merit, reward and punishment, and helps only those whom God likes or who can do something for God in return; *quid pro quo*! Luther thinks that it is to this God, a God who gives only if you give something first, or even an angry God, where thinking about God 'according to human standards' will lead us. If this is what reason will conclude when thinking about 'spiritual matters', then surely Luther is right to prefer the foolishness of the Cross and the gospel to the wisdom of the world!

In this way, 'reason' and faith will certainly do battle over who God is; who we are; and what we are to think, do and hope for. And as Luther thinks, the devil will perpetually try to make us doubt God and his promises and to look at ourselves and despair, and so this battle will continue. Yet Luther can also write about the renewing of reason in the light of faith. He can point to the traditional account of reason following faith in the line of 'If you do not believe, you will not understand' (*Nisi credideritis, non intelligetis*), the pre-Vulgate version of Isa. 7.9 so cherished by Augustine and Anselm.[22] Likewise, just as the life of faith means that our tongues are now used to praise God rather than curse others, so too can illuminated reason further and advance faith:

> The understanding, through faith, receives life from faith; that which was dead, is made alive again; like as our bodies, in light day, when it is clear and bright, are better disposed, rise, move, walk, &c., more readily and safely than they do in the dark night, so it is with human reason, which strives not against faith, when enlightened, but rather furthers and advances it.[23]

Study questions

1. What do you find helpful in the two stories at the start of the chapter when thinking about faith? What do you find unhelpful about them?

---

[21]Luther, 'Commentary on Galatians', p. 132.
[22]Martin Luther, 'On the Papacy in Rome, Against the Most Celebrated Romanist in Leipzig', in Eric W. Gritsch (ed.), trans. Eric W. and Ruth C. Gritsch, *Luther's Works*, vol. 39 (Philadelphia: Fortress Press, 1970), pp. 49–104 (63).
[23]Martin Luther, *The Table Talk of Martin Luther*, ed. and trans. William Hazlitt (London: Bell & Daldy, 1972), CCXCIV, p. 144.

2. What do you think is the relationship between faith, freedom and love?

3. Does Luther's distinction about reason's different abilities in 'matters above' and in 'matters below' actually work?

Further reading

Luther, Martin, 'Preface to the New Testament', in Timothy F. Lull (ed.), *Martin Luther's Basic Theological Writings* (Minneapolis: Fortress Press, 1989), pp. 112–117.
———, 'The Freedom of a Christian', in Timothy F. Lull (ed.), *Martin Luther's Basic Theological Writings* (Minneapolis: Fortress Press, 1989), pp.595–629.

8

Faith as Knowledge, Assent and Trust: Protestant Scholasticism

What is Protestant Scholasticism?

Roman Catholicism is not the only branch of Western Christianity to have had a scholastic period. Protestantism enjoyed its own flowering of scholastic thought from the sixteenth to the eighteenth centuries (roughly from between 1560 and 1800). Just as their Roman Catholic counterparts, the Protestant Scholastics employed and developed the language and logic of Aristotle, presented and refuted their opponents' positions, appealed to certain set authorities and principles and had a predilection for making ever finer and more precise distinctions. Though bound together by the claims of the various Reformations and the scholastic method, the theology and teaching of Protestant Scholasticism should not be thought of as one homogenous block. The two dominant and often contending branches of this movement were made up of Lutheran and Reformed theologians, but one could also say that there were Anglican and Arminian Scholastics. Even the Lutheran and Reformed branches of this period could be divided up into smaller contesting groups.

As for their understanding of faith, the Protestant Scholastics quickly identified and settled upon faith having three different aspects: knowledge (*notitia*), assent (*assensus*) and trust (*fiducia*). Generally speaking, knowledge and assent were thought to be matters of the intellect, while trust or confidence was a matter of the will or affections. There were some disagreements: assent could be thought to concern the will; the chief element of faith was usually trust but sometimes assent; and at times trust or confidence was not technically part of faith but consequent upon it. In general, however, there was a remarkable consensus on this issue with some squabbling over minutiae. While all three of these different aspects of faith can be found in earlier Reformers such as Luther, Calvin and Zwingli, it was their immediate followers who provided this view of faith that would come to characterize Protestant Scholasticism.

The Lutheran Scholastics

Luther was not a systematic theologian in our contemporary sense. He never wrote a systematic theology, and most of his theology is found in his biblical commentaries, sermons and catechisms. It is his follower Melanchthon who is often taken as the first systematizer of Luther's insights. It was the precocious Melanchthon who quite early on produced the earliest 'systematic theology' of Protestantism in his *Loci communes* (1521), written when he was twenty-four years old. No less than with Luther, Melanchthon emphasizes that faith is a matter of trust in the promises of the gospel: 'Faith is thus nothing other than trust in the divine mercy which is promised to us in Christ.'[1] Faith is not only a knowledge of certain historical events (*fides historica*), but contains a personal trust which expects mercy, help and consolation from God. Faith is trust in God's promises in Christ. Likewise, in his *Apology to the Marburg Confession* from some ten years later, Melanchthon argues that historical knowledge does not yet exhaust the nature of faith, for faith also entails an assent to the promise that our sins are forgiven in Christ and a desire to receive these promises.[2]

While all of the pieces of faith as knowledge, assent and trust are there in Melanchthon, it is usually thought that Martin Chemnitz (1522–1586), one of Melanchthon's followers, was the first theologian to systematize this way of handling faith. In Chemnitz's *Loci theologici*, itself a commentary and expansion upon Melanchthon's *Loci communes*, we find this statement:

> [F]aith in the article of justification must be understood not only as knowledge and general assent, stating in a general way that the Gospel is true, but that at the same time it includes the activities of the will and the heart; that is, it is a desire and trust which, in the struggle with sin and the wrath of God, applies the promise of grace to each individual, so that each person includes himself in the general promise given to believers.[3]

Faith, then, has three aspects or modes. As knowledge, faith understands the gospel. As assent, faith holds the gospel to be true. As desire and trust, faith accepts that the promises of the gospel include oneself. Faith is a full confidence and persuasion that the promises of the gospel are true. Chemnitz also thinks the triad of knowledge, assent and trust applies not only to the New Testament's understanding of faith but to the Old Testament's use of 'believe' and 'trust'.

Understanding faith to be knowledge, assent and trust filtered down into later Lutheran Scholastics, including Johannes Andreas Quenstedt (1617–1688) and David Hollaz (1648–1713). Quenstedt, for instance, even sees this triad of faith expressed in Jn. 14:10–12. While the Greek verb used in all three verses is the same (*pisteuo*), Quenstedt says that verse 10 refers to faith as knowledge, verse 11 to faith as assent and verse 12 to faith as trust or confidence.[4] Hollaz can put the matter fairly simply, noting 'Faith is in the intellect with respect to knowledge; and assent,

---

[1] Phillip Melanchthon, *Loci communes (1521): Lateinisch-Deutsch*, trans. Horst Georg Pöhlmann (Gütersloh: Mohn, 1993), pp. 218–219.

[2] Philip Melanchthon, 'Apology of the Augsburg Confession', in *The Book of Concord: The Confessions of the Evangelical Lutheran Church*, ed. By Robert Kolb and Timothy J. Wengert, trans. Charles Arand, Robert Kolb, Timothy Wengert, Eric Gritsch, William Russell, Jane Strohl, James Schaaf (Minneapolis: Fortress Press, 2000), pp. 107–294.

[3] Martin Chemnitz, *Loci Theologici*, trans. J. A. O. Preus, vol. 2 (St. Louis: Concordia Publishing House, 1989), p. 493.

[4] Heinrich Schmid, *The Doctrinal Theology of the Evangelical Lutheran Church*, trans. Charles A. Hay and Henry E. Jacobs (Philadelphia: United Lutheran Publication House, 3rd ed., 1899; reprint, Minneapolis: Augsburg Publishing House, 1961), p. 414.

in the will with respect to confidence'.[5] Both Quenstedt and Hollaz also find this account of faith in the venerable triad of *credere Deum*, *credere Deo* and *credere in Deum*, which can be found in Augustine, Peter Lombard and Thomas Aquinas. [6] As Quenstedt sees it, *credere Deum* means to believe that God exists; *credere Deo* means to believe that what God says is true; and *credere in Deum* means to love and cling to God.[7]

The Reformed Scholastics

The idea that faith entails knowledge, assent and trust was also taken up by most Reformed Scholastics, including James (Jacobus) Arminius.[8] In this regard, they not only had Melanchthon's *Loci communes* for their inspiration, but even the later editions of Calvin's *Institutes of the Christian Religion*. In the 1559 edition of the *Institutes*, for example, Calvin complains about earlier Roman Catholic Scholastics who have gone entirely astray when identifying faith 'with a bare and simple assent arising out of knowledge, and leave out confidence and assurance of heart'.[9] Throughout his remarks on faith, Calvin charges his Roman Catholic opponents, perhaps unfairly, with understanding faith to be solely knowledge and assent (and so a matter of the intellect), and thus neglecting faith as trust and confidence (as also a matter of the heart). There is some small irony here, for the earlier editions of Calvin's *Institutes* tended to interpret faith primarily as knowledge. Some scholars have argued that the growing emphasis on faith as heartfelt trust in God's promises in the later editions is due to the influence of Melanchthon's 1536–1537 *Loci communes* on Calvin.[10]

The Swiss theologian Johannes Wolleb (1589–1629) offers a fine example of both the use of Aristotelian terminology as well as this account of faith. In his *Compendium theologiae christianae* (1626), for instance, Wolleb notes that the 'efficient cause' of faith is God and that its 'instrumental cause' is the preaching of the gospel. Generally speaking, the 'matter' or 'object' of faith is the Word of God, but more particularly it is the free promises of Christ. The 'form' of faith, finally, is knowledge, assent and trust. For Wollebius, knowledge means understanding all that is necessary for salvation; assent means firmly believing that these things are true; and trust means that the believer holds that the gospel's promises apply to herself or himself.[11]

---

[5]Schmid, *Doctrinal Theology of the Lutheran Church*, p. 414.

[6]Also from Augustine, although in inchoate form, is the threefold distinction of *credere deo*, *credere deum* and *credere in deum*: see *Sermo* 61.2. For Peter Lombard, see *Sentences* III, 23 C & D. As for Thomas Aquinas, see *Summa theologica*, II–II, q. 2., a. 2.

[7]Schmid, *Doctrinal Theology of the Lutheran Church*, p. 414.

[8]James Arminius, *The Works of James Arminius*, ed. James Nichols, vol. 2 (London: Longman, Bees, Orme, Brown, and Green, 1828), pp. 400–401.

[9]Calvin, *Institutes*, III.II.33, p. 581.

[10]Richard A. Muller, *The Unaccommodated Calvin: Studies in the Foundation of a Theological Tradition* (Oxford: Oxford University Press, 2000), p. 163.

[11]Johannes Wollebius, 'Compendium Theologiae Christianae', in *Reformed Dogmatics: J. Wollebius, G. Voetius, F. Turretin* (ed. and trans. John W. Beardslee III, (New York: Oxford University Press, 1965), pp. 26–262 (162–163).

The highly influential Swiss-Italian theologian Francis Turretin (1623–1687) also highlights faith as a multifaceted reality. In his *Institutes of Elenctic Theology* (1679–1685), which became widely used as a textbook, Turretin notes that faith is not just one simple habit and that it involves both the intellect and the will. Faith is a varied and composite reality, and when theologians consider faith to have just one aspect (assent), or two (knowledge and assent) or three (knowledge, assent and trust), they are attempting to unfold and describe a complex reality. Faithful to his own insight regarding the complexity of faith, Turretin develops no less than seven different aspects of faith (perhaps only outdone in sheer number by Hermann Witsius, who identifies nine).[12] He does think, however, that these seven can be referred to the traditional three.

The first three acts of faith which Turretin discusses are the familiar knowledge, assent and trust. As knowledge, faith understands all the things to be believed, either of God or of humanity's misery. As 'theoretical assent', faith believes the above to be true. As 'practical assent' or 'fiducial assent', faith is fully persuaded that God is the highest good and thus worthy of love and desire. It is when he reaches the fourth through seventh acts of faith that Turretin richly expands its affective element. The fourth act of faith is 'the act of refuge', which means fleeing to Christ as the one who forgives sins and to whom one is to be united. The fifth is the reception of Christ, which means being united with him such that 'we are bone of his bone and flesh of his flesh and one with him'.[13] The soul flees to Christ and Christ offers himself and all his benefits and blessings. One participates in the blessings of Christ inasmuch as one is united with him: 'From this union of persons arises the participation in the blessings of Christ, to which (by union with him) we acquire a right (to wit, justification, adoption, sanctification, and glorification).'[14] The sixth act of faith is reflexive. Having been united with Christ and having received his blessings, believers know that Christ belongs to them, and they to Christ, and that nothing can separate them from his love. The seventh act of faith is consolation and confidence, and is characterized by joy, tranquillity, peace and delight. Confident and assured of having been united to Christ, the believer rejoices in him, overcomes adversity and continues to go about doing good works, confident that the one who began them will also perfect them (Phil. 1.6).

The aftermath

The general decline of Protestant Scholasticism from its theological dominance near the end of the eighteenth century has been linked to the effects of pietism, rationalism and historical-critical methods of interpreting Scripture. In Germany and Prussia in particular, the language and logic of Aristotle was largely replaced by

---

[12]Herman Witsius, *The Oeconomy of the Covenants between God and Man*, trans. William Crookshank, vol. 1 (Edinburgh: Turnbull, 1803), III.VII.VIII–XXVII, pp. 379–389.

[13]Francis Turretin, *Institutes of Elenctic Theology*, ed. James T. Dennison Jr., trans. George Musgrave Giger (New Jersey: Presbyterian and Reformed Publishing, 1994), p. 563.

[14]Turretin, *Institutes of Elenctic Theology*, p. 562.

that of Kant, Hegel and the Romantics. Yet even those theologians who attempted to mediate between Protestant thought and the philosophies of the Enlightenment often dealt with faith as knowledge, assent and trust, even if critically. The so-called 'modern theologians', such as Albrecht Ritschl (1822–1889) and Wilhelm Herrmann (1846–1922), tended to seize upon faith as trust in the promise of God's forgiveness and either criticized or downplayed understanding faith as knowledge or assent. By emphasizing faith as trust, a self-consciously modern Protestant theology could still accept the insights of contemporary intellectual culture, particularly higher criticism of Scripture and secular accounts of church history, while not falling into scepticism or rationalism. Conversely, characterizing faith as knowledge, assent and trust still continued on in influential theologians such as the Dutch Herman Bavinck (1854–1921)[15] and the American Presbyterian Charles Hodge (1797–1878),[16] past principal of Princeton Theological Seminary and leader of the Princeton Theology.

Study questions

1. What does distinguishing faith as knowledge, assent and trust help to illuminate?
2. What does distinguishing faith as knowledge, assent and trust hide or obscure?
3. Which one of these three do you think is the 'principal part' of faith?
4. How might one see faith as one or as unified within this framework?

Further reading

Chemnitz, Martin, *Loci Theologici*, trans. J. A. O. Preus; vol. 2. (St. Louis: Concordia Publishing House, 1989), pp. 490–499.

Melanchthon, Phillip, 'Justification and Faith', from *Loci communes*. One readily available edition is *Melanchthon and Bucer* ed. Wilhelm Pauck (Philadelphia: Westminster John Knox Press, 1969), pp. 88–108.

Turretin, Francis, Institutes of Elenctic Theology, ed. James T. Dennison Jr.; trans. George Musgrave Giger. (New Jersey: Presbyterian and Reformed Publishing, 1994), pp. 560–564.

---

[15]Herman Bavinck, *Reformed Dogmatics*, vol. 4, *Holy Spirit, Church, New Creation*, ed. John Bolt, trans. John Vriend (Grand Rapids, Mich.: Baker Academic, 2008), pp. 126–132.

[16]Charles Hodge, *Systematic Theology*, vol. 3 (New York: Scribner and Sons, 1873), p. 91.

9
Faith and Rebirth: Pietism

Born from above

Jesus answered him, 'Very truly, I tell you, no one can see the kingdom of God without being born from above'. (John 3.3)

Jesus' conversation with the Pharisee Nicodemus in Jn. 3 is full of the language of birth. In the stillness of the night, Jesus tells Nicodemus that he must be 'born from above' (Jn. 3.3), 'born of water and Spirit' (3.7) and simply 'born of the Spirit' (3.8). It is an evocative and elusive set of images. That this conversation is set during the night makes Jesus' talk of light and darkness at the end of the chapter all the more ironic. Jesus is the light of the world (Jn. 8.12) and yet Nicodemus comes to him in the darkness. Nicodemus is a teacher of Israel, and therefore knows that Jesus' signs and deeds can only come from one in whom God is present. Yet his befuddlement at Jesus' talk of being born from above – 'How can anyone be born after having grown old?' (3.4) – seems only reasonable. The familiarity and current use of the phrase 'born again' makes it difficult to recognize how strange and stark these words of Jesus are.

The New Testament is full of notions of rebirth, new creation and the new person, and thus so are the various intellectual and spiritual traditions within Christianity. Rebirth signals the beginning of a process, a beginning of growth. Within the modern period the idea that faith is a rebirth, conversion and regeneration of the mind and especially of the heart can be seen in such different groups as the Reformed English Puritans, the Catholic French Jansenists and the primarily Lutheran Continental Pietists. It is with this last group in particular that we will be concerned in this unit, as the notion of rebirth or conversion has been called 'the central expression for the self-understanding of Pietism'.[1]

Pietism

Ask any historian about Pietism and they will tell you that it was a diverse seventeenth- and eighteenth-century movement that started in Germany as a response to the scholasticism and intellectualism of Lutheran Orthodoxy and was both influenced by and influenced in turn religious movements in England and the

---

[1]Markus Matthias, 'Bekehrung und Wiedergeburt', in Hartmut Lehmann (ed.), *Geschichte des Pietismus*, vol. 4, *Glaubenswelt und Lebenswelt* (Göttingen: Vandenhoeck & Ruprecht, 2004), pp. 49–79 (49).

Netherlands. In order to see how truly influential Pietism has been, however, we need only offer a brief account of what the Pietists generally thought faith and the life of faith to be. Faith is an experiential, personal and practical affair, a matter of the heart. It involves a specific moment of conversion, of going through a crisis. These conversion stories often involve an initial period of youthful vanity and debauchery and then being reborn. Yet being reborn is only the start of a new life characterized by holiness and godly living. This new life is best encouraged by daily personal devotions and Scripture reading, and by meeting in small, unofficial groups in which to pray, practice spiritual exercises and discuss Scripture together. While belief in certain doctrines is good and salutary, all the head knowledge in the world does not matter unless one also feels and trusts in God's mercy in Jesus Christ with one's whole heart. The simple church of the New Testament is an ideal and model to which contemporary believers and churches should always try to return. It is a testament to the influence and attraction of Pietism that most of these ideas and practices sound familiar.

The honour of being the founder of Pietism typically goes to the Lutheran pastor Philipp Jacob Spener (1635–1705), who published his short booklet *Pia desideria* ('Pious Longings') in 1675. *Pia desideria* was a call for reform, or as the subtitle of the book aptly puts it, 'A Heartfelt Desire for a God-Pleasing Reform of the True Evangelical Church, Together with Several Simple Proposals Looking toward this End'.[2] In the first part of the work, Spener deals with the corruptions and defects he sees within the civil authorities, the clergy and among lay Christians. In the second part, Spener argues that better conditions within the church are indeed possible. Here Spener points to the example of the early church, which 'was in such a blessed state that as a rule Christians could be identified by their godly life, which distinguished them from other people'.[3] The early Christians examined and tested the lives of their members, held high standards for one another and exhibited a fervent love among themselves. The Holy Spirit was able to bestow such gifts on the early Christians and is no less able to sanctify believers now.

We meet Spener's 'several simple proposals' in the third part, where he details six practical recommendations for reform. These include a greater use of Scripture in preaching, private reading and in smaller meetings, and increased participation among laypeople, following Luther's priesthood of all believers. Believers should be taught that Christianity is not simply a matter of knowledge, but of practice, most especially love. Religious debates among different groups should be conducted in love and holiness, which seems a sensible recommendation after the Thirty Years War (1618–1648). Ministers should receive better training and ministry schools should be filled with the Holy Spirit rather than being places of worldliness filled with ambition, carousing and brawling. Spener says, 'Study without piety is worthless,'[4] and so both professors and students should strive for growth in holiness, and that students should admonish and encourage each other in brotherly love. Sermons should keep in view ordinary Christians and their edification, for '[o]ur whole

---

[2]Philipp Jacob Spener, *Pia desideria*, ed. and trans. Theodore G. Tappert (Philadelphia: Fortress Press, 1964), p. 29.
[3]Spener, *Pia Desideria*, pp. 81–82.
[4]Spener, *Pia Desideria*, p. 104.

Christian religion consists of the inner man or new man, whose soul is faith and whose expressions are the fruits of life, and all sermons should be aimed at this'.[5]

Another notable figure in the history of Pietism was the count Nikolas Ludwig von Zizendorf (1700–1760). In 1722, Zizendorf offered some land to wandering religious groups who had been persecuted by religious authorities in Moravia and Bohemia (present-day Czech Republic). These Moravians set up a village called 'Herrnhut', which became a kind of asylum for religious groups unwelcome in their respective established churches for one reason or another. As these groups held different beliefs, the practicalities of living together meant that some doctrinal tolerance was necessary. The general gist of the community's guidelines can be seen in the first three points of a document called 'Brotherly Union and Agreement at Herrnhut'. The first is that a work of God has built Herrnhut, and it is not to be a city but an establishment for the 'Brethren'.[6] The second is that the old inhabitants of the village 'must remain in a constant bond of love with all children of God belonging to different religious persuasions'.[7] The community's members are not to judge each other's beliefs or argue about them, but only follow 'the pure evangelical doctrine, simplicity, and grace'.[8] Some of this 'pure evangelical doctrine' is spelled out in the third guideline. Herrnhuters are to confess that their 'awakening and salvation' belong solely to Christ, that they could not stand for even one moment to be without the mercy of God in Christ and that without Christ nothing is of value before God. It also notes that one is not a genuine brother or sister of Herrnhut unless one daily proves that it is his or her full intent to be free from sin; to seek more holiness each day; to grow in the Lord's likeness; to be free of vanity, spiritual idolatry and self-will; and to walk as Jesus did, bearing shame and reproach.

As with many other Pietists, Zizendorf himself emphasized the importance of conversion and rebirth, the imitation of Christ and the joy and assurance which accompany faith, and was suspicious of theological systems. Some of the other distinctive traits of Pietism can also be seen in his reinterpretation of the contrast between *fides implicata* and *fides explicata*. For Zizendorf, *fides implicata* no longer means believing in the general teaching of the church, but an 'affective believing with the heart', which is hidden from others. This inner faith moves from distress over one's sin and present misery to a bold trust and love of the Saviour. It is not reason or logical proofs which can lead to this type of conversion. Instead, implicit faith is

the faith which is God's work in the heart in the middle of our stillness, where we and he have to do with each other alone, where nothing comes between us and him – no man, no book, no knowledge, no learning, not even the most necessary truths – but only the distress, the sinner's shame, and the faithfulness of the shepherd.[9]

---

[5]Spener, *Pia Desideria*, p. 116.

[6]'Brotherly Union and Agreement at Herrnhut', in Peter C. Erb (ed.), *The Pietists: Selected Writings* (New York: Paulist Press, 1983), pp. 325–330 (325).

[7]'Brotherly Union and Agreement at Herrnhut,' p. 325.

[8]'Brotherly Union and Agreement at Herrnhut,' p. 325.

[9]Zizendorf, Count Nicolaus, 'Concerning Saving Faith', in Peter C. Erb (ed.), The Pietists: Selected Writings (New York: Paulist Press, 1983), pp. 304–310 (308).

Fides explicata is the upwelling and pouring out of faith to others. The believer 'in his inmost person' knows the mercy and majesty of the Saviour, who is he and what he has done, and is then able to express outwardly what are the reasons of his heart. This outward expression, both in words and in love, is so confident, convincing and beautiful that it can edify the spiritual lives of all who witness it.

The Puritans

While somewhat different from the Continental Pietists, the English Puritans were also known for their focus on the practical, the importance of regular self-examination, a longing for holiness and a desire for higher standards of morality and attention to duties. Conversion narratives and emphases upon rebirth or being born again are also prominent, as can be seen in the host of personal diaries of Puritans from the seventeenth and eighteenth centuries. The Puritans were a controversial bunch. The name 'Puritan' itself began as negative term, and these fervent believers were also called 'Precisians', for their emphasis upon precise and exacting devotional practices. The fact that they were not always welcome in England meant that Puritans were constantly on the move. This gave them opportunities to spread their understanding of faith and the life of faith. They influenced Reformed thought in the Netherlands, particularly through William Ames (1576–1633), and also left an indelible mark upon religious life in the American colonies. The English Puritan John Winthrop (1588–1649) even received permission to set up a Puritan colony in Massachusetts Bay. Winthrop envisioned that this religious community would serve as a 'City upon a Hill' (Mt 5.14) which could show the nations what a Christian commonwealth truly looked like.[10]

Wesley and Christian perfection

Perhaps the strongest account of the regeneration of the heart was offered by the Anglican minister John Wesley (1703–1791), typically considered the co-founder of the Methodists along with his brother Charles. A prolific preacher, writer and a tireless reformer, Wesley was influenced in significant ways by the Puritans and the Pietists. (Wesley had, in fact, several fateful encounters with Moravians in England and the Colonies, spent several months at Herrnhut and translated some of the hymns of the German Pietists, including Zizendorf, into English.) One of Wesley's most significant legacies is his promotion of the idea of 'Christian perfection', complete sanctification and renewal, a total 'circumcision of the heart' (Rom. 3.29). On Wesley's account, after being reborn, believers gradually die to sin and grow

---

[10]See John Winthrop's famous 1630 sermon preached aboard a ship bound for the New World, 'A Model of Christian Charity', in Wayne Franklin, Philip F. Gura and Arnold Krupat (eds), *The Norton Anthology of American Literature*, vol. A, *Beginnings to 1820* (New York: Norton, 2007), pp. 165–185.

in grace. At some point in their life, whether as a result of a process or in one instantaneous moment, a Christian could be saved entirely from the power of sin by the Holy Spirit and love with a fully renewed heart. 'Christian perfection' was Wesley's term for being made perfect in one's love of both God and neighbour, as thus being made like Christ. While believers may pray and hope for such a blessing from the Holy Spirit, the initiative remains wholly God's: 'the Lord your God will circumcise your heart and the heart of your descendants, so that you will love the Lord your God with all your heart and with all your soul, in order that you may live' (Deut. 30.6). In the words of Wesley, Christian perfection is 'loving God with all our heart, mind, soul, and strength. This implies that no wrong temper, none contrary to love, remains in the soul; and that all the thoughts, words, and actions are governed by pure love'.[11] Wesley thought that Christian perfection was not merely a pleasant idea or a distant hope, but a reality which present-day Christians could experience.

In his sermons and writings on Christian perfection, Wesley often attempts to clear up various misunderstandings regarding his doctrine of Christian perfection. Complete sanctification does not mean that one is infallible or no longer beset by temptations or worldly woes. While Christian perfection means that one is pure in love and in intention, it is not merely a matter of being sincere or simply being really nice. Notions of sincerity or niceness seem too narrow for what Wesley has in mind. Christian perfection is 'love filling the heart, expelling pride, anger, desire, self-will; rejoicing evermore, praying without ceasing, and in everything giving thanks'.[12] Likewise Christian perfection is not some static state, for believers can still grow in perfection and should remain watchful and diligent so as not to lose this gift. While admitting that losing such a perfect love was indeed possible, Wesley always preferred emphasizing the positive aspects of Christian perfection and his hope that '[i]n a Christian believer *love* sits upon the throne, which is erected in the innermost soul; namely love of God and man, which fills the whole heart, and reigns without a rival'.[13] One is reborn so that one can grow into perfection.

Study questions

1. What do you think the relationship between faith, rebirth and conversion is?
2. Which of the characteristics of Pietism seem familiar and which seem strange? Which of their proposals regarding the life of faith seem most helpful and which seem unhelpful?
3. What do you think of the three guidelines for the community at Herrnhut?
4. What do you think of Wesley's proposal regarding Christian perfection?

---

[11] John Wesley, *Christian Perfection as Believed and Taught by John Wesley*, ed. Thomas S. Kepler (New York: Cleveland, 1954), p. 54.
[12] Wesley, *Christian Perfection*, p. 96.
[13] John Wesley, 'On Zeal', in John Emory (ed.), *The Works of the Reverend John Wesley*, vol. 2 (New York: Emory and Waugh, 1831), pp. 287–294 (289).

Further reading

The Gospel of John, Chapter 3.

Wesley, John, 'The Circumcision of the Heart', Sermon XVII in Albert C. Outler (ed.), *The Works of John Wesley*, vol. 1, *Sermons 1–33* (Nashville: Abingdon, 1984), pp. 401–414.

Zizendorf, Count Nicolaus, 'Brotherly Union and Agreement at Herrnhut', in Peter C. Erb (ed.), *The Pietists: Selected Writings* (New York: Paulist Press, 1983), pp. 325–330.

10

Faith Ridiculed: Hume's Bonfire of the Vanities of Christian Rationalism

The wars of faith and reason

Right back to the Middle Ages, proponents of 'faith' and of 'reason' jousted on a fine day. The twelfth-century dispute between the logician Peter Abelard and Abbot Bernard of Clairvaux is a legend. What happened between 1690 and 1740 was epic: a whole society experienced contradiction between faith and reason. Dismissal of faith and adherence to rationalism became commonplace. The turn to rationalism was engineered not by atheists or Deists but by Anglican ministers and pillars of the established Church of England. Bible miracles were taken as evidence that the Bible is God's revelation; the doctrine of the Trinity 'ceased being a mystery of faith and became a problem in theology'.[1] The buzzwords of the epic were 'nature' and 'reason'.

In the 1618–1648 'Wars of Religion', European Catholics and Protestants butchered one another and savaged the credibility of faith. The English Civil War made soldiers of fanatical charismatics, who believed themselves agents of the Holy Spirit. Once in power, Oliver Cromwell's Puritan government abolished Christmas. The Restoration of the Monarchy in 1660 created a blowback against charismatic enthusiasm. The empiricist philosopher John Locke defined 'enthusiasm' as a human attitude

> which though founded neither on reason nor divine revelation, but rising from the conceits of a warmed or over-weening brain, works yet, where it once gets footing, more powerfully on the persuasions and actions of men, than either of those two, or both together … For strong conceit … carries all easily with it, when got above common sense and freed from all restraint of reason … it is heightened into a divine authority.[2]

'Enthusiasm' is getting overheated and acting out fantasies of direct divine inspiration. It had caused a lot of trouble in the Continental Wars of Religion and the English

---

[1]Philip Dixon, *'Nice and Hot Disputes': The Doctrine of the Trinity in the Seventeenth Century* (London: T&T Clark, 2003), p. 1.
[2]John Locke, *An Essay Concerning Human Understanding*, ed. Roger Woolhouse (London: Penguin Books, 1997), IV.XIX.7, pp. 616–617.

Civil War. It seemed like a good idea after all that religiously instigated turbulence to tether faith tightly to reason; but it is difficult to meditate deeply on God without the inspiration of the Holy Spirit.

Satire

The 1662 Press Act opened English printing presses to publish satirical tracts, and even religion was included in the mockery. Ironically, for a hundred years after the legalization of freedom of speech, a main method of disputation was irony, that is, the use of indirect speech, saying the opposite of what one means, and the satirical adoption of one's opponent's position, to reduce it to logical absurdity. One cannot see the true face of a writer masked in irony. What did Jonathan Swift (1667–1745) mean when, in 'An Argument against Abolishing Christianity', he argued that abolishing the Established Church would sink the Bank of England?[3] Swift's tract mocked the rationalist Unitarian John Toland (1670–1722), but its surface, at least, mocks Anglicanism. Swift was the dean of St. Patrick's Cathedral in Dublin. He wrote a tract proposing to alleviate Irish food shortages by consuming Irish babies. In Swift's fantasy novel *Gulliver's Travels*, the hero lives among super-rational horses, the Houyhnhnm, whose perennial foes are degraded human beings, Yahoos. 'Houyhnhnm' is onomatopoeic, representing an equine neigh: it means, in their language, 'the perfection of nature'. Did their author regard the Houyhnhnm as ideal creatures or monsters? Swift's double-talk and irony make his writing opaque. Most people think that David Hume was on the side of the demons, not the angels, when he claimed in ironic tones that it takes infused faith to believe in miracles. Hume pronounced what Christians had always believed. They were not amused.

Socinianism

The turn to rationalism started long before the Wars of Religion, when the Italian Anabaptists Lelio Socinus and his nephew Faustus Socinus (1539–1604) assumed leadership of the Polish Brethren. The Brethren were a non-magisterial Protestant sect who later became known as Socinians. Lelio and Faustus disavowed belief in the eternal divinity of Christ and in the Trinity *on the grounds that these traditional articles of faith cannot clearly be reasoned out of Scripture*. By 1601 Faustus' ideas were enshrined in the Racovian Catechism, which states that reason 'is…of great service, since without it we would neither perceive with certainty the authority of the sacred writings, understand their contents…nor apply them to any practical purpose. When…I stated that the Holy Scriptures were sufficient for our salvation…I certainly assumed its presence [the presence of reason]'. The Socinians were Protestants who took the *sola Scriptura* principle to a logical conclusion. In so

---

[3]Jonathan Swift, 'An Argument against Abolishing Christianity', in Claude Rawson and Ian Higgins (eds), *The Essential Writings of Jonathan Swift* (New York: W. W. Norton, 2010), pp. 135–145.

doing, they replaced faith with 'what can be reasoned out of Scripture'. What had hitherto been termed, variously, the rule of faith, the light of faith and the articles of faith now for the first time was equated with what a rational individual can get out of a literal perusal of the Bible. Socinianism was identified with Unitarianism, that is, anti-Trinitarian theism. But the core of it is rationalist Bible-literalism. Anglican apologists attempted to put paid to Unitarianism with the weapons of reason and the Bible.

So Socinianism influenced the Established Church of England. Disputing Catholic claims that one needs the faith of the Church to recognize Scripture as divine revelation, the Anglican archbishop William Laud (1573–1645) argued that reason can by its own lights recognize the divine origin of Scripture: 'for though this truth, that Scripture is the word of God, is not so demonstratively evident *a priori*, as to enforce assent; yet it is strengthened so abundantly with probable arguments, both from the light of nature itself and human testimony, that he must be very wilful and self-conceited that shall dare to suspect it.'[4] Laud affirmed that '[t]his assent is called faith' which agrees to what reason can find in or deduce from Scripture about human salvation. Faith is assenting to what reason can get from the Bible, says Laud. But what exactly can be seen in or deduced from Scripture? Is the Trinity in Scripture? The divinity of Christ? The fall of Adam? Original sin? Anglicans had inadvertently set themselves the task of demonstrating the Trinity out of Scripture read without the light of the Holy Spirit, and without the perspectives of ecclesial faith.

Is the Trinity easily intelligible?

The problem is that religions are not based on what their sacred texts say, but on what believers think these texts say. Unless one already believes in the Trinity by other means, say, because it is the historical faith of the church expressed in the creeds, one will not find the Scriptures speaking of Father, Son and Spirit as the three Persons of one God. Anglican apologists committed themselves to a circular argument. The Bible's miracles, especially the miracles Jesus performed, were thought to give the Bible rational credentials for being God's revelation. If we think it implausible that God's revelation would contain any unreasonable propositions, we would have to think the doctrine that God is three Persons in one substance *is reasonable* in order to find it in Scripture. Works of Catholic apologetics pointed out that it is 'as equally unreasonable and as seemingly repugnant, to say that One is Three, as to say a Body is not what it appears', that is, to say that the bread consecrated by the words 'This is my body' has become the body of Christ.[5] Ironic Catholic interjections about the equal difficulty of finding the Trinity and Transubstantiation in Scripture played into these debates. In *An Answer to a Late Dialogue between a new Catholick Convert and a Protestant, to Prove the Mystery of the Trinity to Be as Absurd a Doctrine*

---

[4]*Relation of the Conference*, quoted in Jason E. Vickers, *Invocation and Assent: The Making and Remaking of Trinitarian Theology* (Grand Rapids, Mich.: Eerdmans, 2008), p. 44.
[5]*A Dialogue between a New Catholic Convert and a Protestant*, cited in Dixon, '*Nice and Hot Disputes*', p. 78.

of Transubstantiation (1687), the Anglican William Sherlock observes that his faith will not stomach 'that which is unreasonable and absurd'. He claimed the Trinity was above reason, but not contrary to it.[6]

Sherlock later tried to present 'a very easie and intelligible Notion of a Trinity in Unity'.[7] Unfortunately, Sherlock's description of the three Persons of the Godhead as three minds or centres of consciousness was mocked by Deists and Unitarians as effectively Tritheist. Under the cover of criticising three Roman deities, the Unitarian-Deist Matthew Tindal (1653–1733) satirized a Trinity consisting of three separate minds:

> Had the Heathen believ'd God to have been a purely spiritual, invisible Being, they could never have supposed him visible to Mortals; or have thought that an unlimited Being cou'd appear under the limited Form of a Man ... or that an Omnipotent Being cou'd any more be present in one Place, or Creature, than another; or that such a Being cou'd be confi'd to a small Spot of Earth, while another equally omnipotent was in Heaven, and a third descending from thence &. Or that one God cou'd be sent on the Errand of another God, after the Manner that God *Mercury* was by God *Jupiter*; tho' there was nothing to absurd for the Heathen to believe, after they had destroy'd the Unity of God.[8]

Tindal was pretty much a Houyhnhnm in his conception of religious symbols.

The alpha Houyhnhnm, though, was John Locke (1632–1704). Locke demonstrated that faith contains nothing unreasonable by defining it as dutifully obedient to reason. In his *Essay Concerning Human Understanding* (1689), he contends that the 'object of faith' is what God has revealed, and reason must be the judge of knowing exactly *what* God has revealed: '*nothing that is contrary to and inconsistent with the clear and self-evident dictates of reason, has a right to be urged, or assented to, as a matter of faith.*'[9]

Reason, says Locke, is 'the discovery of the certainty or probability of such propositions or truths, which the mind arrives at by deductions made from such ideas which it has got by the use of its natural faculties, viz. by sensation or reflection'. Reason works on *ideas*, which emerge from *sensations*. It deduces proposition from ideas which originate in sensations. Faith, by contrast, does not derive from deductions from ideas. Rather, says Locke, '*Faith* ... is the assent to any proposition ... upon the credit of the proposer, as coming from God in some extraordinary way of communication. This way of discovering truths to men we call *revelation*'.[10] Rather than buying the item 'cash down' on the basis of ideas emerging from sensations, one buys the truths of faith *on credit* from God. But why is it reasonable to buy truths on credit from God? What makes it rational to *believe* the Bible is God's Word? Locke's *The Reasonableness of Christianity* (1695) claims that

---

[6]Dixon, '*Nice and Hot Disputes*', pp. 81–82.
[7]William Sherlock, *Vindication of the Doctrine of the Trinity*, cited in Dixon, '*Nice and Hot Disputes*', p. 101.
[8]Matthew Tindal, *Christianity as Old as Creation* (London: Routledge, 1995), pp. 74–75.
[9]Locke, *Essay*, IV.18.10, p. 613.
[10]Locke, *Essay*, IV.18.2, p. 608.

the 'proposer' is Jesus Christ in the Gospels, and the *evidence* Jesus offers, making it rational for us to credit that he is God's emissary, is his miracles and fulfilment of Old Testament prophecy. Jesus' miracles are his credit card, making rationally credible his claim to speak on God's behalf. Jesus showed himself to be the Messiah by his miracles and by claiming the prophesied Kingdom of God had come. Locke does not think Jesus said he was the Messiah, but he thinks the Gospel writers say so. Locke's 'article of faith' is that Jesus was the Messiah. It is reasonable to have faith that the Bible is God's revelation because in it Jesus the Messiah performs miracles, acts which are evidence that he was on a mission from God.

For Locke, Jesus is the Messiah, but is he the second Person of the Trinity? If, on Locke's account, we make an inference *from Jesus* to God, then Jesus is not God. *The Reasonableness of Christianity* does not mention the Trinity. When called on this, Locke both denied that he was a Unitarian and sarcastically demanded to see a different Bible, one which refers unequivocally to the Trinity:

My Lord, my Bible is faulty again; for I do not remember that I ever read in it either of these propositions in these precise words, 'that there are three persons in one nature, or, there are two natures in one person'. When your Lordship shall show me a Bible wherein they are set down, I shall then think them a good instance of propositions offered me out of Scripture…they may be drawn from the Scripture: but I deny that these very propositions are in express words in my Bible.[11]

Scripture exegesis becomes the test which faith must pass, and we know in advance that Scripture will not offend our reasoning minds by deciding to read it as a string of literal propositions. Faith does not, according to Locke, assent to any proposition it does not understand, and here he had the Reformers' rejection of any type of *fides implicata* on his side.

The representative doctrine of perception

Locke's writings proved an inspiration to such Deists as John Toland and Matthew Tindal. A year after Locke's *The Reasonableness of Christianity*, Toland published *Christianity not Mysterious* (1696). Like Locke, Toland thinks of 'ideas' as high-class sensations. He follows Locke in maintaining the 'representative theory of perception', whereby the objects of our thoughts are mental representations, not things outside of our consciousness. Locke somehow lost sight of the intentionality of thought, its orientation towards and absorption in things outside of consciousness. Toland states, 'By the word IDEA…I understand *the immediate Object of the Mind when it thinks, or any Thought that the Mind employs about any thing.*'[12] If the Idea is the 'Immediate Object of the Mind', and not, rather, the mediate object of the mind, the object by which realities are mediated to it, then our objects of perception

---

[11]John Locke, Letter 3, cited in Dixon, *'Nice and Hot Disputes'*, pp. 158–159.
[12]John Toland, *Christianity not Mysterious* (London: Routledge, 1995), p. 11.

are representatives or emissaries from the world of sensible things. We shall have to make an *inference* from our sensations and ideas to realities outside of ourselves.

Certainty will then be sought and founded in qualities of the conscious mind itself, such as its reasonability. Disavowing the presence of miracle or mystery in the Scriptures, Toland claims, '*Reason* is the only Foundation of all Certitude, and … nothing reveal'd … is more exempted from its Disquisitions, than the ordinary Phenomena of Nature. Wherefore, *there is nothing in the Gospel contrary to Reason, nor above it; and that no Christian doctrine can be properly call'd a Mystery.*'[13]

David Hume (1711–1776): satirical 'Catholic atheist' and champion Yahoo

Hume set light to the bonfire of vanities of Bible-rationalism by asking on what evidence anyone believes in the Gospels' miracles. Hume's 'Essay on Miracles' opens by discussing the difference between the Anglican theologian Dr. Tillotson's attitude to the 'real presence' and to eyewitness testimony. Dr. Tillotson disavows the Catholic doctrine of the 'real presence' of Christ in the consecrated Eucharist as contrary to the evidence of the senses: no Scriptural reference can demonstrate what runs counter to the senses of every rational man. Scripture is above reason but not contrary to it! But Dr. Tillotson owns eyewitness testimony as backing Bible miracles. Hume nails Tillotson to the mast of his refutation of the 'Papist' doctrine of transubstantiation: if sensation and experience rule out the real presence, then how much more should they exclude belief in the testimony of the Gospel writers to miracles? Our concurrence in the reality of an event on the say-so of others, that is, on the basis of testimony, will always be 'weaker' than our concurrence in the veracity of what we experience for ourselves. Testimonies are merely 'probable' evidence in comparison with the direct *proof* of our own experience. And miracles run counter to our own experience: no testimony can outweigh our direct experience that the course of nature runs smooth and straight. For miracles to authorize Scripture, the occurrence of miracles would have to be credible. Otherwise, as Hume says, '*I should not believe such a story were it told me by Cato* … The incredibility of a fact, it was allowed, might invalidate so great an authority.' If it is a matter of authority, our own experience trumps testimony in reasonability.

Hume notes other irrationalities in the proposal that Jesus' miracles authorize the reasonableness of assent to Scripture as God's Word. Why is this host of miracles isolated and elevated above the miracles of the Muslims and Hindus as the sole showing of divine revelation? Why, within Christianity, are the Bible miracles isolated and elevated above the host of miracles claimed by Papists for their saints?

Hume concludes that it is a sheer miracle that anyone believes the Bible miracles:

the *Christian Religion* not only was at first attended with miracles, but even at this day cannot be believed by any reasonable person without one. Mere reason is insufficient to convince us of its veracity; and whoever is moved by *Faith* to assent

---

[13]Toland, *Christianity not Mysterious*, p. 6.

to it, is conscious of a continued miracle in his own person, which subverts all the principles of his understanding, and gives him a determination to believe what is most contrary to custom and experience.[14]

With these words, Hume, speaking as a kind of Catholic atheist, restated the traditional doctrine that faith is a supernatural virtue, a gift of the Holy Spirit.

Two stories

As moderate Anglicans saw it, reason first demonstrates that God exists from the apparent design of the universe. Reason is then led, on the evidence of Jesus' miracles, to accept the Bible as the revelation of this designer God. There are two stories to this building: reason the foundation, and revelation as the floor stacked upon it. Joseph Butler declared, 'Reason can, and it ought to judge, not only of the meaning, but also of the morality and the *evidence* of revelation.'[15] Few of Jesus' miracles make prosaic sense, so not many were impressed by the claim that the miracles make it rational to take the Bible as God's revelation. Counter-attacking the moderate Anglican would-be rationalists, countless Deist tracts mock the sheer *irrationality* of Jesus' miracles, such as cursing the fig tree for not blossoming when figs were not in season. Why take *anything* on credit when we can get cash down in nature for a religion of reason? Tindal noted, with sardonic irony, that if Scripture is as reasonable as the Anglican apologists claim, '[t]he truly illuminated books are the darkest of all'.[16]

The Houyhnhnm philosophers had hung too much weight on inference. In *The Dialogue Concerning Natural Religion* (1750–1776), Hume asks how one can *know* that a domesticated Designer stands at the end of a chain of causal inference from design in the cosmos to its producer. Mediaeval Christians who argued to the existence of God avowedly knew by faith for whom they were looking. As Hume notes, his contemporaries suppose themselves simply to know, by analogy, that the Designer of the Universe would, like the designer of a house, reside at the end of the chain of causal inference. Cleanthes, one of Hume's characters, professes himself 'scandalised … with this resemblance, which is asserted between the Deity and human creatures; and must conceive it to imply such a degradation of the supreme Being as no sound theist could endure'.[17] Hume's argument shows that the two stories or floors of faith and reason do not work unless they mutually reinforce each other.

---

[14]David Hume, 'Of Miracles', in L. A. Selby-Bigge (ed.), rev. P. H. Nidditch, *Enquiries Concerning Human Understanding and Concerning the Principles of Morals* (Oxford: Oxford University Press, 3rd ed., 1975), pp. 109–131 (113).

[15]Joseph Butler, *The Analogy of Religion: Natural and Revealed to the Constitution and Course of Nature*, part II, chap. 3. Available on Christian Classics Ethereal Library, http://www.ccel.org/ccel/butler/analogy. html. Accessed 25 March 2014.

[16]Matthew Tindal, *Christianity as Old as Creation*, p. 23.

[17]David Hume, 'Dialogues Concerning Natural Religion', in J. C. A. Gaskin (ed.), *Principle Writings on Religion Including Dialogues Concerning Natural Religion and the Natural History of Religion* (Oxford: Oxford University Press, 1993), pp. 29–130 (49).

On the English Empiricist account, sensations are also the beginning of a long line of causal inferences. For Hume, 'without the authority either of the memory or of the senses our whole reasoning would be chimerical and without foundation'. Every testimony to which we give credence can be traced back to a sense impression. For instance, our belief that Julius Caesar 'was kill'd in the senate house on the ides of March' traces back to our sense impressions of the history books in which we have read the eyewitness testimonies to this event.[18] We cannot know for sure what causes these impressions: it could be the direct action of God (as the Occasionalists say) or physical objects, or something else. Like Locke, Hume subscribes to the representative theory of perception. He states, '...'twill readily be allow'd, that...nothing is ever really present to the mind, besides its own perceptions.'[19] Hume does not think of impressions or ideas as *mediating* realities to us, but, as it were, of substituting for realities in our consciousness. Unlike Locke, Hume grasps the consequences of this. Since we do not know what is the real cause of our impressions or what lies beyond them, *believing* in the veracity of some impressions and not others, or the reality of some external objects and not others, cannot be a matter of *rationality*. The first act judgement makes is to *believe*. Ideas are simply weak impressions, while beliefs are very strong impressions. Hume did not only eviscerate Bible-rationalism but struck at the foundations of rationalism, arguing that 'all probable reasoning is nothing but a species of sensation'. ''Tis not solely in poetry and music, we must follow our taste and sentiment, but likewise in philosophy. When I am convinc'd of any principle, 'tis only an idea, which strikes more strongly upon me.'[20] It follows then that *belief* is the source of all of our ratiocination. All reasoning rests on belief.

Study questions

1. Who was more reasonable in his attitude to Jesus and his miracles, Locke or Hume? Who was more rational?

2. Do the miracles of Jesus make it reasonable to believe that the Gospels are divine revelation? Or would we have to believe the Gospels are true in advance of accepting their accounts of miracles?

3. Can reason alone give an account of God as three Persons in one Being?

4. Was it a good idea for eighteenth-century Christians to try to disprove Socinianism on rational grounds? If not, what should they have done instead?

5. How did the conception of faith change in the seventeenth and eighteenth centuries?

6. Do the miracles in the Gospels make it more plausible or less plausible that they rest on eyewitness testimony?

---

[18]David Hume, *A Treatise of Human Nature: Being an Attempt to Introduce the Experimental Method of Reasoning into Moral Subjects*, vol. 1, *Of the Understanding*, 2nd ed., ed. L. A. Selby-Bigge; rev. P. H. Nidditch (Oxford: Oxford University Press, 1978), p. 83.
[19]Hume, *A Treatise of Human Nature*, p. 197.
[20]Hume, *A Treatise of Human Nature*, p. 103.

Further reading

Dixon, Philip, *'Nice and Hot Disputes': The Doctrine of the Trinity in the Seventeenth Century* (London: T&T Clark), 2003.

Hume, David, 'Of Miracles', *Enquiry Concerning Human Understanding*, 3rd ed., ed. L. A. Selby-Bigge; rev. P. H. Nidditch (Oxford: Oxford University Press, 1975), pp. 109–131.

Redwood, John, *Reason, Ridicule and Religion: The Age of Enlightenment in England 1660–1750* (London: Thames & Hudson, 1976).

Vickers, Jason E., *Invocation and Assent: The Making and Remaking of Trinitarian Theology* (Grand Rapids, Michigan: Eerdmans, 2008).

11

Pure Religious Faith: Immanuel Kant

A Copernican Turn

People in ancient times believed that the Earth was the motionless centre of a universe composed of transparent spheres of various sizes seamlessly fitted into one another. This vast system of spheres was believed to be in a constant spherical motion, each moving sphere having one of the planets (the Sun and the Moon included) as its lodestar. This geocentric worldview was substituted by the heliocentric, or sun-centred, view only after the publication of Nicolaus Copernicus' *On the Revolutions of the Heavenly Spheres* in 1543. The change took at least two centuries to gain the unanimous approval of leading scholars. When we believe today that the Sun moves only apparently through the ecliptic and that in reality it is the Earth that circles around the Sun, we can thank the great Polish astronomer of the late Middle Ages for this recognition.

In philosophy we also speak of a 'Copernican Turn' in an analogical sense. This turn is attributed to the German philosopher Immanuel Kant (1724–1804), who realized the sterile dogmatism of theology and philosophy in the midst of the rapid development of the natural sciences. Triggered by Hume's skepticism, Kant realized that human knowledge must have a more solid foundation than mere belief. In order that philosophy and theology may gain a new foundation and begin their development, Kant proposed a radically new approach to traditional philosophical and theological questions. According to his 'Copernican Turn', in order to understand what reality is we need first to clarify the nature of our understanding. Reality is out there, but what we perceive as real is always determined by the structures of our understanding. So Kant thought that the main task of philosophy was to develop an overall theory of mind. Once we had an insight into the working of mind, we might better grasp what is presented to us as reality. Kant himself understood the 'Copernican Turn' in philosophy as the turn to the human mind which ensures the proper understanding of understanding itself.

Are the old arguments for the existence of God still valid?

Kant's main objective is clearly given in his epoch-making work, *Critique of Pure Reason* (1781): 'I therefore had to deny knowledge in order to make room for faith.'[1] Kant especially targets so-called theoretical reason, the reason designed to know empirical reality and unable, Kant claimed, to go beyond the limits of possible experience. To show the bad use of theoretical reason, Kant takes as an example the traditional arguments for the existence of God. First, he identifies theories of our knowledge of God as 'transcendental theology', because this knowledge transcends the everyday physical world. Transcendental theology is of two kinds. 'Cosmotheology' refers to the kind of argument which takes as its basis the general experience of the external world and concludes with the existence of God. 'Ontotheology' refers to the kind of argument which concludes with the real existence of God merely from the fact that we possess the notion of God. Kant attempts to refute first the ontotheological argument by pointing out that it is illogical to conclude with the real existence of God from our notion of God, just as we cannot conclude with the real existence of hundred dollars in our pocket from the mere fact that we have the notion of hundred dollars in our mind. On the other hand, cosmotheological arguments cannot logically arrive at the insight of the real existence of God either, because such arguments illegitimately apply the category of causality beyond the limits of the empirical world. Even if we start with the experience of design in the world – such as the well-arranged and functional structures of living organisms – the best result we can reach is merely the probability of the existence of an ultimate designer, but not God in the Christian sense. Finally, Kant explains that every cosmotheological argument logically presupposes the validity of the ontological one, so if the ontological argument is mistaken, as it is according to Kant, no cosmotheological argument can be considered valid. There is no way to prove the existence of God by the use of theoretical reason. Nevertheless, Kant argues, theoretically it is equally impossible to *disprove* God's existence.[2]

Was Kant an atheist?

Kant was not an atheist. He merely wanted to rebuild the entire tradition of philosophical theology and change it into 'natural theology', a theology having human morality as its basis. Even Kant recognizes that we possess the idea of God in our mind. In fact, we necessarily possess the reasonable notion of God, but this notion alone does not allow us to conclude with God's real existence. The idea of God only provides the theoretical mind with the highest principle of its activities by regulating our theoretical knowledge of the world. Besides theoretical reason, however, we possess practical reason as well. Practical reason is what coordinates moral action. The core of practical reason is the unconditional practical law or, as Kant calls it, the 'categorical imperative'. This imperative 'commands' human persons to act in a certain way if they want to act morally. This imperative is 'categorical' as well, because it does not give us concrete commandments, but only a universal rule to follow in every situation. The first formula of Kant's categorical

---

[1]Immanuel Kant, *Critique of Pure Reason*, ed. Paul Guyer, trans. Allen Wood (Cambridge: Cambridge University Press, 1998), B xxx.
[2]Kant, *Critique of Pure Reason*, B 611/A 583–B 670/A 642.

imperative runs like this: 'Act only according to that maxim by which you can at the same time will that it should become a universal law'.[3] Since this rule is fundamental and every human being is aware of it, Kant in fact transcends the limits of empirical experience and enters the domain of morality. The awareness of the universal moral law is 'the fact of reason', a fact stronger and more fundamental than the external world.

Kant quickly arrives at an entirely new kind of argument for the existence of God. This kind is called a moral argument and is based on Kant's notion of a 'postulate'. For Kant, a postulate is that which we necessarily presuppose if we think or do something. For instance, it is a necessary postulate of our use of human language that there is a community of reasonable beings capable of understanding language. There is no point in having and using a language if there are no reasonable beings capable of understanding our language. Similarly, God as a postulate is logically necessary in the context of morality. As Kant shows, every human being strives for happiness. Happiness is the possession of the highest good. Moral action aims at the realization of goodness and, through goodness, happiness. There is a logically necessary connection between happiness and goodness in the sense that we understand that, in principle, good people must be happy. Nevertheless, this is not what we experience day by day. On the contrary, we see that moral action often provokes hatred, that good people are punished for their goodness and that evil ones flourish at the same time. The 'fact of reason', or the power of morality, is nevertheless so great that we understand that the proper relationship between goodness and happiness must exist in some form. We understand that, in spite of our daily experience, morally good people must possess happiness in a certain way. Thus Kant gains the insight that good people, even if they suffer in this world, must have their due reward in another, morally just world. However, the existence of another, morally just world – a genuine afterlife – presupposes that there is a morally just judge, an absolute moral authority, who punishes evil and rewards good. Thus we have the postulate: *the necessary existence* of an absolutely just being. We understand that there is a God as absolute goodness, perfection and the eternal keeper of the proper relation between goodness and happiness. Kant even goes so far as to say that this God is absolutely holy, happy and wise, and has omnipotence, omniscience, omnipresence and perfect goodness.

How can we genuinely believe in God?

This notion of God is reasonable or rational, that is to say, we logically understand the necessity of his existence. If Kant really intends to 'make room for faith', he needs to tell us what kind of faith we may have in God. Kant offers an analysis of various kinds of faith, one unparalleled in the philosophy or theology of his time. Kant's logical starting point is the contrast between 'historical' and 'pure' faith. Historical faith is based on historical facts of a certain age and a certain culture recorded in a certain language and it possesses a number of constraints which make it difficult

---

[3]Immanuel Kant, *Grounding for the Metaphysics of Morals* (Indianapolis: Hackett, 1993), p. 30.

to understand its real meaning. For instance, if we want to understand what 'faith' meant in the Old Testament, we need to know the Hebrew language and possess a great amount of additional knowledge of historical circumstances. Those with historical faith are unable to communicate their faith without explaining carefully the historical, cultural and linguistic conditions under which the concrete events, the objects of faith, took place. As opposed to this restricted kind of communication, pure faith is reasonable: it is universally understandable and communicable to every rational person. It is pure faith because it is not bound up with beliefs in accidental historical circumstances; it is pure faith because it is purified from such eventualities. And it is pure faith because, as Kant shows, there are universally understandable and logically well-formed arguments in favour of maintaining such faith.

The background to Kant's argument about the notion of pure faith is his understanding of radical evil. 'Radical evil' refers to the fact that in every human being there is a tendency of intending and doing evil, even serious or 'diabolical' evil.[4] Human beings naturally form political communities, but these political communities are thus formed by the very same human beings who possess the tendency of radical evil. In such a community, co-existence is secured by the rule of law issued by some political authority. In the strict sense, such a community cannot be called ethical, because it exists in the natural juridical state of following positive law; it is a state of 'everybody's war against everybody' in a latent fashion, controlled by the rule of law. This natural state of a community is 'brutish' and is characterized by inner immorality.[5] However, the state of genuine ethical community is reached when the community recognizes the existence of a transcendent ethical ruler, God, who knows everybody's heart and rewards everybody in accordance with his or her merit. In other words, the beginning of a genuinely ethical community is given in a theocratic state in which the people are God's moral people as opposed to the 'band under the evil principle – a union of those who side with that principle for the propagation of evil'.[6]

Kant suggests that God's moral people can become the bearer of pure religious faith only as a 'church'. That is, for Kant, political existence and the existence of the church are intrinsically linked to one another. On the other hand, this church must be a *universal church* based on pure religious faith, that is, a church existing beyond the limits of historical faith. Historical faith can be properly understood only by pure religious faith. The criterion of historical faith is Scripture, which can be properly interpreted only by the bearers of the pure reasonable religion and its objective and scholarly developed exegesis.[7]

Kant describes the essence of historical faith with these words:

> We must believe that there once was a human being (of whom reason tells us nothing) who has done enough through his holiness and merit, both for himself (with respect to his duty) and for all others (and their deficiency as regards their

---

[4]Immanuel Kant, *Religion within the Boundaries of Mere Reason*, ed. and trans. Allen Wood and George di Giovanni (Cambridge: Cambridge University Press, 1998), pp. 55–61.
[5]Kant, *Religion within the Boundaries of Mere Reason*, p. 108.
[6]Kant, *Religion*, p. 110.
[7]Kant, *Religion*, p. 111.

duty), to hope that we ourselves can become blessed in the course of a good life, though only in virtue of this faith.[8]

On the other hand, the essence of pure faith is summarized as follows:

> We must strive with all our might after the holy intention of leading a life well-pleasing to God, in order to believe that God's love for humankind (already assured to us by reason) will somehow make up, in consideration of that honest intention, for humankind's deficiency in action, provided that humankind strives to conform to his will with all its might.[9]

The contrast is formulated as that between 'slavish' or 'mercenary faith' as opposed to 'free' or 'genuine faith'.[10]

For Kant, then, it is possible to have faith in God, yet this faith is only secondarily historical, empirical or ecclesiastical faith; primarily it is pure religious faith. Those of pure faith form a genuine ethical community, a church, the establishment of which, as Kant suggests, is 'a work whose execution cannot be hoped for from human beings but from God himself'.[11] This 'moral people of God' is, nevertheless, continuously attacked by the 'band (or gang) of the evil principle', so that this band apparently overcomes God's moral people in certain situations. The reason for such a defeat is the creation of the possibility of a higher renewal of God's people, a stronger realization of pure religious faith as a faith in God's eternally compensating love. This realization of pure religious faith is a faith which has a sacred and mysterious character. Although the very fact of a mystery seems to exclude the reasonableness of pure religious faith, Kant points out that mysteries may still belong to pure religious faith.[12]

It is in this context that Kant clearly addresses the difference between the notion of faith as based on divine grace ('divinely dispensed' faith) and the 'pure faith of reason'. Kant intends to limit his investigation to rational faith but acknowledges that even the foundation and ultimate end of rational faith are mysterious. As an analogy he offers the fact of human free will, a faculty every human being is aware of. We are able to talk about and consider human free will in a rational way because it is publicly observable in each of us. However, the ultimate ground and end of free will cannot be rationally talked about and considered and are in this way mysterious. Similarly, the mystery of faith belongs to the grounds and ends of pure faith, a faith designed to support the intention of moral action.[13]

Kant's idea of a pure religious faith is a philosophical idea. His new kind of philosophy, which focuses on the structures of the mind as underlying objective reality, revolutionized modern philosophical thought. In Kant's work, this 'Copernican' revolution leads to the reformulation not only of arguments for the

---

[8]Kant, *Religion*, p. 126.
[9]Kant, *Religion*, p. 126.
[10]Kant, *Religion*, p. 122.
[11]Kant, *Religion*, p. 111.
[12]Kant, *Religion*, p. 126.
[13]Kant, *Religion*, p. 126.

existence of God but more importantly to the new notion of pure religious, or reasonable, faith. Kant's deep faith in God, moral goodness and the holy calling of the faithful in the world cannot be questioned. As a philosopher, Kant attempted to interpret the mainly Protestant traditions of faith and developed an understanding which has become fruitful during the subsequent centuries. His main merit consists in that, based on his analysis of the historical and ecclesiastical notions of faith, he recognized the need for a new form of faith which responds to the challenges of the Age of Enlightenment. This new faith is pure religious faith, a faith having as its guide the universal rule of the categorical imperative.

Study questions

1. What is the importance of Kant's use of the phrase of the 'Copernican Turn' with respect to his own thought?
2. What are the main points of Kant's criticism of the traditional arguments for the existence of God?
3. Was Kant an atheist? If yes, in which sense? If no, what kind of argument does he offer for the existence of God?
4. What is 'pure religious faith' according to Kant?

Further reading

Kant, Immanuel, *Critique of Pure Reason* (Cambridge: Cambridge University Press, 1998), Introduction (as in the second edition), trans. Paul Guyer and Allen W. Wood, pp. 136–152.

———, *Religion within the Boundaries of Mere Reason*, ed. and trans. Allen Wood and George Di Giovanni (Cambridge: Cambridge University Press, 1998), pp. 31–191.

Guyer, Paul, *The Cambridge Companion to Kant and Modern Philosophy* (Cambridge: Cambridge University Press, 2006).

Scruton, Roger, *Kant: A Very Short Introduction* (Oxford: Oxford University Press, 2001).

12
Faith and Feeling: Friedrich Schleiermacher

Romanticism

Romanticism began near the end of the eighteenth century and flowered in the middle of the nineteenth. Inasmuch as some of the main themes of Romanticism still resonate so powerfully within us, some have said that Romanticism as an era has never really ended, but that we are still living in it. In early German Romanticism, we can find the impression that the infinite saturates the finite and temporal; an emphasis upon feeling and intuition as opposed to cold and calculating rationalism; a view of nature as a dynamic and living whole rather than a large mechanism or congregation of dead and inert parts (against eighteenth-century French materialism); the praise of passionate and romantic love; and the valorization of creativity, the figure of the genius and 'sensitive souls'.

Within such a context, the emotional and affective life came to the centre of theology. The theologian who put it there was Friedrich Schleiermacher (1768–1834). The young Schleiermacher studied in a Moravian Pietist school and their piety created a lasting impression on him. At a fairly early age, however, he started to doubt much of what passed for traditional Christianity. Nevertheless, despite his criticisms of much traditional theology, he could still call himself a 'Moravian of a higher order'.[1] Having completed his exams in theology and spending some time as a tutor, Schleiermacher served as a chaplain in the Charité hospital in Berlin. His leisure time was devoted to the salons of the cultural elite and to writing for *Athenaeum*, the literary magazine in the vanguard of the early Romantic movement in Germany.

It was during his time in Berlin as a chaplain that his cultured and Romantic friends asked him to write a book on religion. A thirty-year-old Schleiermacher published, albeit anonymously, *On Religion: Speeches to Its Cultured Despisers* in the summer of 1799. The work was seized upon by both advocates and detractors, and so Schleiermacher revised it before the second edition of 1806, and added lengthy 'Explanations' to some of the more problematic passages in 1821.[2] The *Speeches* brought early Romanticism and idealism into conversation with Christianity, and did so in a creative and sophisticated way which proved highly alluring. Schleiermacher gave feeling, intuition and affectivity a prominent place within Christian life and

---

[1] Letter to George Reimer, 1802.
[2] It was also republished in 1831.

theology. Others had done so before him, but Schleiermacher gave this stream of reflection his own distinctive mark.

The *Speeches* are an apology or defence of religion before these cultured elites who view religion as fear of God or as a selfish wish for immortality. Schleiermacher's defence of religion clears away misunderstandings held by the friends and foes of Christianity alike. He also reinterprets or translates traditional Christian categories into the language of Romanticism and idealism. Schleiermacher speaks about Christianity in the voice of Romanticism and yet says things which they themselves would never say. He sometimes goes on the offensive, and even maintains that science and morality, two outstanding concerns of his readers, could not be 'true science' and 'true morality' without religion and piety.

The five 'speeches' that make up *On Religion* are not sermons, academic essays or philosophical arguments. They are more like literary performances done in true Romantic style. The 'speeches' could also be seen as dialogues. Throughout the speeches, Schleiermacher directly addresses religion's 'cultured despisers' as 'you', and presents their ideas on religion, morality and metaphysics. This was a book that had to be written, and if not by Schleiermacher then by someone less gifted. At the time, there was a growing separation between 'high' and 'low' culture. Eighteenth-century cultural elites saw popular culture, practices and habits as vulgar, backward and superstitious. Popular religion was thus at odds with the higher ideals of the Enlightenment and refined art, literature and music which they themselves embodied.[3] The *Speeches*, then, speak the language of Romanticism and idealism and speak it to Christianity's 'cultured detractors'.

In his 'Second Speech', Schleiermacher tries to uncover the essence of religion, or piety. Piety is neither knowing nor doing, nor a mixture of the two, but feeling. Piety is not knowledge of the world, or even of God. One can know many interesting facts about the world, or about what Christianity says God is, and can even grasp these facts very well, but we still would not recognize this as piety. As Schleiermacher succinctly puts it, 'quantity of knowledge is not quantity of piety'.[4] Piety is not a matter of activity, of doing good deeds or even performing a special set of duties and actions towards God. Piety seems to be a kind of surrender.[5] Piety is not a mixture of knowing or doing, as in knowing many titbits about God and performing religious acts. It seems, then, that alongside knowing and doing, alongside perception and operations, alongside metaphysics and ethics, there is a third thing: piety, feeling, sensation and thus religion. Yet while we can distinguish knowing, doing and feeling, we cannot completely separate them.

Schleiermacher defines piety or religion as a 'sense and taste of the infinite'.[6] It is a feeling of the infinite and eternal within the finite and temporal, and the feeling of the finite and temporal within the infinite and eternal. It senses that everything (the

---

[3]See Harry C. Payne, 'Elite versus Popular Mentality in the Eighteenth Century', *Historical Reflections/ Réflexions Historiques* 2:2 (1976), pp. 183–208.

[4]Friedrich Schleiermacher, *On Religion: Speeches to Its Cultured Despisers*, trans. John Oman (New York: Harper & Row, 1958), p. 35.

[5]Schleiermacher, *Speeches*, p. 37.

[6]Schleiermacher, *Speeches*, p. 39.

All) lives and moves within a unified whole, a unified totality (the One). Piety can feel the presence and working of God, or the infinite, within both the small and the grand, the sacred and the ordinary.[7] These 'pious feelings' can take a variety of forms and Schleiermacher can even call religion 'the sum of all the higher feelings'. All feelings that are not diseased or unhealthy are a feeling of the divine. His examples of such feelings include awe, love, affection, compassion, contrition, humility and gratitude. These feelings come directly from the infinite, from God. So they are not a matter of any knowing or perceiving of the world, or about acting in any certain way. For Schleiermacher, saying that everyone has 'sense and taste of the infinite' is another way of saying that we all are in relation to God, that we feel how everything is in relation to God and that these relations are basic to what we are.

This account of piety provoked some controversy. Particularly worrisome was Schleiermacher's view that piety or religion is not related to consciously having the idea of a personal God. Piety finds expression in different ways and in different concepts, including God as personal or non-personal (impersonal is another matter). Piety can appear both in those who have an idea or concept of a personal God and those who do not, provided that each feels the immediate presence of God within them.[8] The young Schleiermacher had been influenced by both Spinoza and Kant. His remark in the *Speeches* that Spinoza, widely condemned as a pantheist or an atheist, 'was full of religion, full of the Holy Spirit'[9] shocked some of his contemporaries and he had to fight off accusations of pantheism. His response was that he thought it more generous and Christian to see piety wherever it may be found. Matters were also not helped by the various names Schleiermacher used for God or for the unity of the universe in God: *the Infinite*, *the World-Spirit*, *the World* and *the All and One*. Schleiermacher can even deny that God is some type of highest being or first cause 'outside of' or 'behind' the world itself. The living God lies beyond all the types of oppositions and contrasts we find around us, like 'outside', 'beyond' and 'behind', and so Schleiermacher does not think that describing God's relation to the world in these ways is helpful or edifying.

The Christian Faith

Published in 1821, with a second edition in 1830, *The Christian Faith* was aimed at a different audience. It was the first systematic theology put forward for the sake of the newly formed Prussian Union of Churches (1817), which brought together the Lutheran and Reformed churches in Prussia. While many of Schleiermacher's ideas from the *Speeches* are retained, there is a gain in precision, clarity and scope as he drops the dreamy language of Romanticism and discusses a range of Christian doctrines.

---

[7]Schleiermacher, *Speeches*, pp. 45, 84.
[8]See Julia A. Lamm, *The Living God: Schleiermacher's Theological Appropriation of Spinoza* (University Park, Penn.: Pennsylvania State University Press, 1966), pp. 103–108.
[9]Schleiermacher, *Speeches*, p. 40.

Asking what the church really is, Schleiermacher once again raises the question of piety. [10] The church, he argues, is a communion or fellowship of religion and piety, and the church's business is to strengthen and maintain this piety. Once again piety is neither a knowing nor a doing, but a feeling. By 'feeling' Schleiermacher means one's 'immediate self-consciousness', one's existential state, like experiencing joy or sorrow. Feeling is not a matter of 'objective self-consciousness', an existential state which arises from analyzing one's self, like self-approval or self-reproach (for here the self becomes the object of one's self-consciousness). Feelings are direct changes in my self-consciousness, or existential state. They happen when the world, people and events affect me. Feeling is thus 'immediate' and receptive.

Conscious of the accusations that he is a subjectivist or a pantheist, Schleiermacher tries harder than he did in his *Speeches* (or in the first edition of his *Christian Faith*) to distinguish the feeling or self-consciousness which arises from my being in the world and that which arises from my being in relation to God. There is always reciprocity as regards my feeling or self-consciousness which arises from the world. I act and am acted upon, effect and am affected. As regards the world, then, I feel myself to be *partly* free and *partly* dependent. I am not utterly free, as there is always a world and people around which affect me, and I am not utterly dependent, as I can also affect the world and others around me in turn, even simply by existing or being there.

Matters are different in my feeling or self-consciousness of being in relation to God. Defining piety and of being in relation to God, Schleiermacher states, 'the common element in all howsoever diverse expressions of piety, by which these are conjointly distinguished from all other feelings … is this: the consciousness of being absolutely dependent, or, which is the same thing, of being in relation with God'.[11] A feeling of absolute freedom cannot exist, for I am always aware of being in relation to a world and having not created myself. Along with my consciousness of being partially free and partially dependent, there is also the feeling of absolute dependence. This feeling is the consciousness that my whole existence – both passive and active – comes from some other source. In fact, it is the feeling that this whole universe of acting and receiving comes from a source which is not itself. It is the consciousness that all this activity and spontaneity, this receiving and affectivity, both of myself and the world as a whole, has a 'whence', a 'from where' (in German *Woher*), a 'from some other place'. This feeling of utter or absolute dependence is not one particular feeling amongst others; nor is it caused by any particular object within the world. Instead, it is a feeling which accompanies both my action upon the world and its action upon me. The name for this 'whence', the source of the world and myself, is God. The feeling of absolute or utter dependence is an immediate and direct awareness of God, of my being in relation to God, the source of everything. The measure of one's piety is the extent to which this feeling of absolute dependence upon God, or 'God-consciousness', saturates all of one's self-consciousness, in both its active and passive moments.

---

[10]Friedrich Schleiermacher, *The Christian Faith* (Berkeley: Apocryphile Press, 2011), §3.
[11]Schleiermacher, *The Christian Faith*, §4, p. 12.

Piety, or God-consciousness, becomes the recurring theme in what Schleiermacher says about God, creation, humanity, sin, redemption and reconciliation, and the church. This definition of piety arose in the introduction to the work, in the course of a discussion of the church. It is technically a 'proposition' or claim which theology 'borrows' from ethics. The source of this idea of piety, however, only becomes clearer later. In a somewhat dramatic reversal, Schleiermacher says that this seemingly general account of the feeling of absolute dependence is actually an 'abstracted' version of what Christian self-consciousness experiences in fellowship with the Redeemer.[12] It is a particularly Christian self-consciousness or piety, one which is completely derived from an experience of fellowship with Jesus, which serves as the source for this general account of piety. Yet this 'abstracted' or 'derived' account of piety still serves an important regulative role in describing Christian self-consciousness. The criterion for what we say about our relationship to the Redeemer is that it strengthens and increases the feeling of absolute dependence within us.

Within this framework, faith becomes a matter of being certain about the feeling or consciousness of God. Faith cannot create this relationship or feeling for it always and everywhere exists, even when the feeling of God-consciousness is resisted by sin. Faith holds this feeling to be true, and so faith is an 'assenting certainty'.[13] Faith is about the 'truth' of one's religious feeling, and is less one particular feeling than a confidence which accompanies all of one's pious feelings. What faith believes is not any particular doctrinal formulation, but the truth of one's pious feelings. In fact, there are a variety of doctrinal formulations which will 'fit', 'correspond to' or be 'adequate to' these feelings. There are also ones that contradict them.

Faith in Christ is certainty in the experience or feeling that the Redeemer has removed sin, has communicated his own perfect God-consciousness and blessedness and has assumed one into a new corporate life characterized by piety which replaces one's old corporate life of sin and misery. This faith in Christ, or in one's feelings about Christ, is aroused by the community's preaching, in which Christ himself is present and active.

Schleiermacher thinks he is simply describing what Christians mean when they speak of piety, God and faith. The task of theology for him is not a matter of deduction or speculation, but recognizing and bringing to light the connections and relations that are already there but which are misunderstood. In order to bring these connections to light, Schleiermacher believes that he can 'borrow' propositions from other disciplines, including ethics, philosophy of religion and apologetics. As these disciplines or wider intellectual currents change, so too will the language of theology change. Yet Schleiermacher believes that his theology is not founded upon any one philosophy or worldview, but is actually based on the consciousness of the believer who enjoys Christ's blessedness and God-consciousness within the communal life the Redeemer created and sustains.

---

[12]Schleiermacher, *The Christian Faith*, §62, p. 262.

[13]Robert Merrihew Adam, 'Faith and Religious Knowledge', in Jacqueline Mariña (ed.), *The Cambridge Companion to Schleiermacher* (Cambridge: Cambridge University Press, 2005), pp. 35–51 (42).

Study questions

1. Is Schleiermacher right in thinking that 'piety' or 'religion' is neither a knowing nor a doing?
2. Does the Schleiermacher of the *Speeches* sound like a pantheist?
3. Does faith seem more like certainty about our feelings and experience or a feeling or experience itself?
4. Could the same 'pious' or 'religious feelings' be expressed in differing doctrinal formulations? In ones that even seem to conflict with each other?

Further reading

Schleiermacher, Friedrich, 'First Speech: Defense', in *On Religion: Speeches to Its Cultured Despisers*, trans. John Oman (New York: Harper & Row, 1958), pp. 1–21.

———, *The Christian Faith*, ed. and trans. H. R. Mackintosh and J. S. Stewart (Berkeley: Apocryphile Press, 2011), §§3–4, pp. 5–18; §62, pp. 259–262.

13

Faith and the Absolute: Georg Wilhelm Friedrich Hegel

'If Kant was the one who brought about the revolution in philosophy that is its modern achievement, Hegel was the one who made the event explicit'.[1] Whether the work of Georg Wilhelm Friedrich Hegel (1770–1831) may be qualified as a 'titanic synthesis', in which God is constructed out of the particular,[2] or as a 'Gnostic return in Modernity' may be left open for the time being. Hegel has great merits which are recognized even by his sternest opponents. For instance, Hans Urs von Balthasar acknowledges Hegel's closeness to the patristic author St. Maximus the Confessor.[3] Even Hegel's philosophical critics, such as Eric Voegelin, recognize his unusual philosophical genius and intellectual power.[4] Gislain Lafont concedes that Hegel restored the intellectual nature of theology and redirected human knowledge to the half-forgotten objective of universality. Moreover, Hegel re-established the intellectual importance of the doctrine of Trinity by making its interpretation the foundation of his own philosophical work.[5]

A precise description of Hegel's notion of faith would require an analysis of most of his works. Since that is impossible here, let us consider only three perspectives under which his notion of faith can be approached.

Hegel and the Christian notion of faith

Unlike Kant, Hegel rejected the idea that human knowledge must be restricted to empirical reality and that the notion of God, by going beyond the empirical, cannot be the object of knowledge. For Hegel, faith is intrinsically linked to knowledge, because one must know what one believes. Faith is doctrinal in the basic sense for Hegel and the doctrines of faith are the doctrine of Christianity. *Dogmatics* is the discipline that treats the contents of faith and these contents are expressed in the *symbols* (or creeds) of the Church. In Protestantism, as Hegel emphasizes, the

---

[1]David Walsh, *The Modern Philosophical Revolution* (Cambridge: Cambridge University Press, 2008), p. 76.

[2]Hans Urs von Balthasar, *Cosmic Liturgy: The Universe according to Maximus the Confessor*, trans. Brian E. Daley, S.J. (San Francisco: Ignatius Press, 2003), p. 282.

[3]Von Balthasar, *Cosmic Liturgy*, p. 17, and especially p. 95.

[4]Eric Voegelin, *In Search of Order* (Columbia: University of Missouri Press, 1999), pp. 69–85.

[5]Ghislain Lafont, *Histoire théologique de l'Église catholique* (Paris: Du Cerf, 1994), ch. 2.

doctrines are supposed to be based on the Bible; thus the fundamental notion of faith, for Hegel too, is biblical.

It is the story of Jesus that is indicative of the biblical meaning of faith. Jesus' life story is itself *the* symbol of history. Jesus' life, death and resurrection contain the central message of the Bible, a message not mythological but real and sensible, which is at the same time human and divine:

> Not only [is there] this outward history, which should only be taken as the ordinary story of a human being, but also it has the divine as its content: a divine happening, a divine deed, an absolutely divine action. This absolute divine action is the inward, the genuine, the substantial dimension of this history, and this is just what is the object of reason. Just as a myth has a meaning or an allegory within it, so there is this twofold character generally in every story.[6]

In the Bible, the simple meaning of faith is faith in the miracles of Christ. To believe a miracle, however, is merely a beginning of religious faith and Hegel shows some understanding of the Enlightenment criticisms of the biblical stories. As he emphasizes, the words of the Bible constitute an unsystematic account; they are Christianity as it appeared at its birth. Christianity, however, further developed and elementary belief evolved into more mature faith. Hegel quotes the famous words of St. Paul, according to which, 'For the letter kills, but the Spirit gives life' (2 Cor. 3.6). Hegel sometimes tacks on to this verse the words of Jesus: 'The Spirit will lead you into the truth'.[7] The biblical account of faith itself, then, leads to a spiritual conception of truth, a conception inspired in the believer by the Holy Spirit.

Hegel's use of the doctrines of Christianity, especially that of the Holy Trinity, permeates his entire thought. His focus on the 'Spirit' derives from the Gospels' emphasis on the Holy Spirit, the 'Spirit of truth' (Jn. 16.13).[8] The unity of the Father, the Son and the Spirit is mirrored in the course of history in such a way that each important period of human history can be considered as an expression of one of the persons of the Trinity (Father, Son and Spirit). Hegel does not want to say that history produces the Trinity. All he claims is that God as Trinity is meaningfully – that is to say, not aimlessly or only aesthetically – reflected in his creation. This meaningful reflection is present not merely in physical nature or in human beings but beyond them in history as a process culminating in the advent of Christ.

As Hegel writes in the *Encyclopaedia of the Philosophical Sciences*, the Absolute Spirit exhibits itself (1) as eternal content which remains within itself even in its manifestation; (2) as the distinction of the eternal essence from its manifestations, and this difference becomes the world into which the content enters; and (3) as infinite return to, and reconciliation with, the eternal being – the withdrawal of

---

[6]G. W. F. Hegel, *Lectures on the Philosophy of Religion*, ed. Peter C. Hodgson, trans. R. F. Brown et al. (Los Angeles: University of California Press, 1984), p. 399.

[7]Hegel, *Lectures on the Philosophy of Religion*, p. 338.

[8]G. W. F. Hegel, *On Christianity: Early Theological Writings*, trans. T. M. Knox and Richard Kroner (New York: Harper, 1948), p. 205.

the eternal from the phenomenal into the unity of its fullness.[9] That is to say, God the Father represents the universal aspect of the Absolute Spirit; this universality becomes particular with the Incarnation of Christ. Finally, with the death of the particular (Jesus in the Gospels), the Son is reunited with the Father in the unity of the Holy Spirit. In the central doctrine of Christianity, then, one finds the necessary features of the reality of the Absolute Spirit.[10]

Hegel's discussion of his contemporaries' view

Hegel developed his philosophy in a continuous dialogue with the main figures of his age. In *Faith and Knowledge*, Hegel offers a thorough-going criticism of the thought of Kant, Jacobi and Fichte. These philosophies conceive faith in terms of an isolated subjectivity, isolated from its real content, God, and isolated from the counterpart of faith, reason. Kant's pure faith has merely a postulate for its object and is restricted to the objective side of subjective reason, that is, to the structures of the mind. Jacobi develops a general account of faith in which faith is identical with the emphatically subjective side of the human mind, that is, perception. For Jacobi, sense perception is an act of faith receiving God's revelation. Finally, Fichte offers a synthesis of the notion of faith in the two previous authors and develops an objective view of faith as a moment of knowledge.[11]

Hegel criticizes Kant's notion of faith as subjective. It is the notion of the 'postulate' that Hegel finds hopelessly detached from the real content of faith, which is something absolute, namely God. It is impossible to arrive at God through the subjective and limited act of postulating, and thus it is impossible to conceive the proper object of faith in this one-sided way. Faith is connection to the absolute, as Hegel claims, not only in its content but also in its form, the act of believing. For Kant, however, precisely this act of believing, based on the postulate of morality, remains unable to attain its content, which is God. Hegel is even more critical of Jacobi's notion of faith as all-pervasive certitude of human cognition, because, in Hegel's eyes, 'faith is the relation of an absolute finitude to the truly absolute'.[12] Finally, Hegel also criticizes Fichte inasmuch as the latter thinks that the absolute, God, can be conceived of only by faith and not by knowledge as well. Indeed, Hegel understands faith on the basis of a difference between humanity and God, and he concludes that Fichte developed a fully ideal form of faith as the only means of our access to God in our finitude.[13]

---

[9] G. W. F. Hegel, *Philosophy of Mind*, Part 3 of the *Encyclopaedia of the Philosophical Sciences* (1830) (Oxford: Clarendon, 1971), § 566.

[10] See Jon Stewart, 'Kierkegaard and Hegel on Faith and Knowledge', in Stephen Houlgate and Michael Baur (eds), *A Companion to Hegel* (Oxford: Blackwell, 2011), pp. 501–519.

[11] G. W. F. Hegel, *Faith and Knowledge*, ed. and trans. H. S. Harris and Walter Cerf (Albany: SUNY Press, 1977), p. 62.

[12] Hegel, *Faith and Knowledge*, p. 137.

[13] Hegel, *Faith and Knowledge*, p. 172.

Hegel's notion of faith in his own system

Hegel's understanding of faith is fairly consistent throughout his mature output: faith is always considered to be the perception of the absolute accompanied by the lack of articulate knowledge. This perception is understood as certitude, and thus Hegel continues the long tradition of interpreting faith in terms of individual certainty. In particular, faith is not certainty in a conceptually articulate way, but rather only as feeling, an emotional surety of the fact that God exists:

> Certainty is termed 'faith' partly inasmuch as it is not immediate sensible certainty and partly inasmuch as this knowledge is also not a knowledge of the necessity of this content … I do not need to believe what I see before me, for I know it. I do not believe that a sky is above me; I see it. On the other hand, when I have rational insight into the necessity of a thing, then, too, I do not say 'I believe'.… Faith is a certainty that one possesses apart from immediate sensible intuition, apart from this sensible immediacy, and equally without having insight into the necessity of the content.[14]

Faith in God is grounded on authority: we often accept other persons' faith as authoritative for us. Second, we accept this faith because others offer *witness* about their faith: they confess their belief in God. This confession is based on external and historical verification, such as the existence of the Bible and the Church. Ultimately, faith is grounded on 'the witness of the Spirit', as Hegel suggests, that is to say, on the direct influence of the Holy Spirit in our soul. This witness is given to each of us in a way appropriate to our spiritual and intellectual position and desires: 'My spirit knows itself, it knows its essence – that, too, is an immediate knowledge, it is the absolute verification of the eternally true, the simple and true definition of this certainty that is called faith.'[15]

Feeling is an important aspect of faith; it is Schleiermacher's notion of faith that Hegel targets here. In feeling, we have certainty on a low level and in a subjective way; we know of God emotionally and directly, but this presence of God in our feeling is inarticulate. It is intellectual and volitional, that is, I have a conception of God and I consent to this conception by my will. Yet this is not real knowledge of God. Faith is only the entrance of knowledge; while faith belongs to knowledge, it is still limited and subjective. The content of my faith on this level has objectivity, yet objectivity here is undeveloped. For Hegel, faith must develop into 'representation', that is a higher level objectivity. Representation takes many forms, such as pictures, individual and collective acts and works of art, and in this way faith acquires sensible publicity and objectivity. Faith thus develops into a perception of the divine in sensible forms and, already at this point, takes the form of knowledge. Faith and knowledge are not each other's opposites but rather form separate moments of an identical development, the development of the totality of God. Yet even the

---

[14]Hegel, *Lectures on the Philosophy of Religion*, pp. 387–88.
[15]Hegel, *Lectures on the Philosophy of Religion*, p. 389.

knowledge of God is still something indirect and in God's full totality all these moments – feeling, representation and knowledge – are organically linked to one another.[16]

Faith and knowledge are part and parcel of God's self-revelation as the full deployment of God's reality which takes place in God himself and real history at the same time. The history of salvation, as we know it from the doctrine of the Church, is a reflection of God's self-revelation. This reflection is not a meaningless appearance of God's reality but is rather constitutive of God. In this way, Hegel's notion of faith is related to the absolute inasmuch as it is always conceived as a certain stage – philosophical, theological or historical – in the absolute and dynamic reality of God.

Hegel struggles with the correct description of how God's self-revelatory reality is absolute in itself and, at the same time, has the history of salvation as its own constitutive movement. This difficulty has led to various difficulties in grasping properly Hegel's notion of faith. One of these difficulties is the charge that Hegel suggested the attainability of full knowledge of God. In fact, Hegel never proposes that such a full knowledge is attainable for any human being. He even points out the secondary character of all knowledge in contradistinction to God's *reality*. Yet Hegel could not dispel the suspicion that he considered at least himself, the philosopher, as a person capable of gaining full knowledge of God. This ambiguity rightly raises the impression that Hegel's notion of faith is a one-sided rationalistic account of what we can properly approach only in the realm of mystery.

Study questions

1. What is the main merit of Hegel according to Gislain Lafont?
2. What are the main ideas of Kant, Jacobi, Fichte and Schleiermacher which Hegel criticizes in his account of faith?
3. How would you characterize Hegel's notion of faith in his system?
4. Why is Hegel's notion of faith ambiguous?
5. In your opinion, did Hegel have faith in God?

Further reading

Desmond, William, *Hegel's God: A Counterfeit Double?* (Aldershot: Ashgate, 2003).
Singer, Peter, *Hegel: A Very Short Introduction* (Oxford: Oxford University Press, 1983).
Taylor, Charles, *Hegel* (Cambridge: Cambridge University Press, 1975).

---

[16]Hegel, *Lectures on the Philosophy of Religion*, p. 414.

14

Faith and Paradox: Søren Kierkegaard

Foolishness to the Greeks

In 1 Cor. 1.23 Paul declares the Cross to be foolishness to the Greeks. Instead of choosing the wise, powerful and noble of the world, God chose what is foolish, weak and despised. The foolishness of the gospel according to the wisdom of the world is dramatically performed in Paul's speech on the Areopagus to the learned Athenians, whom the text identifies as Epicurean and Stoic philosophers. While some in the audience believe Paul's preaching about the crucified and risen Jesus, others scoff at the raising of the dead (Acts 17.16–34).

Several Christian thinkers are well known for revelling in the foolish or paradoxical nature of Christianity. While the Roman apologist Tertullian (160–225) did not actually say, 'I believe because it is absurd', as is commonly thought, this striking line fairly summarizes some of his assertions. Even the Benedictine monk Peter Damian (c. 1007–1072/1073) claimed that Jesus did not choose philosophers as disciples, but mere fisherman. Finally, there is Blaise Pascal's famous option for 'the God of Abraham, God of Isaac, God of Jacob, not of philosophers and scholars'.[1] For Pascal (1623–1662), the heart finally outruns reason: 'this faith is in the heart, and makes us say not *Scio* [I know], but *Credo* [I believe].'[2]

The best-known modern advocate of the foolishness and paradox at the heart of Christianity was the Danish thinker Søren Kierkegaard (1813–1855). For Kierkegaard, the distinguishing mark of Christianity is the 'absolute paradox' it places before us in the figure of the God-man Jesus Christ. He is a 'paradox' as he is the walking unity of apparent contradictions. The transcendent, eternal, infinite God became this earthly, temporal and finite man without ceasing to be God. To speak of Jesus, we need to combine impossibly contradictory things both of which are necessary to his single reality.

As a paradox, the Incarnation is an offense to reason in terms of both its 'loftiness' and its 'lowliness'.[3] Jesus Christ appears as a homeless peasant, but speaks as God does, forgives sin and demands that we give our all to him. This lowly man speaks

---

[1]Blaise Pascal, *Pensées*, trans. Roger Ariew (Indianapolis: Hackett, 2004), p. 266.
[2]As quoted in Michael Moriarty, 'Grace and Religious Belief in Pascal', in Nicholas Hammond (ed.), *The Cambridge Companion to Pascal* (Cambridge: Cambridge University Press, 2006), pp. 144–164 (155).
[3]See Søren Kierkegaard (Anti-Climacus), *Training in Christianity and the Edifying Discourse Which 'Accompanied' It*, trans. Walter Lowrie (Oxford: Oxford University Press, 1941), pp. 86–108.

and does 'lofty' things. Conversely, the doctrine of the incarnation claims that the Creator of all known and unknown universes, dimensions and times became just this one person who lived long ago in a distant place, gathered a few followers, gave them some cryptic sayings and died on a Cross at the hands of his creatures. The majestic God speaks and does 'lowly' things. Even more offensively, Jesus expects all the billions of people in the world, scattered through all times and places, to learn about him from a slow oral transmission, rather than constantly and clearly broadcasting it across the skies for all to see.

Kierkegaard eagerly underlined the paradox of Christianity because he thought it needed to be harder to be a Christian. In nineteenth-century Denmark, Christianity was the official state religion. So any Dane was automatically a Christian. Having faith was the norm. There was also 'the System', meaning Hegel's thought, in which everything – God, the Cross, the Napoleonic wars, you, that tree – had a rational place within the sweeping unfolding of reason. In response to both Christendom and 'the System', Kierkegaard highlighted the difficult and arduous process of *becoming* a Christian. For his contemporaries, *being* a Christian meant *being* born into their society. Kierkegaard pointed at *becoming* a Christian by accenting its paradoxes and offensiveness. He said the individual matters.

One tactic Kierkegaard adopted for making faith once again be faith was 'indirect communication'. Christianity's claims about Jesus Christ and the response of faith in him are not like other forms of knowledge and reception, as when a chemistry professor writes a chemical pathway on the board and her class scribbles it down. Having faith in Jesus is not like knowing one more interesting fact about the world. Religious or existential concerns cannot be 'communicated directly', as they aren't like chemistry equations but require passion, subjective appropriation and attuning one's whole life to this truth. How, then, can the presentation match the content? How does one talk about matters of life and existence in a way which causes people to stop and reflect upon the course and future of their lives and not simply adopt what someone else says? 'Indirect communication' is what it takes.

To speak indirectly, Kierkegaard developed full-blown personas with their own viewpoints about life and then wrote works from their perspectives or even staged conversations between them within his books. Readers of Kierkegaard's works will meet a cast of characters: Johannes Climacus, Vitor Heremita, Johannes de Silentio, Hilarius Bookbinder, Johannes Anti-Climacus, Vigilius Haufniensis, Constantin Constantius, Judge William, the Young Man and more. (As Kierkegaard published whole books under the name of some of these characters, it is important to remember who the stated 'author' of the work is, as one cannot always assume that the viewpoint is Kierkegaard's own.) Each one of Kierkegaard's personas or 'masks' has a different, serious and well thought-through view on life, even the ones who think that the pursuit of enjoyment and entertainment is the highest and best type of life. This style of writing, forcing one to come to grip with different ways of life and thinking, generates reflection on how to live and to exist.

Kierkegaard's most outstandingly paradoxical characters are Johannes Climacus, the 'author' of *Philosophical Fragments* and *Concluding Unscientific Postscript*, and Anti-Climacus, the 'author' of *Training in Christianity* and *The Sickness unto Death*. The relationship between Johannes Climacus and Anti-Climacus, and between them and Kierkegaard himself, is complex. Johannes Climacus (John the Climber) says that he would not call himself religious (which is somewhat strange given that he is named for a sixth-century monk who wrote *The Ladder of Divine Ascent*), but is absorbed in the difficulty of becoming a Christian. Anti-Climacus, on the other hand, represents for Kierkegaard a kind of 'ideal' yet almost inhuman type of Christianity. Kierkegaard notes that Anti-Climacus has a bit of 'the demonic' in him, but still insists that his portrayal of the Christian ideal is 'sound'. (In his *Journals* Kierkegaard places himself higher than Johannes Climacus but lower than Anti-Climacus.)

Johannes Climacus calls the idea that the eternal God became one particular man 'absurd'.[4] Climacus is also responsible for Kierkegaard's well-known line that 'truth is subjectivity'. This does not mean that if one believes hard enough, then everything and anything can be 'true'. This commonplace view would not be very paradoxical or interesting. Furthermore, Climacus also says that Christianity actually thinks that subjectivity is 'untruth' on account of sin. So perhaps we should not trust our own thoughts, passions and desires too much. But Climacus does think that there is more 'truth' in the pagan's passionate worship of an idol than in a Christian's uncaring recitation of the creed. By giving utter devotion to his god of stone and wood, the pagan grasps that religious existence is a matter of surrender and self-giving. It grasps the whole individual. The absolute paradox of Christianity generates this kind of impassioned and suffering believing or *pathos* (passion). In doing so, the paradox creates an individual. It invokes within a person concerned about external beauty (aesthetics) or external obligations (ethics) a tumultuous 'inwardness' or subjectivity (religion). The paradox does this because the paradox can neither be finally comprehended nor gotten rid of: 'Faith *must not be satisfied* with incomprehensibility, because the very relation to or repulsion from the incomprehensible, the absurd, is the expression for the passion of faith.'[5] It is this 'passion of faith' which snatches the individual from being just another unthinking part of 'the System' or from assuming that faith is natural or easy.

Fear and Trembling contains Kierkegaard's most famous account of faith. It is 'written' by Johannes de Silentio (John the Silent), who repeatedly concedes that he is not Christian. He says he wants to understand Abraham, and especially the faith and anxiety Abraham must have felt when told to sacrifice his only son Isaac (Gen. 22.1–19). The tale of the binding of Isaac is fascinating because its laconic and matter-of-fact narration of these strange events leaves so many questions unanswered. *Fear and Trembling* begins with four short retellings of the story. In each retelling the events are broadly those of the biblical text, but Johannes de Silentio adds different twists and revelations of the characters' thoughts and feelings. The results are haunting, and their effect is to make this 'father of faith', who trusted God and did what God had commanded him, a paradoxical and enigmatic figure.

When he pursues three ethical questions about the story, Johannes de Silentio introduces two similar yet finally very different figures: the 'tragic hero' (or 'knight of resignation') and the 'knight of faith'. Johannes de Silentio brings up three tragic

---

[4] Søren Kierkegaard (Johannes Climacus), *Concluding Unscientific Postscript*, trans. David F. Swenson and Walter Lowrie (Princeton: Princeton University Press, 1968), p. 188.
[5] Kierkegaard (Johannes Climacus), *Concluding Unscientific Postscript*, p. 540.

heroes whose stories seem similar to that of Abraham. Agamemnon is told to sacrifice his daughter Iphigenia so that the goddess Artemis could be appeased and his ships could sail to Troy. Jephthah in the Old Testament makes a vow to God for victory in battle and then sacrifices his own daughter when she unexpectedly greets the victorious Jephthah first. Junius Brutus of Rome promises to hunt down all traitors and in the end must kill his own sons for treason. As Johannes de Silentio sees it, in each case one set of ethical duties, the ethical relationship between parents and children, is suspended or broken for the sake of a higher set of ethical duties, the city or society as a whole. These figures thus remain within 'the ethical' and 'the universal'.[6]

Johannes de Silentio adds that in 'paganism' the universal and the ethical are the divine, the highest and eternal order of things. The tragic hero is able to renounce and surrender the finite and the temporal (e.g. one's children) and focus on the infinite and the eternal (the ethical and universal). This surrender is not an easy matter, but requires commitment, courage and loss. The knight of resignation, or even 'infinite resignation', accepts this loss, and finds comfort in the universal and eternal, meaning the ethical nature of things.

Abraham is not a tragic hero, but a knight of faith. Abraham does not exchange one set of ethical duties for another, but moves beyond the ethical and the universal altogether. In fact, 'the ethical' exists for him as a kind of temptation. Being a good father to his son, following one's parental duties, would in this case mean disobeying the command of God. Abraham moves beyond the sphere of the ethical entirely. He can do so because of his faith and trust in God. Abraham believes that God can and will return Isaac to him, not in the hereafter, but in this life. He trusts the God who can bring back the dead (Heb. 11.18) and who will bring Isaac back to him. It is by Abraham's faith that an act which should be reckoned as attempted murder becomes a holy act, one pleasing to God. It is because of Abraham's willingness to sacrifice his son that Abraham is then given Isaac back. Faith is, accordingly, a 'prodigious paradox'.[7] It makes the individual (Abraham) higher than the universal (the ethical). It puts the individual directly into contact with the absolute (God), rather than having the relationship between the individual and the divine mediated through the universal (the ethical).

The tragic hero has one movement. He renounces the temporal and the finite for the sake of the eternal and infinite. In the eternal and infinite, the tragic hero finds consolation and joy. Abraham's faith has two movements. The first is like that of the tragic hero. Abraham renounces the world by giving up Isaac, the promised child through whom he would become a father of many nations. Thus the tragic hero's resignation is 'half way' to faith and serves as a kind of transition step. Yet the second movement is that Abraham believes that he will get Isaac back in the here and now. In this movement, the knight of faith leaves the consolation of the eternal and infinite and returns to the finite and temporal. Johannes de Silentio thinks that the first step, the renunciation of the temporal, can be done. It is difficult, but it is within one's powers. The second step, however, Johannes thinks, is not within any

---

[6]Søren Kierkegaard (Johannes de Silentio), *Fear and Trembling* ed. C. Stephen Evans and Sylvia Walsh, trans. Sylvia Walsh (Cambridge: Cambridge University Press, 2006), pp. 50–51.
[7]Kierkegaard, *Fear and Trembling*, p. 46.

person's powers to achieve by themselves. One can weep for the tragic hero, but before Abraham, the knight of faith, one can only feel a kind of terrible awe.

Two of Johannes de Silentio's targets here are Kant and Hegel. Kant thought that the principles of reason – including those of practical reason, or ethics – were universally binding and necessary truths. Any reasonable person, regardless of time or place, could reflect upon life and come to certain necessary and universal truths about ethics. Hegel thought that Kant's ethics were too abstract and general to be of much use within life. For Hegel reason is manifested, or mediated, through the demands of law, social customs and intuitions, which can change over time. Within this short story from Genesis, however, we find a divine command addressed to one specific individual, not a social custom or something true for every reasonable being. We find a man who believes in the absurd and paradoxical, that Isaac will be returned to him, and this man goes on to be called the father of faith.

In the true style of indirect communication, the positions of Anti-Climacus, Johannes Climacus and Johannes de Silentio should not be thought of as 'objective knowledge' which we can just adopt as our own. In their very plurality and disagreements with each other they are supposed to be spurs for own reflections upon existence. Kierkegaard's own thought remained in motion even after publishing these pseudonymous works. Kierkegaard later began to publish various 'edifying discourses' under his own name. These discourses seem less concerned about provoking 'infinite subjectivity' or 'inwardness' than consoling and encouraging Christians who suffer on account of following Christ. While the notion of offence remains, faith also becomes a matter of confidence, of expecting victory in sorrows and sufferings: the theme of love becomes heightened. (In his *Journals*, Kierkegaard even criticizes Luther for saying that we can only love our neighbour and have faith in God, rather than being able to love God as well.)

Scholars still argue about whether Kierkegaard is an irrationalist. In his *Journals*, Kierkegaard noted that 'when the believer has faith, the absurd is not the absurd – faith transforms it'.[8] The exact phrase 'leap of faith' cannot be found in either Kierkegaard's pseudonymous works or those published under his own name.[9] Even his style of indirect communication is an impetus to thought about existence and even to modes of existence which thought might have difficulty understanding, but not faith.

Study questions

1. Is the Incarnation 'paradoxical' or 'foolish'?
2. Does faith ever lose its paradoxical or apparently foolish nature? Should it?
3. Is the individual higher than the universal/ethical?
4. Does Kierkegaard's method of 'indirect communication' seem helpful or just confusing?

---

[8] Søren Kierkegaard, *Journals and Papers*, ed. and trans. Howard V. Hong and Edna H. Hong, vol. 1 (Bloomington: Indiana University Press, 1967), 10, p. 7.
[9] As pointed out by Alastair McKinnon, 'Kierkegaard and the Leap of Faith', *Kierkegaardiana* 16 (1993), pp. 107–125.

Further reading

Gen. 22.1–19; Judg. 11.29–40; Heb. 11.1–19.

Kierkegaard, Søren, 'Blessed Is He Whosoever Is Not Offended in Me', sections A, B, C of part II of *Training in Christianity*, trans. Walter Lowrie (Princeton: Princeton University Press, 1944), pp. 79–123.

———, 'Tuning Up' and 'A Tribute to Abraham', in C. Stephen Evans and Sylvia Walsh (eds), trans. Sylvia Walsh, *Fear and Trembling* (Cambridge: Cambridge University Press, 2006), pp. 7–11; 12–20.

15

The Limits of Reason II: Vatican I

Divi Filius: Church and State

In ancient times, each Roman emperor was *Divi Filius*, a 'son of God': the 'divine' Caesars persecuted the early Christians for refusing them a pinch of incense. The French Revolution saw a reversion to ancient attitudes. The aftermath of the revolution witnessed a revulsion against 'classical' rationalism in favour of sentiment, history and even tradition. 'Traditionalism' was a form of pietism, which became very popular in France in the nineteenth century: Traditionalists held that *all* of our knowledge of God derives from an original revelation by God, which has been filtered through the Chinese whispers of human transmission. It was a period of reaction against intellectualism, for the devout held that Enlightenment rationalism was to blame for the French Revolution, in which countless clerics, aristocrats and simple lay Catholics were murdered. Hard-core traditionalists rejected the scholastic apparatus of rational proof for the existence of God and insisted that it is only by Tradition, which traces back to God's original revelation, that we can know about God. Louis Bautain (1796–1867) was one such traditionalist. A professor at the University of Strasbourg, he taught, like some Church Fathers, that Christianity is the only true philosophy, and indeed, that only Christian faith makes philosophy possible at all.

Felicité de Lamennais (1782–1854) was another traditionalist. From studying the traditions of human civilization, Lamennais came to think that people are naturally religious and would continue to worship God outside of the protection of State establishment. Lamennais advocated the disestablishment of the French Church because he thought it the best way to avoid the subjugation of the Church to the State. His initiatives were rebuffed by Pope Gregory XVI in 1834, with *Mirari vos*. The encyclical denounces Lamennais' notion of disestablishment as a mirage which would not result in the spread of Christian faith, but in mass indifference to religious claims.

Realistic anxieties about governmental pursuit of control over the Church played a role in the development and clarification of Catholic teaching about faith and reason in the nineteenth century. If Christianity is said to be *purely* a matter of *faith*, and faith is defined as private opinion, then there are no good grounds for why it should have any public influence or for why its own institutions should not be governed by people with better credentials to be called reasonable. When religion is seen as a matter of private opinion most people become indifferent to it, since more people are interested in truth than in other people's private opinions. On the other hand, if Christianity is said to be a matter of reason *alone*, then it would make more sense for its activities to be determined by reasonable people such as a government's civil servants rather than by an esoteric club of clergy and ministers.

Prussian governments pursued the logic of State domination of the Churches by drawing ever more tightly the boundaries of what may rationally be said. In France it was the traditionalists and Jansenists who tended to marginalize the Church from public influence. Nineteenth-century encyclicals' denouncing of rationalism and indifferentism denote these errors as causes of 'civil strife'.

Doctrines only develop after some implicit Christian thinking is explicitly denied. The new possibilities for controlling institutions (like universities, churches, monasteries, religious orders and courts of law) which emerged in the nineteenth century led to socially influential redefinitions of faith and reason. The Church had to defend itself against being absorbed into the secular State. So it had to deny the absolute claims of reason. The Church also had to remind believers that God is mysterious. By denying the right of the State to define everything on secular terms, the Church defended its own existence.

Over the top about faith or reason

The respective standings of faith and reason were a big question in this era. The claims of faith and reason were seldom stated in a balanced way. For some, like the traditionalists, our only access to God is through belief in tradition: such beliefs, they said, are impervious to reason. For others, like the Belgian Georg Hermes (1775–1831), practical reason can adjudicate the claims of divine revelations to count as public knowledge. Anton Günther (1783–1863) argued that the Tri-Unity of God can be validated at the bar of reason. The nineteenth century was the era of big systems and the engine of these grand narratives tended to be a single big idea. The great narratives were usually driven exclusively either by faith or by rationality, for their purpose was to capture everything within a single idea.

Papal teaching began to push back against extreme 'faith-ism' and rationalism in the 1830s. In 1835, Gregory XVI issued a 'Brief' (one notch below an encyclical) called *Dum acerbissimas* against Hermes' incorporation of 'positive doubt' into theological method and against his claim that Kantian-style moral or practical reason can adequately discriminate in favour or against the claims of historical divine revelation. In the same year, Bautain was summoned to Rome and induced by rational Jesuit persuasion to modify his traditionalism. By 1840, Bautain conceded that the original revelation given by God to humanity and passed on through tradition was sufficient to allow human beings to evolve linguistic means of speaking about and arguing rationally for God's existence.

Pius IX

Pius IX's first encyclical was *Qui pluribus* (*On Faith and Religion*, 1846). It calls for moderation in the extreme claims made by the parties of 'faith' and of 'reason':

> although faith is above reason, no real disagreement or opposition can ever be
> found between them: this is because both of them come from the same greatest

source of unchanging and eternal truth, God. They give such reciprocal help to each other that true reason, shows, maintains, and protects the truth of the faith, while faith frees reason from all errors and wondrously enlightens, strengthens, and perfects reason with the knowledge of divine matters.[1]

The encyclical criticizes those who speak

> as if religion … were … a philosophical discovery which can be perfected by human means. The charge which Tertullian justly made against the philosophers … 'who brought forward a Stoic and a Platonic and a Dialectical Christianity' can … aptly apply to those men … Our holy religion was not invented by human reason, but was … revealed by God; … religion … acquires all its power from the authority of God who made the revelation, and … can never be arrived at or perfected by human reason.[2]

This is directed against those who sought to shore up the 'public' character of Christian revelation by showing that it meets the officially pervasive criteria of Kantian moral or practical reason. In an era of rising doubt, the temptation to be too apologetical is hard to resist.

Anton Günther was an Austrian philosophical theologian who wanted to defeat Hegel and pantheism. He sought to demonstrate the reasonableness of faith in the Trinity. In *Singulari quidem*: *On the Church in Austria*, Pius IX singles out rationalism for disapprobation.[3] Pius IX criticized Günther in his 1857 Brief *Eximiam tuum* for making faith so reasonable that reason and faith become modes of the same intellectual act. The 1864 *Syllabus of Errors* (which, contrary to popular belief, does not list electric light as one of the errors of modernity) has as an appendage *Quanta cura*, which stigmatizes pantheism, indifferentism and rationalism.

Vatican I (1869–1870): *Dei Filius*

The teachings of Gregory XVI and Pius IX thus already sketch most of what will be promulgated at the ecumenical Council Vatican I. Vatican I (or the First Vatican Council) will promulgate two decrees. The first, *Dei Filius*, deals with faith and reason, while the second deals with the Church and defines the conditions of papal infallibility. The authors of *Dei Filius* drew upon the above-mentioned Briefs and encyclicals. In its original drafting, by J. B. Franzelin, *Dei Filius* was directed in an obscure philosophical way against the intricacies of metaphysical systems, like emanationism (a recondite version of pantheism which gave seminary professors a headache). After this draft was rejected, it was rewritten by Joseph Kleutgen (1811–1883) so as to address the great contemporary problems of atheism and agnosticism. *Dei Filius* was written by clear-minded Thomists to defend Christianity

---

[1] Pius IX, *Qui pluribus: On Faith and Religion*, §6.
[2] Pius IX, *Qui pluribus*, §7.
[3] Pius IX, *Singulari quidem: On the Church in Austria* (1856), §6.

against those who would redefine it as 'private opinion' or permit it only to speak in the moderate tones of a scientific civil servant-university professor.

The Prologue to *Dei Filius* gives a 'declinist' history of the present-day dilemmas. Reformation Protestantism has devolved into 'a multiplicity of sects', leaving many without faith in Christ and regarding the Bible as 'the inventions of myth'. This gave rise to 'rationalism or naturalism', which denies that anything exists outside and above 'nature'. The denial of the supernatural then spawned 'pantheism, materialism and atheism', which generate irrationalism and immoralism.[4]

Chapter 1 of *Dei Filius* affirms that God created the world 'by an absolutely free plan'. The god of pantheism creates by a necessity of his nature, or simply because that is how such a god rolls. The Christian God creates 'to manifest his perfection', and does so freely.[5] Chapter 2 is 'On Revelation'. It asserts that God 'can be known with certainty from the consideration of created things, by the natural power of human reason'. It does not prescribe any particular proof of the existence of God. It does not affirm that human beings might potentially be able to prove that God is. Rather, it says that God 'can be *known* with certainty' from 'created things'. We can know God by rational inference from 'things', like human beings, dogs and stars. Since the chapter is 'On Revelation', these remarks mean that as God is revealed to human reason through God's creation, like an author is revealed by his work, so God can be *known* from created things (here the Decree cites Rom. 1.20). The opening sentences of the Decree are about *natural* revelation, or God's *creation*.

It goes on to speak about *supernatural revelation*, or those things exhibited to faith. In the first Question of the *Summa*, Thomas Aquinas notes that even those things about God which can in principle be known by reason were supernaturally revealed by God. Effectively paraphrasing Thomas' article, the Decree adds that God 'reveal[ed] himself to the human race by a ... supernatural, way ... It is ... thanks to this divine revelation, that those matters concerning God which are not of themselves beyond the scope of human reason, can, even in the present state of the human race, be known by everyone without difficulty, with firm certitude and with no intermingling of error'. Just as Thomas does, the Decree notes that the purpose of God's revealing even those things which pagans could have guessed at about God is that the purpose for which the human race was made – to see God – transcends their natural powers.[6]

God reveals to the eyes of faith even some things which reason could know. The Decree states that 'one must hold revelation to be absolutely necessary' to humanity because 'God directed human beings to a supernatural end'. This is against diminishing the human journey to a path which we could naturally reason our way through. The purpose of humanity is to transcend itself and know the supernatural God, who exceeds anything which we could see or know naturally.[7]

Moderns are interested in the psychology of faith. Focusing on the psychology of faith, or as faith as something interesting *about me*, can come *at the expense* of considering faith as a *gift*, or as something *from God*. This loses sight of the truth

---

[4]Decrees of the First Vatican Council, *Dei Filius* (1870), Prologue, §§5–7.
[5]*Dei Filius*, I.3.
[6]*Dei Filius*, 2.1–4. Compare Thomas Aquinas, *Summa theologica* I, q. 1, a. 1.
[7]*Dei Filius*, 2.4.

that I cannot *give myself* faith, I can only *open myself to it* or *co-operate* with it. If faith is not natural but a *supernatural* way of knowing and seeing *the supernatural* being of God, then I cannot leap or jump into it for myself. I cannot even pick it up and find it for myself, like poor Gollum with his 'birthday present' of a ring. God is too weird, too transcendent to be picked up for ourselves. Chapter 3 of *Dei Filius* states that faith is a 'supernatural virtue', that is, a virtue given by the grace of the Holy Spirit. By 'means' of this supernatural virtue, 'we believe to be true what He has revealed, not because we perceive its intrinsic truth by the natural light of reason, but because of the authority of God himself, who makes the revelation and can neither deceive nor be deceived'.[8]

This assertion is balanced by the affirmation that the 'internal assistance' of the Holy Spirit, that is, supernatural grace, is 'linked' to 'external indications', especially the 'miracles and prophecies' of 'Moses, and the prophets, and especially Christ our Lord himself'.[9] *Dei Filius* did not intend to forfeit the external evidence for Christianity or to withdraw Christian faith from history.

The point here is to avoid defining faith purely on internal grounds, as a private sensation or conviction: 'the assent of faith is by no means a blind movement of the mind', the decree states; rather, we keep our eyes open and observe natural things and historical facts in the very act of believing the supernatural God. And 'yet, no one can accept the gospel preaching in the way necessary for achieving salvation without the inspiration and illumination of the Holy Spirit, who gives to all facility in accepting and believing the truth. And so faith in itself…is a gift of God'.[10] No one can 'achieve justification', nor 'attain eternal life', 'without faith'.[11]

So far, most of *Dei Filius* has been about theological epistemology: it is about how we know God, by faith and by reason. In Chapter 4, 'On Faith and Reason', we find a distinction between *how* we know, the *source* of our knowledge and belief and *what* we know, the *object* of knowledge and belief. It states, 'there is a twofold order of knowledge, distinct not only as regards its source but also as regards its object. With regard to the source, we know at the one level by natural reason, at the other level by divine faith'.[12] Knowledge of God occurs at two levels, through reason and through faith. 'With regard to the object, beside those things to which natural reason can attain, there are proposed for our belief *mysteries* hidden in God.'[13] The text moves beyond theological *epistemology* to the *metaphysics* which determines it: natural reason cannot tell us all we wish to know about God because God is *mysterious*. Therefore, some things about God must simply be *believed*, and cannot be known or proven.

Reason can 'achieve by God's gift some understanding…of the mysteries, whether by analogy from what it knows naturally or from the connexion of these mysteries with one another': so theology is never wholly in the dark about God. Nonetheless, natural human 'reason is never rendered capable of *penetrating* those mysteries' in

---

[8]*Dei Filius*, 3.2.
[9]*Dei Filius*, 3.4–5.
[10]*Dei Filius*, 3.6–7.
[11]*Dei Filius*, 3.9.
[12]*Dei Filius*, 3.2.
[13]*Dei Filius*, 3.3.

the way it can get inside natural objects. Even revealed mysteries of their nature (of the nature of God) remain impenetrable: 'they remain covered by the veil of that same faith' which 'accepted' them, and 'wrapped … in a certain obscurity'.[14] This must refer to the mystery of the Holy Trinity. We can give analogies for the Trinity, as Augustine did with his triad of memory, will and knowledge, but such analogies must not be engineered to explain the Trinity or include it within some rational and total narrative. It makes us think of Winston Churchill's description of Russia as 'a riddle, wrapped in a mystery, inside an enigma'. In the case of the Trinity, faith does not make us see more, but it makes us see that we see less, that is, makes us recognize a mystery when confronted with one.

Reason and faith are different ways of knowing. Reason and faith know God under distinct aspects. But they know *one and the same God* so that what faith knows about God and what reason knows about the same God cannot contradict each other. Both creation (reason) and grace (faith) issue from the same God: 'Even though faith is above reason, there can never be any real disagreement between faith and reason, since it is the same God who reveals the mysteries and infuses faith, and who has endowed the human mind with the light of reason.'[15]

Dei Filius was not aimed against secular philosophies. It was written to warn Christians against being conformed to the mind of the age. It reminded Christian thinkers that faith and reason are distinct, balance one another and work in harmony.

Study questions

1. Why did many nineteenth-century French people become traditionalists after the French Revolution?
2. What is the key concept in *Dei Filius*?
3. Is *Dei Filius* directed more against rationalism or against traditionalism?
4. Can Christianity influence public life if it cannot make evidential and argumentative claims about its truth?

Further reading

Aidan Nichols, O.P., *From Hermes to Benedict XVI: Faith and Reason in Modern Catholic Thought* (Leominister: Gracewing, 2009).
'Dogmatic Constitution on the Catholic Faith: Dei Filius', in Norman P. Tanner (ed.), *The Decrees of the Ecumenical Councils: Volume II: Trent to Vatican II* (London: Sheed and Ward, 1990).

---

[14]*Dei Filius*, 4.4.
[15]*Dei Filius*, 4.5.

16

Faith and the Faithfulness of God: Karl Barth

For I am not ashamed of the gospel; it is the power of God for salvation to everyone who has faith, to the Jew first and also to the Greek. For in it the righteousness of God is revealed through faith for faith; as it is written, 'The one who is righteous will live by faith'.
(Romans 1.16–17)

There is an intriguing phrase here: 'through faith to faith' (*ek pisteōs eis pistin*), sometimes also translated as 'from faith to faith'. How is the righteousness of God revealed through faith and for faith? Does 'faith' mean the same thing in both cases? And whose 'faith' is in view here? As Luther explains in his commentary on Romans, some past theologians and commentators have seen in this phrase a reference to the faith of those in the Old Testament and the faith of those in the New.[1] Others have seen this phrase as a reference to believer's growth in faith, following the line of being changed from 'glory to glory' in 2 Cor. 3.18. Luther also mentions Augustine's interpretation from *On the Spirit and the Letter*, which sees in the phrase references to those who confess the gospel and those who hear and receive it.

Commentary on Romans

In 1919 a young Swiss pastor named Karl Barth (1886–1968) published a commentary on Romans. In true scholarly style, Barth provided his own translations of the verses before he commented on them. His own translation seeks to remove some of the ambiguity of the verse by considering what Paul is speaking about here and elsewhere in the Epistle to the Romans: the righteousness of God. Barth translates Rom. 1.17 in this way: 'For the righteousness of God is revealed in it: from (His) faithfulness to the faith (of humans).' The translation of Paul's *pistis* as 'the faithfulness of God' occurs in other places in Barth's 1919 commentary. In his translation of Rom. 3.27–28, for instance, boasting is excluded 'by the law which is fulfilled by the faithfulness of God. For we maintain that man is justified by the

---

[1]Martin Luther, *Commentary on Romans*, trans. J. Theodore Mueller (Grand Rapids, Mich.: Zondervan, 1954), pp. 41–42.

faithfulness of God, apart from the actions which the law demands'.[2] Likewise, Rom. 14.23, usually translated as 'whatever does not proceed from faith is sin', becomes in Barth's commentary 'whatever does not proceed from the faithfulness of God is sin'.[3]

This way of translating some instances of *pistis* offers a significant shift in focus. Instead of human faith being the subject of the verse, or the primary agent of the action, the emphasis is placed upon God and his faithfulness to his promises. The novelty of some of these translations did not escape some of the premier biblical scholars of the early twentieth century in their reviews of Barth's commentary. Their reaction to it, however, was mostly negative.

Barth heavily revised his 1919 commentary (which has not been translated into English) and published it again in 1922 (the edition used for the English translation). In his preface to the work, Barth responds to his critics regarding his decision to translate *pistis* as 'the faithfulness of God'. Barth notes that this way of rendering *pistis* was suggested to him in a letter from Rudolf Leichtenhan, a pastor and New Testament scholar (and also Barth's cousin). In his letter, Leichtenhan writes to Barth about translating 'from faith to faith' in Rom. 1.17:

> Here I would like to translate the first *pistis* as a *divine* attribute, something for which I can nevertheless offer no *dictum probans* to substantiate. I translate it as 'faithfulness' after the more frequent use of *pistos ho theos* [God is faithful] in 1 Corinthians. It consists in God remaining faithful to the promise given to Abraham and to the good news previously announced by the prophets…Human *pistis* consists of a person confiding in the divine *pistis*.[4]

It seems that Barth thought Leichtenhan was on to something, as Barth takes up Leichtenhan's suggestion not only for Rom. 1.17 but also for other instances of *pistis*. In his Preface, Barth also notes to his critics that he has actually reduced the number of times *pistis* is translated as 'the faithfulness of God' in the 1922 edition, but that he has kept this way of translating it throughout Rom. 3. His conclusion regarding this issue is that something important would be missed if *pistis* were always translated as either 'faith' or the 'faithfulness of God'. Both translations of *pistis* are thus necessary to try to express what Paul is saying. (We should also note that neither Leichtenhan nor Barth were the only or first advocates for understanding 'from faith to faith' in this way. In his own commentary on Romans, Thomas Aquinas also holds that interpreting 'from faith to faith' to mean from God's promises to human faith is a legitimate understanding of the verse.[5])

---

[2]Karl Barth, *Der Römerbrief (Erste Fassung) 1919*, ed. Hermann Schmidt (Zürich: Theologischer Verlag Zürich, 1985), p. 101.

[3]Barth, *Der Römerbrief 1919*, p. 553.

[4]Karl Barth, *Der Römerbrief (Zweite Fassung) 1922*, ed. Cornelius van der Kooi and Katja Tolstaja (Zürich: Theologische Verlag, 2010), p. xvii.

[5]See Michael Waldstein, 'The Trinitarian, Spousal, and Ecclesial Logic of Justification', in Matthew Levering and Michael Dauphinais (eds), *Reading Romans with St. Thomas Aquinas* (Washington: Catholic University of America Press, 2012), pp. 274–287 (275–276).

Barth at this time thought that much of nineteenth-century theology, and in particular the theologians who followed Schleiermacher, was more concerned with the pious believer than with the righteous God. For these theologians, the faith of the believer had become more interesting than the faithfulness of God as described in Scripture. In both editions of his Romans commentary, Barth attempted to place the emphasis upon God and not upon the person's response to or feeling about God. Barth thought that this emphasis in his commentary was necessary because it was also where Paul placed his emphasis: the promises of God to Jews and Gentiles and God's faithfulness to these promises in Jesus Christ. In order to follow Paul and Paul's concerns, one needed to see that sometimes *pistis* for Paul meant the divine faithfulness and not human faith.

How Barth changed his mind

It took Barth time to come to this conclusion. Before the outbreak of the First World War, Barth was a student of the 'modern theology'. Broadly speaking, this movement consisted of followers of Schleiermacher and Albrecht Ritschl. For the younger, so-called 'liberal' Barth, faith was primarily a matter of trust (*fiducia*). In some of his earliest essays, he tried to offer a creative synthesis of Melanchthon's ideas of trust and knowing the benefits of Christ and Schleiermacher's idea of feeling. In this way, the young Barth hoped to bypass Kant's criticisms of traditional ideas of God, revelation and metaphysical realities. This Barth also criticized the Protestant Scholastics for their accounts of faith as assent (*assensus*) or knowledge (*notitia*). He thought that understanding faith in this way was a kind of return to an intellectualist voluntarism common in Roman Catholicism. Here an individual is given a list of things to believe and wills to believe it. The wilful acceptance of a collection of truths or historical facts is a form of works righteousness. Faith is trust of the heart, the feeling of Jesus Christ within the believer, the experience of the inner life of Jesus within me.

During the First World War, Barth the Swiss pastor soon came to think that this account of Christian faith was inadequate for reading Scripture, for preaching in troubled times, for resisting the dangers of national idolatry, for avoiding the use of religion for well-intentioned yet finally malicious ends and simply for talking about the God of Jesus Christ. Barth returned to the text of Romans in order to rethink the modern or 'liberal' theology that he had inherited from his primarily German theological teachers. What he found in Romans, and in Scripture more generally, was a living, faithful and transcendent God who proved his faithfulness and continual presence to humanity in the life, death and resurrection of Jesus Christ.

Faithfulness of God, not human beings

This emphasis upon the faithfulness of God and faith as an acceptance and confession of this faithfulness would continue in Barth's mature account of faith in the much later *Church Dogmatics* IV (1953). Here faith has its origin and content not in itself, but in its 'object', which is God in Jesus Christ. Faith is the free renunciation and abandonment of being oriented and based upon oneself in favour of being oriented and based upon Jesus Christ. Faith is an awakening by the Holy Spirit, the creation of a new person who follows Jesus Christ and lives within the community Jesus Christ created and still guides: the church.

Barth describes the act of faith by using three variants of the German word *kennen* (to know): *acknowledgement, recognition* and *confession* (*anerkennen, erkennen* and *bekennen*). The act of faith is a free and spontaneous human act, and yet it is a free human act which is always a response. Acknowledgement, recognition and confession are all types of responses. One can only acknowledge, recognize and confess something. Without that which is acknowledged, recognized or confessed, we are not left with anything interesting or substantial. Faith acknowledges the presence and call of Jesus Christ as he makes himself known in and through the Christian community. Faith recognizes who Jesus Christ is and what he has done. It recognizes that Jesus Christ accomplished what the believer never could and that the work of Jesus Christ is *pro me*, for me, and *pro nobis*, for us. It is thus not only recognition of Jesus Christ but is also self-recognition, for I too am affected by what he has done. Faith is confession, a public and visible standing with Jesus Christ and his community. It confesses that Jesus Christ is the basis of its faith, hope and love, and that it exists and lives only because of him. It confesses that who Jesus Christ is and what he has done matters not only for Christians or the church but is of import to everyone.

Barth's sense is that even when we talk about ourselves and our faith, we are not really talking about ourselves or our faith. When discussing Christian faith, we are always talking first and foremost about God and his faithfulness and then secondarily about ourselves. Faith knows that it lives only from its 'object', from Jesus Christ. It can also see, then, that the only advantage of the Christian over those who might one day be Christian is that the believer can be actively for Jesus Christ. Nevertheless, the believer also knows that Jesus Christ is for everyone, for the whole world. The one who has faith knows that God is faithful to all.

In the language of the Protestant Scholastics, Barth argues that assent (*assensus*), or acknowledgement and recognition in his terms, proceeds knowledge (*notitia*). Certainly one must understand what is being claimed about Jesus Christ before one can have faith in him and follow him in free obedience. Yet Barth is worried that by 'knowledge' the Protestant Scholastics had in mind 'an abstract acknowledge of all kinds of truths which a man may amass and enjoy without its having any further relevance to him'.[6] As we have seen, some of the Protestant Scholastics were also worried about this possibility and so made the 'primary' aspect of faith trust (*fiducia*) in God's promises (Barth even admits this). Nevertheless, Barth wants to emphasize that the 'assent' of acknowledgement and recognition is an obedient following of Jesus Christ, not a neutral or detached contemplation. We might say that here the Reformed Barth is following Calvin's line that 'all right knowledge of

---

[6]Karl Barth, *Church Dogmatics* IV/1, *The Doctrine of Reconciliation*, ed. G. W. Bromiley and T. F. Torrance, trans. G. W. Bromiley (Edinburgh: T. & T. Clark, 1961), p. 765.

God is born of obedience'.[7] Two different images might help for getting at Barth's concern. The situation of humanity is not like that of scientists in a laboratory who make hypotheses and run experiments in a sterile environment, peacefully and autonomously considering the results. Instead, the situation of humanity is more akin to a group of prisoners made hopeless and inhumane by their detainment in a prisoners of war (POW) camp. The life of faith then becomes a long and perilous journey away from the camp, of constantly following the rescuers who lead the way even if the prisoners themselves do not know where they are headed.

Like the other figures in the 'modern theology' who came before him, Barth was strongly opposed to natural theology and to making philosophy a basis for theology. This was as true of the 'liberal' Barth as of the mature Barth. Generally speaking, natural theology means thinking about God solely from the general features of the cosmos, or our moral intuitions and daily experiences, or our logic about how reality must be. But if God has revealed both who God is and who humanity is through Jesus Christ, then it seems strange to go looking elsewhere to know who God and humanity are. Barth is nervous about what we will dream up when we look around the world and think about who God is without taking Jesus Christ into account. Perhaps we will imagine a wrathful or absent God. What seems likelier, though, is that we will imagine that God is just like us, so that God likes the people and things we like and hates the people and things we hate. Another name for this type of natural theology is idolatry, and it is fully reasonable and justified for theology to ignore it and look to God in Christ. Barth will readily admit that we must always speak about God from the ideas and language that we already have, from the perspective of our own philosophies about the world. For what would the alternative be? Philosophy, then, is inevitably present in all our theologies, and surely some natural theology will creep in as well. The important thing, nevertheless, is to always look to the faithfulness of God in Christ in order to think about who God is and who we are.

Study questions

1. What do you think 'from faith to faith' means in Rom. 1.16–17?

2. Do you think Barth's criticisms of Schleiermacher are fair?

3. In what ways are acknowledgement, recognition and confession more or less illuminating as descriptions of faith than knowledge, assent and trust?

4. Are Barth's worries about natural theology justified?

Further reading

Prefaces to the first and second edition of Barth's, *The Epistle to the Romans*, 1–15.
Barth, Karl, *Church Dogmatics IV/1, The Doctrine of Reconciliation*, ed. G. W. Bromiley and T. F. Torrance, trans. G. W. Bromiley (Edinburgh: T. & T. Clark, 1961), pp. 757–779.

---

[7]Calvin, *Institutes*, I.VI.2, p. 72. Barth, *CD* IV/1, p. 761.

17

The Dynamics of Faith: Paul Tillich

Tillich's place in theology

Paul Tillich (1886–1965) was, more than anybody else, a philosopher of faith. Or shall we rather say he was a theologian? He came from a family of Lutheran pastors, began his career as a pastor himself and till the end of his life maintained the habit of composing and giving sermons in Protestant churches. His main work is entitled, characteristically, *Systematic Theology*, and yet his theology is so deeply speculative and philosophical that he certainly counts as one of the most philosophically courageous theologians in recent history. While he never belonged to any theological or philosophical school, he himself created a powerful school, a philosophical-theological current which can still be felt in contemporary thought. It is not enough to say that Tillich was an important thinker, because he certainly was in some respects even a very important thinker; we must concretely see what this importance consisted in and what kind of validity we can attribute to it today.

The most important currents in early twentieth-century Germany, where Tillich was born, were liberal Protestantism, exegetic theology and the neo-orthodoxy of Karl Barth. In philosophy, phenomenology and existentialism dominated academic life. On the periphery of German academia (and in the centre of many French universities), there appeared the influence of an invigorated Neo-Scholasticism. In a sense, Tillich belonged to liberal Protestantism, because he sought to articulate new perspectives in the interpretation of dogmatics and church history; on the other hand, Tillich was deeply influenced by the mystical thought of F. W. J. Schelling (1775–1854). Tillich was open to Catholic mysticism as well and, later in his life, to the mystical contents of the world religions. He was liberal and mystical simultaneously, which determined his intellectual position close to the Christian socialism of his time. Moreover, Tillich was impressed by the existential philosophies of Martin Heidegger (1889–1976) and Karl Jaspers (1883–1969), who emphasized the ultimate importance of the fact of individual personhood. As a thinker standing relatively close to liberal socialism, Tillich was a natural enemy of the emerging National Socialism in Germany, which led to his emigration to the United States in 1933. His career in America as the main representative of 'existential theology' may overshadow the fact that Tillich was one of the most profound interpreters of faith in the history of Western thought.

Approaches to faith

Tillich attempts to approach the reality of faith in several ways. In his *Systematic Theology*, his explanation of faith is based on what he calls 'Spiritual Presence'.[1] Spiritual Presence is the concrete spirit permeating reality and reveals itself in the human soul in two basic forms: in faith properly so called, and in love. Both are centred in the new life of Christ, a life in which human beings are invited to participate. When faith is defined as the influence of Spiritual Presence in the midst of the ambiguities of life, we have a non-reductionist notion of faith. Tillich's notion of faith is non-reductionist inasmuch as he sought to understand faith as a matter of ultimate importance. As Tillich emphasizes, faith as the concrete form of Spiritual Presence is not a mental function of human beings; neither is it the recognition of the authority of God, because any acceptance of authority calls for a further instance of authority *in infinitum* to authorize the previous authority. Faith is not a 'will to believe', it is not obedience, and, following Hegel's criticism of Schleiermacher, it is not the mere feeling of dependence. Faith is a sui generis reality which entails an acknowledgement of authority, wilful obedience to a divine witness and intellectual assent. However, faith cannot be reduced to any of these features of human beings, because it is something autonomous and ultimate. We are aware of its presence in our soul as the greatest power overcoming the loss of being and the ambiguities of life.

In a systematic context, faith is intimately connected to love. Like faith, love is a matter of ultimate importance expressed in various mental activities. For instance, love is not merely a feeling, it is certainly not an instinct and it is not even an intellectual attitude. Love is again the overcoming of distinction, a striving to unity in an ontological sense; love is ultimate truth. Love focuses everything in the centre of energy of human personhood and motivates everything towards its ultimate end, the realization of Spiritual Presence. Love as *agape*, the New Testament's central expression for love, is the creation of newness in divine unity. In this sense, *agape* unites itself with faith and faith develops into *agape*; their relationship is mutual and pervasive.[2]

Here it is already clear that for Tillich faith is not merely *fides qua*, or the act of faith. Equally important for him is the *fides quae*, the content of faith, which he defines as a divine–human encounter in Christ. While maintaining a philosophical interpretation of the traditional doctrines of Christianity, Tillich makes it clear that his thought is Christ-centred. Tillich's *Systematic Theology* offers a thorough-going explanation of the central Christian tenets on the basis of his existential thought and aims at an overall vision of the history of salvation which culminates in the Kingdom of God.[3]

---

[1]Paul Tillich, *Systematic Theology*, vol. 3 (Chicago: University of Chicago Press, 1963), p. 8.
[2]Tillich, *Systematic Theology* III, pp. 134–138.
[3]Cf. Tillich, *Systematic Theology* III.

Faith as ultimate concern

While Tillich offers a grandiose summary of philosophical theology in the above-mentioned book, it is in his two shorter works, *The Dynamics of Faith* (1957) and *The Courage to Be* (1952), that he explores the paramount significance of faith. In *The Dynamics of Faith*, Tillich develops a full-fledged phenomenology of faith which he calls here 'the ultimate concern'. The connection between 'faith' and 'ultimate concern' may seem unintelligible at first glance, but we must take into consideration that Tillich's mother tongue was German. The origin of the English expression was *Das, was uns unbedingt angeht*, an expression which may be better translated as 'what unconditionally comes upon a person'. By this Tillich does not only mean faith but also the core of religion: religion is about our engagement in what is most essential for us. The purest form of ultimate concern is Christianity's notion of faith as it developed from its ancient and Middle Age sources through mysticism and the Protestant Reformation until the nineteenth- and twentieth-century philosophical and theological movements. In this process, as Tillich points out, the biblical notion of faith becomes more articulate; leaving behind partial conceptions, such as faith as virtue or as an act of intelligence and will, we arrive at the emergence of the Protestant principle, for which faith is defined as the central act of a person. Tillich is, nonetheless, somewhat critical of the developments of Protestant theology in which faith was often understood as mere trust, firmness or feeling. He is also critical of Hegel for trying to dissolve faith in intellectual knowledge.

In Tillich's succinct definition, 'Faith, nevertheless, is the state of being ultimately concerned'.[4] We are ultimately concerned whether we know it or not, but being aware of our being ultimately concerned is the beginning of a way leading to personal and communal fulfilment. We need to give ourselves totally and unconditionally to what presents itself as of ultimate concern, namely to the presence of the divine in the concrete form of Christ. Nevertheless, human persons are unable to realize an ideally perfect state of their being ultimately concerned, because sinfulness, forgetfulness, and physical, moral and intellectual fragility hinder them in realizing what they recognize as ultimately important. Thus faith is permeated with doubt even in its purest moments; doubt is actually an organic part of faith and those who are conscious of their being ultimately concerned must live through the torments of doubt so that a deeper level of faith may be attained.

Faith as courage to be

This leads us to the second main realm of Tillich's notion of faith, his 'existentialism', which he explains in detail in *Systematic Theology*.[5] Existentialism was originally a reaction to Hegel's total philosophy and so it emphasized the concretely existing

---

[4]Paul Tillich, *The Dynamics of Faith* (New York: Harper, 1957), p. 1.
[5]Paul Tillich, *Systematic Theology*, vol. 2 (Chicago: University of Chicago Press, 1957), pp. 19–28.

human individual as opposed to overarching ideal and historical structures. Existentialism sought to expose being to fundamental questions but renounced giving definitive answers. Christian theology also needs existentialism because it seeks to understand human persons and their questions so that a renewed formulation of the Christian message – that 'Jesus is the Christ' – may be offered.[6]

Existentialism in Tillich's view is about the grasping of being in the form in which human personhood discloses it, in human misery as well as in human grandeur. A person is always a synthesis of both, and the proportion of misery and greatness changes from time to time and from one person to another. Still, we are able to realize the one *in* the other: grandeur in misery and misery in greatness. A human person is both a believer and an unbeliever, having faith as ultimate concern and forgetting the ultimate call of being. This ambiguity is the expression of the haziness of being, of being exposed to the threat of the dark nothingness of non-being.

Faith as 'the courage to be' is the attitude a human person is called to assume in face of such nothingness. In *The Courage to Be*, Tillich describes the history of the notion of courage from Plato through Thomas Aquinas to Nietzsche so that he can show the development of this notion until it reaches an ultimately personal meaning. The second important notion is that of anxiety. Tillich identifies anxiety as the effect of non-being in the realm of being. Fear and anxiety emerge from the conflict of being and non-being, and since human existence is openness to being, it entails openness to non-being as well.[7] Thus, anxiety is not only a formal output of an ontological tension but also the lived experience of human persons facing physical, moral and intellectual collapse. Through the experience of persons, anxiety becomes the fundamental feature of culture, and a feature of modernity in particular, when the ontological conflict becomes more violent than ever. The cultural, political, moral and intellectual crises of our age, Tillich says, are only symptoms of an unfathomable divergence in being, a divergence unfurling gradually in the course of Christian history. It is the essence of human vocation to overcome divergence in the act of faith as the courage to be.[8]

What actually happens in faith? Human persons are apparently defenceless beings: they are born naked and helpless, live in societies which are often unjust and exploitive and are surrounded by a nature which is always apt to unleash destruction. Yet human persons do not give up and so organize themselves into societies, develop science and technology, take care of the weak and the sick, defend themselves against the extremities of nature and sometimes even revolt against repressive regimes. More importantly, they pray and build churches. They realize the courage to be on the cultural and political level. In faith properly so-called, human beings bring about the courage to be on the existential level of being. Facing the abysmal darkness of non-being, human persons turn to being and give themselves to the renewing power of life. Faith is the courage to be on the transcendental level, by which we accept our being accepted into the productive source of being, which is God. Ultimately, faith originates in this source of being, and if humans become capable of having faith,

---

[6]Tillich, *Systematic Theology* II, pp. 118–137.
[7]Independently of Tillich, we find this notion in the important mystical writings of the Hungarian philosopher László Gondos-Grünhut written in the 1930s: *Die Liebe und das Sein* (Bonn: Bouvier, 1990).
[8]Paul Tillich, *The Courage to Be* (New Haven: Yale University Press, 1952).

being courageous in view of non-being, it is only because the gracious power of being *encourages* them to turn against death and choose life.[9]

Faith is a Christian phenomenon, but in latent forms it is present in other religious structures as well, such as in Daoism, and also in various forms of non-theistic humanism. Tillich's broad ontology of courage makes him able to speak of faith in cases where no obvious religious connotation can be discovered, such as in atheistic humanism. Tillich can be generous because he was generously supplied with so many fruitful insights. Such an insight, originating in the thought of Schelling, concerns the end of theism and the notion of 'God above God'. Tillich realizes that traditional forms of theism are linked to a terminology hardly capable of describing the ontological and existential situation of humankind during the second half of the twentieth century. Thus he thinks that a superficial theism must be transcended and a new kind of awareness is to be acquired. In the total movement of faith, in 'absolute faith' as Tillich names it, shallow forms of theism are overcome so that we may discover 'God above God': 'The courage to be is rooted in the God who appears when God has disappeared in the anxiety of doubt.'[10]

In spite of his unusual terminology, Tillich remains faithful to Christian faith: he labours to abandon idolatrous notions of God and trusts himself to the God whose faith he was given after all his struggles against the demons of non-being, anxiety and self-annulment. Indeed, as Tillich's thought proves, the demons remain the same, but God is forever new.

Study questions

1. What are Tillich's approaches to the notion of faith?
2. What is the meaning of 'ultimate concern' for Tillich?
3. What is 'the courage to be' in Tillich's thought?
4. Can an atheist have faith according to Tillich?
5. Is the notion of 'God above God' identical with atheism?

Further reading

Dulles, Avery, *The Assurance of Things Hoped For* (Oxford: Oxford University Press, 1994), ch. 6.
MacIntyre, Alasdair, 'God and the Theologians', *Encounter* 21:3 (September 1963), pp. 3–10.
Re Manning, Russell (ed.), *The Cambridge Companion to Paul Tillich* (Cambridge: Cambridge University Press, 2009).
Wright, Eliott, Paul Tillich as Hero: An Interview with Rollo May. See: http://www.religion-online.org/showarticle.asp?title=1617. Accessed 15 March 2014.

---

[9]Tillich, *The Courage to Be*, p. 160.
[10]Tillich, *The Courage to Be*, p. 190.

18

Kenotic Faith:
Hans Urs von Balthasar

The trilogy

Hans Urs von Balthasar (1905–1988) wrote a multi-volume trilogy. Part I, *The Glory of the Lord: A Theological Aesthetics*, is about the revelation of the *beauty* of God in the crucified and resurrected Christ. Part II, the *Theo-Drama*, is about the expression of the *goodness* of God in Christ and through him in the economy of salvation. Part III, the *Theo-Logic*, is about the truthfulness of God as manifested to the Church by the Holy Spirit.

Von Balthasar wrote a *trilogy* about beauty, truth and goodness because the disunified way in which people of today approach beauty, goodness and truth bears some of the blame for the modern disjunction between faith and reason. Beauty, truth and goodness each in its characteristic way relies upon *faith* to be acknowledged. So, for instance, truth is not just seized in a dispassionately intellectual way, but rather requires that we put our *faith* in someone else's testimony, and that we be *genuine* in our intellectual commitments, making ourselves *trustworthy*, so that we can personally 'stand in' for what is lacking in evidence. 'The declaration of truth', von Balthasar says, 'implies the ethical characteristic of truthfulness…there is a corresponding *faith* on the part of the receiver. Without this faith, any exchange of truth between free entities is unthinkable'.[1]

Faith and philosophy

Von Balthasar does not agree with Aquinas that one cannot simultaneously know and believe something. Knowledge and faith are not mutually exclusive. There is no zero-sum game between knowing and believing, because one cannot *know* without accepting the testimony of others, that is, without belief. Knowledge relies upon belief. Even when it achieves certainty, such belief is not knowledge, because it is a 'response' to an 'existential proof'.[2] Belief in another's testimony is recognizing that

---

[1]Hans Urs Von Balthasar, *Theo-Logic: Theological Logical Theory*, vol. 1, *The Truth of the World*, trans. Adrian J. Walker (San Francisco: Ignatius Press, 2000), p. 96.
[2]Von Balthasar, *Theo-Logic* I, p. 178.

he serves it with his life. Belief in another's testimony is seeing that his life is lovingly poured out for it. Believing in others belongs to our human quest for truth, so that ultimately, having faith in God is our natural *modus operandi*. Faith in God is not submitting to an alien Commanding Officer, but to our own *m.o.*

There is an inner philosopher in all of us who asks, 'why?'. Faith in God will answer the philosopher's endless questions, patiently listening to all of them, and allowing the believer to remain a philosopher who asks. Faith does not dispossess our inner philosopher. But the knowledge of God which faith brings has this proviso: the more we know about God, the more we believe. Just as faith answers questions and deepens knowledge, so knowledge of God deepens our faith.

Like Vatican I, von Balthasar distinguishes between what reason or philosophy can know about God and what faith in divine revelation is shown about God. He says that this is like the distinction between knowledge of the Creator *God* (reason/philosophy) and seeing God in his Triune 'interiority' (faith/revelation). 'Natural knowledge of God inexorably comes to a halt before the intimacy of God's personal life. And it requires a new revelation of grace...to open man in faith and to communicate to him – in abiding mystery – what God is in his innermost being.'[3] Von Balthasar compares the act of trying to seize knowledge of God unbidden to the 'serpent's malice in presenting God's truth...as if it could be attained by knowledge alone, without the attitude of faith'.[4]

Theological faith

It is human nature to be receptive. Because (and not 'although') faith fulfils the desire for truth innate in human beings, faith is not brought about by us, by our 'Open Sesame', but by God. The study of divine *beauty* is the study of God's free self-manifestation in the world; otherwise it would be aesthetics, the study of worldly beauty, as distinct from *theological* beauty: 'if we can speak of a *theological* aesthetics it is only because it is *on his own initiative* and independently of man's particular anthropological structure that God takes form and allows himself to be seen, heard, and touched.'[5] The one who moves the plot and the characters in *theology* is God, and von Balthasar conceives of God as the author of the human act of faith in the sense that it is God's self-revelation which brings it about. We put our trust in another human *person* when he reveals his personality as loving, self-giving and thus trustworthy. We put our faith in God as he reveals Who He Is. It is God's self-revelation as love which engenders our faith. Von Balthasar says that, in a sense, since faith fosters knowledge of God, so it must foster *experience* of God. But faith is experiential in the sense of being absorbed in the object of experience, not in the mere having of experiences. It does not look back at itself, at its experiences, but at whom the experiences are moving towards: 'experience...does not have the least thing in common with "feeling" (in Schleiermacher's sense)...because that towards

---

[3]Von Balthasar, *Theo-Logic* I, p. 102.
[4]Von Balthasar, *Theo-Logic* I, p. 262.
[5]Von Balthasar, *Glory of the Lord* I, p. 311.

which existence is "travelling"…through God's grace is the objective, Trinitarian reality of God, which has "first"…had mercy on us.'[6]

Seeing the form

Since the eighteenth century, the figure of Jesus Christ has been studied by text-critics, ancient historians, philosophers, archaeologists and millions of ordinary people who have asked, 'who is he?' How can we even see who he is, through the jumble of different pictures of him thrown by the Gospels, 1500 years of lofty Christian icons and a hundred years or so of atheist portraits of a humanist Jesus? How can we hear him over the cacophony of biblical critics and believers, philosophers and bishops? How can we put together the pieces of the puzzle or mystery which is Jesus Christ? For von Balthasar, faith consists in seeing Christ as he truly is, seeing the inner 'form' of his personality expressed in the unique historical form of his life and self-sacrifice. Unless God gives us the faith to illuminate Christ, he will remain for us what one biblical critic called, 'a stranger and an enigma'.[7] Even the disciples and Apostles, Jesus' followers and friends, were baffled by him. Peter, who had recognized that Jesus is the Messiah, ran away and denied him when he realized that the Romans would crucify him. Who could blame him? Who could see the form of God in a bleeding man nailed to a wooden cross? It is, von Balthasar says, the Holy Spirit who allows us to see God's enduring radiance and beauty and thus the 'Form' of God in the crucified Christ. The Holy Spirit enables us to see God's self-giving love poured out by Jesus on the Cross. It is through the Holy Spirit that Who He Is is revealed by the Cross. God's love creates our faith in Jesus and enables us to see him for who he is.

Von Balthasar insists that this is not a 'special' sort of seeing which looks over and beyond the actual historical person of Jesus. Faith is a real, sensory seeing of the bodily, historical events of Jesus' life, and which perceives the form of God in and through those unique circumstances. Faith helps us to see with our own eyes, not with anyone else's. When we get to know another person, it is not because we have spied and stalked our way into their private life, but because they want to be friends and chose to open themselves to us. Just so, in the act of faith, we see what Jesus communicates of himself, by the grace of the Holy Spirit. For von Balthasar, the 'Preface' said at Mass on Christmas day sums up the meaning of faith as 'vision' of Christ's form: *Because through the mystery of the Incarnate Word the new light of your brightness has shone into the eyes of our mind; that knowing God visibly, we might be snatched up by this into the love of invisible things.* We see Christ's 'form', and we see God's act of self-communication. God opens a door to us: 'For this particular perception of truth…a "new light" is expressly required which illumines this particular form, a light which…breaks from within the form itself…the "new light" will…make seeing the form possible and be itself seen along with the form.'[8]

---

[6]Von Balthasar, *Glory of the Lord* I, p. 229.
[7]Albert Schweitzer, *The Quest of the Historical Jesus: A Critical Study of Its Progress from Reimarus to Wrede*, trans. W. Montgomery (London: Adam and Charles Black, 1910), p. 399.
[8]Von Balthasar, *Glory* I, p. 119.

The Christ-Form in the body of Christ

In order to see the Christ-Form, one has to become the kind of person who *could* see the form of Christ. One has to become the kind of person to whom self-giving love instinctively makes sense and hangs together. To see God's crucified love as the most solid form of love, one has to become like Christ. So 'seeing the form' of God in Christ crucified and becoming 'another Christ' are inseparable: one will not come to see and know the form of God in Christ without becoming like Jesus. Theory (or seeing and aesthetics) cannot be separated from practice (or doing and ethics). For von Balthasar, this is part of the meaning of St. Paul's idea that the Church is the 'body of Christ': every member of Christ's body receives the form of Christ, and goes on to continue Jesus' own mission of love in the unique way intended for each particular person. Von Balthasar states,

> For Paul, this contemplation of the image of Christ is both theoretical and practical: it is the im-pressing of the form upon the memory and the understanding (*gnosis*) of the believers, so that it will determine … their life, which must come to bear the form of Christ. The relative invisibility of the Head has its ground in the divine economy, to the end that he might become visible in the body of the Church ('it is good for you that I go', Jn 16.7); the person who truly lives through Christ's Holy Spirit sees Christ.[9]

Faith consists in receiving the form of Christ into one's life, abandoning one's desires and plans for how to shape one's own life and instead letting the form God wants take shape through one's life. Faith is entrusting one's life to God to shape it through and through with the form of the crucified Christ.

> [F]aith is nothing other than this: to make the whole man a space that responds to the divine content. Faith attunes man to this sound; it confers on man the ability to react to this divine experiment, preparing him to be a violin that receives just this touch of the bow, to serve as material for just this house to be built, to provide the rhyme for just this verse being composed.[10]

In the lifelong act of faith, God acts on us like a potter, remaking us in the image of Christ, sculpting human beings to 'correspond totally to God according to the archetype of Christ and in imitation of him'.[11]

Von Balthasar sees Christ both as the object of our faith and as the model for faith, who by example teaches us how to have faith in God the Father. The Scriptural motif behind von Balthasar's thinking about faith is Paul's saying, 'I have been crucified with Christ and I no longer live, but Christ lives in me' (Gal. 2.20). So faith is 'kenotic': the believer empties himself or herself in order to make room for Christ, taking like him the 'form of a servant' (Phil. 2). Faith means dispossessing ourselves

---

[9]Von Balthasar, *Glory* I, p. 319.
[10]Von Balthasar, *Glory* I, 220.
[11]Von Balthasar, *Glory* I, p. 220.

of our imagined selves in order to become our real selves, so that God's love can be expressed through us, as it is expressed through Christ. Christ is absolutely, divinely trustworthy in the testimony to God which he gives on the Cross. He perfectly and genuinely represented the truth of which he spoke: he *was* that truth. Since Christ is faithful to the end in the mission his Father gave him in sending him to empty himself, become Incarnate and die for human sin, so human faith is a sharing in Christ's own faithfulness to the Father.

Faith has an objective and a subjective side to it. The self-giving love which generates our faith is objectively 'out there', and external to us. But this love is also internal to us, shaping our relationship with God the Father, through Christ the Son. When we know an object, our objective knowledge is interiorized, becomes part of us and thus 'subjective'. The Holy Spirit is the objective love of God, outside of us, binding the Father to the Son. But it is also the Holy Spirit who gives us the interior, subjective convincing vision of the crucified Son as the very heart of God. The Holy Spirit is both the 'objective' love of God and the means of our corresponding, subjective love for God. Faith in God is thus objective and subjective love of God: it is the love of *God* (the objective Spirit) and the love *of* God (the Spirit as subjective, speaking within us).

Von Balthasar's conception of faith is 'kenotic' because he conceives of faith as self-giving, other-directed love. Seeing the form of the crucified Christ is nothing else than *loving* God. And this love for God is enabled by the outpouring of love for us by Christ, in his Incarnation, crucifixion and resurrection. So faith, as von Balthasar explains it, is the mutual love of God and his creatures, the wedding of God and his bride, the Church.

Study questions

1. Does it make sense to define faith as love?

2. In what ways does von Balthasar treat God as analogous to human persons? Is this legitimate?

3. Is God really beautiful? How can we say God is beautiful if God is non-material and therefore invisible?

4. What is the relation between faith and reason according to von Balthasar?

5. Read Phil. 2 and say what you think it tells us about God and about faith.

Further reading

Balthasar, Hans Urs von, *Does Jesus Know Us? Do We Know Him?* (San Francisco: Ignatius Press, 1983).
———, *Truth Is Symphonic: Aspects of Christian Pluralism*, trans. Graham Harrison (San Francisco: Ignatius Press, 1987).
———, *Love Alone Is Credible* (San Francisco: Ignatius Press, 2005).

19

Anonymous Faith: Karl Rahner

Karl Rahner's place in theology

'Karl Rahner [1904–1984] is universally recognized as important, but often lightly dismissed.'[1] Indeed, the outstanding formal feature of Rahner's thought is that it is difficult to follow. Dismissing it lightly often seems easier than doing the heavy reading it requires. Rahner's thought is deeply rooted in German philosophy, the authors of which, such as Kant and Hegel, offered difficult readings from the outset. In particular, the transcendental approach which we find in Rahner's writings belongs to a period in the history of Western thought when down-to-earth realism began its victorious world domination over the artistic, and often artificial, thinking about the conditions of possibility of such realism. To understand Rahner philosophically, we must know Kant and his followers. To understand Rahner theologically, we must see the development of modern theology in the work of such towering figures as Joseph Maréchal (1878–1944), Henri de Lubac (1896–1991) and Hans Urs von Balthasar (1905–1988).

In 1950 von Balthasar considered Rahner to be 'our only hope', one whom 'we must support'.[2] On the one hand, the main formal feature of von Balthasar's thought is his overall reinterpretation of traditional dogmatic propositions in the context of the rich history of European culture: the graphic arts, music, literature and philosophy. In its contents, von Balthasar sought to demonstrate the truth of traditional doctrines based on the common elements of culture and theology embedded in the dynamism of a providential guidance of the loving God of history. In nature as well as in culture, the glory of God shines forth as the ultimate proof of the eternal renewal of the transcendent order. On the other hand, Rahner emphasized a conceptual approach to the tradition, especially Thomism, an approach methodologically congruous with the transcendental logic of German philosophy. Rahner's important thoughts, such as 'supernatural existential', 'transcendental revelation' or 'anonymous faith', cannot be properly understood without mapping out this epistemological legacy which, especially in the thought of Martin Heidegger, became an overall and theologically resonant ontology. The soil which produced the systems of Maréchal, von Balthasar and Rahner had been the same: 'the modern philosophical revolution'.[3] In his own words, von Balthasar chose Goethe instead of

---

[1]Karen Kilby, *Karl Rahner: Theology and Philosophy* (London: Routledge, 2004), p. 1.
[2]Quoted in Rudolf Voderholzer and Michael J. Miller, *Meet Henri de Lubac* (San Francisco: Ignatius Press, 2007), p. 64.
[3]Cf. Walsh, *The Modern Philosophical Revolution*.

choosing Kant. Indeed, we find in Goethe the awareness of history and culture and also, in a nutshell, later developments of German philosophy.[4]

Réginald Garrigou-Lagrange's article of 1946 formulated some of the important objections of the old school against the *Nouvelle théologie*, which was, at least partially, the homeland of Rahner. In Garrigou-Lagrange's view, substituting the Thomistic formula 'truth is the adequation of things and intellect' with the formula 'truth is the real adequation of life and human mind' by the new theologians leads to a subversion of traditional doctrine.[5] However, for the theologians in question the problem did not primarily concern the 'things' or the 'intellect' but rather the meaning of 'adequation'. As Rahner points out in *Hearers of the Word* (1941), that which is known, according to St. Thomas, is the ontological reality of the mind and not a mere composition of a thing and a thing-like intellect. Thomas' important notion of 'the subject's return into itself' is the key to the understanding of reality. What we know is mind-like, because reality is mind-like, in a sense more real than anything given in the senses.[6] Rahner's approach entails his emphasis on the subject, the overall nature of divine–human relationship, with special reference to his inversion of a legendary maxim: if theology is anthropology, as Feuerbach claimed, then anthropology *is* theology.[7]

The paradox of grace

In accordance with the most important theological tradition throughout the Christian millennia, Rahner's notion of faith presupposes his understanding of divine grace as the utmost and concretely active presupposition of faith. Rahner offers a reinterpretation of the notion of grace, which he considers the inner core of the Thomistic conception of the 'natural desire to see the essence of God'.[8] Along with his colleagues in the *Nouvelle théologie* movement, Rahner sought to overcome the dualism of modern theories of grace originating especially in the teaching of Francisco Suárez (1558–1617). This theology emphasized a dualism between God's grace and human nature, thereby offering an interpretation of Thomas Aquinas' teaching on humanity's natural desire to see God. Thomas insisted that human natural desire cannot be satisfied without sanctifying grace. Yet his view of the beatific vision as the object of humanity's natural desire raised the problem whether one can maintain the absolutely supernatural and free grace of God in accomplishing salvation.

---

[4]Cf. Dulles, *The Assurance of Things Hoped For*, ch. 7.

[5]Réginald Garrigou-Lagrange, 'La nouvelle théologie où va-t-elle?', *Angelicum* 23 (1946), pp. 126–145(143).

[6]Karl Rahner, *Hearers of the Word*, trans. J. Doncell; (New York: Continuum, 1994), p. 33.

[7]Rahner, *Hearers of the Word*, p. 142. See also Karl Rahner, 'On the Theology of the Incarnation', in translated with an introduction by Cornelius Ernst (eds), *Theological Investigations* IV (London: Darton, Longman & Todd, 1974), pp. 105–120 (116). The succinct formula is given by Steffen J. Duffy in 'Experience and Grace', in Declan Marmion and Mary E. Hines (eds), *The Cambridge Companion to Karl Rahner* (Cambridge: Cambridge University Press), pp. 43–62 (43).

[8]Thomas Aquinas, *Summa theologica* I–II, q., 3, a. 8.

Rahner's solution is contained in his notion of 'uncreated grace'. Uncreated grace is 'God himself, the communication in which he gives himself to man as the divinizing favour which he is himself'.[9] Uncreated grace is 'the triune God himself', the *a priori* horizon of 'created grace', which is grace offered for the created world in the concrete history of salvation. Rahner claims that uncreated grace is mediated by the Persons of the Trinity, yet it is above all 'God's self-communication', 'the goal and ground of those acts which are related to God in himself'.[10] Uncreated grace is the condition of the possibility of created (habitual or particular) grace, yet particular grace is the concrete source of uncreated grace. For the eternal focus of uncreated grace is the highest event of particular grace, namely the Incarnation of the Word of God. The two orders of grace are thus intertwined in God, and Rahner's emphasis on uncreated grace calls our attention to God's eternally gracious being. In this perspective, not only humanity's natural desire to see God is the work of uncreated grace but the whole existence of creation, history and humanity. Every aspect of human life is in a certain sense a direct or indirect, a freely given and a freely received, effect of grace.

Rahner does not wish to abolish the distinction between the natural and the supernatural orders. He finds it important to keep this distinction, yet always in the free context of God's ultimate and unifying being. The 'supernatural existential' is the presence of God's supernaturally salvific will in the natural subject and it expresses the latter's natural capability of the reception of God's uncreated grace.[11] God's love, the concrete form of uncreated grace, ensures the unity of being in and beyond the *real* difference between the creation and the Creator. The emphasis on uncreated grace is the emphasis on God's absolute power which does not abolish creation, sin, fall, the real history of redemption or Christianity as the centre of history and the Church as the visible presence of Christ. Uncreated grace merely offers us the ultimate framework of divine love, in which all these moments are comprehended. There is no aspect of spiritual or material life of human beings, Christian or non-Christian, which is not permeated by uncreated grace in particular and always appropriate ways.

What we find here is certainly a paradox, because uncreated grace does not make particular grace unnecessary; and the necessity of created grace is defined in the ultimate framework of uncreated grace. Their precise relation, because of our meagre comprehension, cannot be fully explained. Rahner, therefore, was often charged either with unorthodoxy or with exaggeration with respect to this uniquely difficult realm of the theology of grace.

Categorical and transcendental revelation

'God's self-communication' is the expression Rahner uses for a general description of God's self-expression in nature and grace, history and salvation. God's self-revelation,

---

[9]Karl Rahner, 'Nature and Grace', *Theological Investigations* IV, pp. 165–188 (177).
[10]Karl Rahner, 'Religious Enthusiasm and the Experience of Grace', in *Theological Investigations* XVI (London: Darton, Longman and Todd, 1979), pp. 35–51 (41).
[11]Karl Rahner, 'Atheism and Implicit Christianity', *Theological Investigations* IX, trans. Graham Harrison (London: Darton, Longman and Todd, 1979), pp. 145–164 (145).

however, is a more concrete expression, because it refers to the Incarnation of the second Person of the Trinity in the person of Christ. In this occurrence God discloses his innermost essence, that is, his loving readiness to sacrifice himself, in the person of his Son, for the salvation of his creation. This divine readiness necessarily entails the real death of Christ and the real event of the resurrection. Just as the teaching, healing and sacramental activity of Christ are expressions of God's will to do everything possible for the sake of humanity, so too are his death and new life. Original sin, which makes the creation not only fallible but, through concupiscence, self-destructive, is used by God to restore a happiness of which humanity never dreamt. God's revelation, ultimately, is 'good news' (*euangelion*), because in the midst of suffering and death it offers the genuine hope of a full restoration of everything lost.

Rahner terms this concrete notion of revelation 'categorical'. Categorical revelation is concrete, historical and verbal revelation. It is 'categorical', because a 'category' is a certain class of propositions which share some essential features. As opposed to the 'categorical', Rahner identifies the trans-categorical or 'transcendental', referring thereby to overall qualities which are present in all classes. Accordingly, transcendental revelation does not merely transcend but ultimately grounds, makes possible and actualizes categorical revelation. Thus, the difference between the categorical and the transcendental parallels the difference between created and uncreated grace. Indeed, transcendental revelation is primarily the act of God's uncreated grace; and categorical revelation is an act of created grace. At the same time, their relationship is not merely the relationship between the general and the particular, the horizon and the thing, or the *a priori* and the *a posteriori*. Categorical and transcendental revelations presuppose each other: categorical revelation necessarily points to transcendental revelation and *vice versa*. Such a view, nevertheless, does not lead to circularity, because a common enrichment results from this reciprocal teleology, an enrichment realizing God's infinite love.[12]

Implicit and explicit faith

Faith is the human response to God's self-communication in general and to his self-revelation in particular. It is an overall response which encompasses the whole personality of the believer. If the traditional understanding of faith focused on the assent of the intellect and will to certain propositions, Rahner emphasizes something more: faith is not merely a partial response involving human faculties, but a response of the whole person in every dimension of life. Thus faith is, first of all, concrete faith in Christ as the realization of God's infinite love. Second, faith permeates not only the positive aspects of existence but the negative ones as well, especially sickness, tragedy and death. In the face of human difficulties, the Christian faithfully turns to God's healing and saving power on the basis of the concrete existence of the Church and its sacramental reality. As an answer to God's call, faith does not originate in itself but is produced, maintained, strengthened and developed

---

[12]Rahner, 'Atheism and Implicit Christianity', p. 145. See also Karl Rahner and Joseph Ratzinger, *Revelation and Tradition*, trans. W. J. O'Hara (Montreal: Palm, 1965).

by God. Faith is a matter of grace in the created as well as in the uncreated sense, in the realization of God's love in one's individual life and, similarly, in the historical life of the Church.

Rahner often uses the expression 'explicit' to describe the concrete faith of Christians (a revision of the notion of *fides explicata*). He also identifies 'implicit' or 'anonymous' faith: this refers to the effects of the universal presence of God's uncreated grace (a revision of *fides implicata*). God is the origin and aim of everything, and there is no aspect of life and no dimension of history in which divine love did not have its presence in some, often hidden, forms. Since God embraces history in its totality – with the focus on the event of the Incarnation – all ages, peoples and cultures are permeated by God's transcendental revelation. We find everywhere the corresponding forms of faith. Anonymous faith is called so because it is distinguished from the explicit and positive faith of Christians. Christianity is the central, yet not the only, achievement of God's love. There are human beings in every part of the world who respond to God's self-communication in accordance with their cultural and historical circumstances. Every human person is born to be an 'anonymous Christian', naturally possessing the *capacity* of faith in God's transcendental self-communication. The more expressly Christianity is aware of this fact, the more it is able to communicate God's categorical revelation to humanity and activate an explicit faith in Christ.[13]

Rahner's central message can be summarized as the discovery of the transcendental dimension of theology in and beyond the categorical realm. By applying this distinction, we can readily interpret many of his important insights. The transcendental, however, is not a logical category for Rahner but rather, just as for Kant, the name for a higher and richer realm of reality which sheds new light on the historical-empirical dimensions. We easily misunderstand Rahner when we do not take his meaning of the transcendental into account. The worst mistake we can make, for which Rahner may be partially responsible, is losing sight of the paramount importance of the positive, the explicit and the categorical. According to Rahner's original intention, transcendentalism *must not* lead to relativism or the neglect of Christian traditions. On the contrary, Rahner hoped to offer a renewed awareness of the importance of Christian traditions by delineating an inclusive approach in which this importance may receive a more profound explanation.

Study questions

1. What is the difference between the mindsets of von Balthasar and Rahner?
2. What is the paradox of grace?
3. What is the difference between categorical and transcendental revelation?
4. What is explicit faith in Rahner's thought?
5. How would you define the notion of 'anonymous faith'?

---

[13]Rahner, 'Atheism and Implicit Christianity'. See also Daniel Donovan, 'Faith and Revelation', in Declan and Hines (eds), *The Cambridge Companion to Karl Rahner*, pp. 83–97.

Further reading

Burke, Patrick, *Reinterpreting Rahner: A Critical Study of His Major Themes* (New York: Fordham University Press, 2002).

Kilby, Karen, *A Brief Introduction to Karl Rahner Crossroad* (New York, 2007).

Rahner, Karl, 'Intellectual Honesty and Christian Faith', *Theological Investigations* vii, 1971, pp. 47–71.

———, 'On the Situation of Faith', *Theological Investigations* xx, 1981, pp. 13–32.

20

Faith in Crisis: Death of God, Auschwitz and Militant Atheism

Three developments

Traditional religious faith was challenged in the twentieth century by three radical developments: (1) the emergence of Death of God theories, (2) the historical tragedy connected to the name of Auschwitz and (3) the birth of militantly atheistic states and the persecution of religion in many countries throughout the world. These developments originate in the process of secularization, which appeared in an intense form during the French Revolution at the end of the eighteenth century. Secularization spread rapidly during the nineteenth century and permeated the culture of most European societies. As a consequence, atheistic theories became popular and Friedrich Nietzsche's famous dictum of 'the death of God' attained unprecedented popularity. The First and the Second World Wars led to cultural chaos, in the aftermath of which traditional faith was difficult to maintain. And the creation of history's first atheistic state in the Soviet Union added a dark shade to this grim picture. The initial success of National Socialism in Germany resulted in the persecution of Jewish people and eventually to the monstrous attempt of an epochal annihilation. After the Second World War, the name of Auschwitz became a symbol referring to the shock many believers, Jew and Christian alike, had to live through when facing the question, Where was God in Auschwitz?[1] This question was formulated in many ways along the lines of the rise of new atheistic states which persecuted all forms of faith. These developments constitute a common history in which faith in God was endangered and even pushed to the brink of disappearance in a number of countries.

Secularization

'Why was it virtually impossible not to believe in God in, say, 1500 in our Western society, while in 2000 many of us find this not only easy, but even inescapable?'[2] Charles Taylor's question points to a fateful change in Western societies during the

---

[1]Elie Wiesel, *Night*, trans. Marion Wiesel (New York: Hill and Wang, 2006). See also Pope Benedict XVI's meditation: http://www.vatican.va/holy_father/benedict_xvi/speeches/2006/may/documents/hf_ben-xvi_spe_20060528_auschwitz-birkenau_en.html. Accessed 18 March 2014.
[2]Charles Taylor, *A Secular Age* (Cambridge, Mass.: Harvard University Press, 2007), p. 25.

past few centuries. However, public unbelief in God was close to being 'virtually impossible' more or less until the First World War. Describing its present forms, Taylor distinguishes three meanings of secularization: (1) public places have been emptied of God or any reference to ultimate reality, (2) religious belief and practice are falling off and (3) 'the shift to secularity consists…of a move from a society where belief in God is unchallenged and indeed, unproblematic, to one in which it is understood to be one option among others, and frequently not the easiest to embrace'.[3] The third meaning of secularization entails the first two. The most striking change in our societies is that today faith in God is rarely part of public discourse and unbelief is accepted as a natural option. In Western culture, faith has become a private matter so that even religious communities do not encourage public representations of their own faith. Anti-secular arguments, such as those of John Milbank, are limited to circles of experts.[4] As a result, faith in God has lost its earlier status and collapsed into a conviction of individuals and small communities in a pluralistic society. In some analyses, the earlier dominance of faith in Western societies is seen as the hotbed of totalitarianism and so the option of freely choosing one's faith today is considered a genuine benefit.[5]

Death of God

An important symptom of secularization has been the birth of Death of God theories during the twentieth century. The notion indicates the most spectacular collapse of faith in the notion of God which meant salvation for millions for thousands of years. Originally one of the central symbols of Christianity, the death of a divine person, Christ, has been enlarged into an existential theory about the experience that 'God is dead; God died of his pity for mankind'; or even that 'we have killed him', as Nietzsche formulated it.[6] Martin Heidegger offered an influential interpretation of Nietzsche's dictum and understood it as pointing to the end of Platonism as the 'beginning of nihilism' when the notion of the God of the biblical revelation has become implausible.[7]

Death of God theories emerged especially in the works of Gabriel Vahanian, Paul van Buren, William Hamilton, John A. T. Robinson, Thomas J. J. Altizer and Rabbi Richard L. Rubenstein. Vahanian's groundbreaking work of 1957, *The Death of God*, was a critical reflection on liberal theology, a theology attempting to face the explosion of a non-Christian secular culture. There have been two characteristic

---

[3]Taylor, *A Secular Age*, p. 26.

[4]John Milbank, *Theology and Social Theory: Beyond Secular Reason* (London: Blackwell, 1993).

[5]For example, see Christopher Hitchens, *God Is Not Great: How Religion Poisons Everything* (Crows Nest: Allen & Unwin, 2007), p. 212. Hitchens emphasizes that not only Judaism and Christianity but every religious form connects 'racism and totalitarianism' with some faith.

[6]Friedrich Nietzsche, *Thus Spoke Zarathustra: A Book for All and None*, ed. Adrian Del Caro and Robert Pippin, trans. Adrian Del Caro (Cambridge: Cambridge University Press, 2006), pp. 5 and 69.

[7]Martin Heidegger, 'Nietzsche's Word: God Is dead', in ed. and trans. Julian Young and Kenneth Haynes, *Off the Beaten Track* (Cambridge: Cambridge University Press), pp. 157–199 (166).

reactions to this development. On the one hand, strong Death of God theologians, such as Vahanian, van Buren or Hamilton, argued for the end of theism, because '[t]he mythological view of the world has gone, and with it went the possibility of speaking seriously of a *Heilsgeschichte*: a historical "drama of salvation", in which God is said to have acted at a certain time in this world to change the state of human affairs'.[8] Weak Death of God theologians, such as Robinson, Altizer, Rabbi Rubenstein and the most influential theologians of the twentieth century, are in line with the diagnosis of the former group, but proceed to a different conclusion, namely the need to renew theology in accordance with the challenges of modern secular culture, especially the post–Second World War situation and the emerging new media world. For some decades, the notion of the Death of God expressed poignantly the collapse of faith in Western societies, a collapse from which most of these societies have not recovered.

Auschwitz

'Auschwitz', the place of the attempted annihilation of the Chosen, has become symbolic of a historic tragedy with devastating effects on religion. The central argument based on the experience of Auschwitz has been this: If there is an infinite and good God, how could he allow the occurrence of such a monstrosity? Some natural answers to this question have been: 'There is no such God'; 'The God of traditional religion is an illusion'; 'If there was a God, he could not have allowed Auschwitz to happen'. Or, as Elie Wiesel put it, 'God is dead, the God of love, of gentleness and consolation, the God of Abraham, Isaac, and Jacob had … vanished forever into the smoke of the human holocaust'.[9]

'After Auschwitz' reflections are closely connected to the Death of God theories. One of the most famous books written about Auschwitz along this line has been Rabbi Rubenstein's *After Auschwitz*.[10] Rubenstein argues that the traditional faith in God and the monstrosity of Auschwitz are incompatible. Beyond Judaism, the mere fact of such a tragedy motivated many people to distance themselves from faith. In a number of cases, the consequence was not only a distance but rather a collapse: faith lost plausibility for many. Instead of a renewed search for faith, whole generations threw themselves into the building up of welfare societies and enjoyed the life offered by technology and consumption. Especially in countries with a long religious tradition and a high level of technological culture, traditional religion has become a rarity and many churches have been turned into social facilities.

The tragedy of Auschwitz has remained in itself one of the greatest challenges religious faith has to face even today. The problem is both theological and

---

[8]Paul M. van Buren, *The Secular Meaning of the Gospel* (New York: Macmillan, 1963), pp. 11–2.
[9]Wiesel, *Night*, p. 23.
[10]Richard Rubenstein, *After Auschwitz: History, Theology, and Contemporary Judaism* (Baltimore and London: John Hopkins University Press, 1992).

philosophical. On the theological level, the burning problem of the vexed relationship between Judaism and Christianity has to be seen in a new light after Auschwitz. Auschwitz happened in a time still permeated by a Christianity not without clear traces of anti-Jewish sentiments. Thus Christianity has some responsibility for the tragedy. Philosophically, Auschwitz raises the question of horrendous evil and the possibility of explaining evil by reference to some greater good. Even if these questions might be solved theoretically, the practical consequence for many was again the loss of the plausibility of faith.[11]

Militant atheism

Marx and Engels were hostile to religion as they considered it 'the opium of the people', but it was only Vladimir Ilyich Lenin (1870–1924) who developed the idea of a merciless fight against all forms of religion. When Lenin grasped power in Tsarist Russia in 1917, the country was deeply religious and the Orthodox Christian faith was taken to be most natural. Only tiny circles of revolutionary thinkers desired to dispose of religion in its official and private forms, but they could not reach their objective before the creation of the Soviet State. This state was the first in known history which considered all forms of religious faith as a lethal enemy. Lenin had a double agenda with respect to religion. In his written statements, such as *Socialism and Religion*, he appeared to be permissive: religion must be a private affair and members of the proletariat, who still have some religious nostalgia, may be allowed to practice their faith. On the other hand, as a leader with political power, Lenin began a crushing war against the Orthodox Church on all levels. This resulted in destroying churches, murdering priests and religious people *en masse* and basing political life on a harsh atheistic propaganda.[12]

In the aftermath of the victory of the Soviet Union in the Second World War, many European countries with a strong religious tradition became victims of anti-religious activity by the new Communist regimes. In China, Korea, Vietnam, Cambodia or Cuba, believers, priests and churches were victimized in violent ways. Faith in God and religion in general had to face a long period of trial, which, in some cases, led to the almost total collapse of faith: in individual persons, in entire societies and even in the churches themselves. Religious organizations had to co-operate with Communist authorities and priests were often paid for contributing to the self-destruction of their own churches. Such an inhuman pressure resulted unavoidably in the disintegration of traditional religious faith. After the end of the Soviet Union in 1992, the lowest church attendance was reported in some of the ex-Soviet countries.[13]

---

[11]Balazs Mezei, *Religion and Revelation after Auschwitz* (New York: Bloomsbury, 2013).

[12]Leszek Kolakowski, *Main Currents of Marxism*, vol. 2, *The Golden Age*, trans. P. S. Falla (Oxford: Oxford University Press, 1978), p. 459.

[13]For Russia, see Zoe Knox, *Russian Society and the Orthodox Church: Religion in Russia after Communism* (London: Routledge Curzon, 2005). Contemporary philosophical atheism never comes close to the ideological and political atheism of the communist countries.

The rebirth of faith

However, one of the most religious Christian countries of our days has been also the result of the Soviet period: Poland. Pope John Paul II's (1920–2005; papacy 1978–2005) unique spiritual legacy has been the fruit of a historic trial religious faith had to face in his homeland. This legacy indicates that after its crises, faith in God still has inexhaustible resources of survival and rebirth. Traditional forms of belief, such as Judaism and Christianity, may return to a period of resuscitation and flourishing.[14] Today the 'Death of God' has already lost its intellectual magnetism and many theorists think now that serious reflection is able to analyze the drama of the twentieth century in sober and theologically satisfying ways.[15] 'After Auschwitz' discussions in Jewish communities led to a number of proposals processing, even if not explaining, Auschwitz in spiritual and theological terms, such as it happens in the works of Emil Fackenheim, Ignaz Maybaum, Eliezer Berkovits and others.[16] In Fackenheim's view, Auschwitz amounts to God's new revelation calling for a full renewal of our faith in God in accordance with what he calls the 614th commandment.[17] This commandment can be best realized in the State of Israel.

After the period of dry positivism and atheism, a new wave of philosophical arguments has emerged since the 1970s which restructured traditional talk of faith in God in ways meeting rigorous scientific and logical standards. As William Lane Craig declared in 2008, 'God is not yet dead'. The related article explains the various developments in Anglo-American philosophical theology which expounded convincing arguments for the existence of God. As a result of the thought of Alvin Plantinga and Richard Swinburne, various schools have risen that now pursue serious philosophical theology.[18] Contemporary efforts by atheist philosophers to overcome versions of the new philosophical theology show that the debate between belief and unbelief cannot be considered terminated.[19] Even under the new circumstances of 'a secular age', the possibility of new forms of faith has returned. It is now the task of believers to live and express their faith in such a way that the fact of the epochal crisis of faith may receive a theologically and philosophically well-formed meaning. For this latter, we need to understand the history of faith in terms of a process in which new forms of faith become attainable after severe periods of tribulation.

---

[14]See the Chapter on John Paul II's encyclical *Fides et ratio* in the present volume.

[15]Johann Baptist Metz, *Memoria Passionis* (Freiburg: Herder, 2006).

[16]Steven T. Katz, Shlomo Biderman, and Gershon Greenberg (eds), *Wrestling with God: Jewish Theological Responses during and after the Holocaust* (Oxford: Oxford University Press, 2007).

[17]Katz *et al.*, *Wrestling with God*, p. 434.

[18]William Lane Craig and W. Sinnott-Armstrong, *God?* (Oxford: Oxford University Press, 2008). Richard Swinburne, *Was Jesus God?* (Oxford: Oxford University Press, 2008). Chad Meister, *Introducing Philosophy of Religion* (London, New York: Routledge, 2009).

[19]See, for example, Daniel Dennett, *Breaking the Spell: Religion as a Natural Phenomenon* (New York: Viking, 2006).

Study questions

1. What are the forms of secularization according to Charles Taylor?
2. Describe the notion of the 'Death of God'.
3. How would you summarize the experience of 'Auschwitz'?
4. What is the most important feature of atheistic Communism with respect to faith in God?
5. Is a rebirth of faith possible after the period of the epochal crises of faith?

Further Reading

Breiterman, Zachary, *(God) After Auschwitz. Tradition and Change in Post-Holocaust Jewish Thought* (Princeton: Princeton University Press, 1998).

Craig, William Lane, *Reasonable Faith. Christian Truth and Apologetics* (Wheaton: Crossway, 2008).

Habermas, Jürgen et al, *An Awareness of What Is Missing: Faith and Reason in a Post-Secular Age* (Cambridge: Polity, 2010).

21
Faith and Science: Beyond Reciprocity

Introduction

'Let us not forget, however, that there is a difference between arguments *from* first principles and arguments *to* first principles'.[1] Aristotle's famous distinction calls our attention to the fundamental difference between two kinds of reasoning usually identified as 'deductive' and 'inductive'. To understand the difference between how faith and science think, we must keep an eye on this distinction. The various relationships between theological and scientific reasoning presuppose this original difference, which we need to understand properly. Of course, science and faith may be variously deductive and inductive in their details. Yet the general fashion of their workings can be delineated as being based either on the universal axiom of the existence of God or on the axiom that axioms cannot be accepted without sufficient empirical evidence. Even though reasoning faith often refers to experiences, historical data and rules of thinking, it cannot avoid making the ultimate postulate of the existence of God as the God of faith. And even though science uses axiomatic mathematics in many of its procedures, its main focus points to the hypotheses produced on the basis of empirical evidence and their measurable testability.

Historically, faith referred to the ultimate truth of divine revelation as the necessary framework in which sciences were allowed to work. The natural sciences made use of empirical evidence in order to fill out, and also to test, the theological framework. A good example of this sort of conflict is the story of Galileo Galilei (1564–1642). When Galileo built his telescope in 1611, the book Copernicus had published on the heliocentric view of the universe was only on the periphery of people's attention. Some version of the geocentric view still appeared to be the best one and was sanctioned by the authority of the Church. When Galileo began to use the telescope and discovered that the Moon looked like an earthly object and the Sun was not an angel-like heavenly body but showed *spots*, he jeopardized the soundness of the framework theology had presupposed for many centuries. Rome's reaction was correspondingly stern: it sentenced Galileo in 1633 for putting forward the mere hypothesis of the Copernican view as a sure truth. Although the Roman inquisition had a number of reasons, including political ones, to judge Galileo's views heretical, what they essentially did was confirm their old deductive system based on the traditions of the Church. And Galileo, in his turn, attempted to change

---

[1] Aristotle, *Nicomachean Ethics*, 1094a. The Greek word of Aristotle for 'argument' is *logos*.

this framework on the basis of the experiences he reached by using the foremost scientific instrument of his age.[2]

Faith and science: Varieties of a relationship

The relationship between faith and science, nevertheless, cannot be accurately described merely by using the story of Galileo as an example. Until the Second Vatican Council, the Catholic Church, and a number of Christian denominations as well, had a complicated relationship with modern science. The history of the sciences teaches us that to develop a more accurate picture we should not focus merely on one given period of a long history. We move closer to the truth if we conceive this relationship in terms of reciprocity: faith contributed to the development of the sciences in many ways, and the latter variously helped faith's self-understanding.

According to John Polkinghorne, the models of this relationship are as follows: (1) conflict, (2) independence, (3) dialogue and (4) integration.[3] The 'conflict approach' considers science and faith as contradictory and therefore mutually exclusive. For instance, as Sam Harris writes, 'The truth…is that the conflict between religion and science is unavoidable. The success of science often comes at the expense of religious dogma; the maintenance of religious dogma always comes at the expense of science'.[4] The 'independence approach' is represented by authors who maintain that faith and science

> answer different questions about the world. Whether there is a purpose to the universe or a purpose for human existence are not questions for science … Science is a way of knowing about the natural world. It is limited to explaining the natural world through natural causes. Science can say nothing about the supernatural. Whether God exists or not is a question about which science is neutral.[5]

The 'dialogue approach' claims that there is no serious clash between faith and science. Some writers on science tend to overemphasize the existing differences in method and content, but the truth is that faith and science are rather compatible. Alvin Plantinga has shown that the real conflict does not lie between faith and science, but rather between faith and 'naturalism' in science, a naturalism which is not necessitated by sound science. It is not science but naturalism, represented by authors such as Richard Dawkins or Daniel Dennett, which is inimical to Christian faith.[6] In the 'integration approach', we find claims about the close historical, methodological and personal connections between faith and science. Religious faith

---

[2]Richard J. Blackwell, *Behind the Scenes of Galileo's Trial* (Notre Dame: University of Notre Dame Press, 2006).

[3]John Polkinghorne, *Science and Theology* (London: SPCK/Fortress Press, 1998), pp. 20–22.

[4]Sam Harris, *Letter to a Christian Nation* (New York: Random House, 2006), p. 21.

[5]From a text issued by the National Academy of Sciences, quoted by Harris, *Letter to a Christian Nation*, p. 21.

[6]Alvin Plantinga, *Where the Conflict Really Lies: Science, Religion, and Naturalism* (Oxford: Oxford University Press, 2011).

contributed to the emergence and development of the sciences importantly, and influential scientists have often confessed their belief in ultimate divine power. The question concerns the concrete ways in which faith and science can cooperate in a mutually beneficial way.[7]

This list of possibilities may be reduced to two important options: the role of faith in science and the role of science in faith.

The role of faith in science

It is non-controversial that faith, or in a more general sense religion, contributed to the development of the modern sciences in many ways. Theologically, the notion of the creation of the universe by God made it possible to demarcate the world as an independent field of investigation. Western Christianity's emphasis on the difference between faith and reason prepared the soil for the emergence of scientific rationality. Christian universities encouraged scientific research and contributed to the propagation of its results. Many influential scientists in Western history, such as Jean Picard (†1682), Giovanni Battista Riccioli (†1671), Francesco Grimaldi (†1663) or Gregor Mendel (†1882), were churchpersons and important scientists at the same time. Isaac Newton (1642–1727) and Charles Darwin (1809–1882) referred to their faith in God in their writings. In the twentieth century, Albert Einstein (1879–1955) had a kind of belief in God, and other leading scientists of that age, such as Werner Heisenberg (1901–1976), offered complex views on the importance of faith for scientific research.[8] Kurt Gödel's (1906–1977) revolutionary 'incompleteness theorem' is closely connected to his 'ontological proof' for the existence of God.[9] The best example is offered by Michael Polanyi's notion of 'personal knowledge'. As he argues, scientific knowledge is based on personal commitment. Scientific truth cannot be reached mechanically. Our personality goes into the sciences, including our emotions, conviction and faith. With reference to Augustine's favourite biblical passage 'If you do not believe, you will not understand' (Isa. 7.9),[10] Polanyi writes, 'We must now recognize belief once more as the source of all knowledge'.[11] In various ways, faith has played a crucial role in the flourishing of the sciences.

The role of science in faith

On the other hand, the breathtaking development of the sciences in modernity has contributed to a critical evaluation of what faith consists in. Pope Benedict XVI's

---

[7]Known representatives of such a view are Historian Lawrence M. Principe or Scientist John Polkinghorne.
[8]See the revelations about his own and Einstein's faith in God in Werner Heisenberg, *Physics and Beyond: Encounters and Conversations* (New York: Harper & Row, 1971).
[9]Hao Wang, *Reflections on Kurt Gödel* (Cambridge, Mass.: MIT Press, 1995), pp. 161, 195.
[10]See also a better translation in ch 1.
[11]Michael Polanyi, *Personal Knowledge: Towards a Post-Critical Philosophy* (London: Routledge, 1962), p. 280.

statement must be kept in mind about 'the supreme good of modernity: tolerance and freedom'.[12] To learn about tolerance and freedom, Christian faith had to go through the purification of modernity and the Enlightenment.[13] The sciences contributed to the development of faith because, as Polkinghorne explains, the structures of theological reasoning and scientific research are similar to one another:

> Birds and human beings look very different on the outside, but when their bone structures are revealed and analysed one can see that wings and arms are morphologically related to each other. In an analogous fashion it is possible to exhibit the basic similarities of truth-seeking strategy that exist between physics and theology through a procedure of attending to accounts stripped down to their essentials.[14]

Modern psychology teaches us that the human psyche is a complicated structure which needs to be studied and clarified in order that a refined notion of faith may be conceived. Modern physics leads us to understand in a more exact fashion the physical nature in which we live. New discoveries in cosmology create new hypotheses about the origin, age and duration of the universe. Biology clarifies the edifice of living organisms which human beings use for their psychic and intellectual functions. Technology has supplied us with the means by which the contents of faith can be explored in ways unavailable for earlier periods of history. Modern and post-modern philosophy elucidates the pitfalls and possibilities of human rationality taken in itself and its relation to mystery. Political science helps us to understand the structure of societies, and thus the society of the church as well, so that important sociological notions, such as that of subsidiarity, may be better used in our social activities. Research on the origins of totalitarianism and its fateful effects on human societies advises us about the value of democracy in which Christians have a better chance to face the challenge the practice of faith poses today. The study of religion teaches us to understand the intellectual and spiritual significance of non-Christian cultures as well and to see the possibilities of a perceptive dialogue. The entire modern drive to create a new universal culture puts Christianity into a context in which the balance of tradition and progress may be better reached and their values appraised. In this context, the chances of a well-formed faith are enhanced in important ways.

Beyond reciprocity

In our present culture, we have a better grasp of what is at stake when we confess our faith in God. Theology as reasoning faith needs to rely on the cultural world, which means it should rely on the sciences as well. However, faith still offers an

---

[12]Benedict XVI, *The Essential Pope Benedict XVI: His Central Writings and Speeches*, ed. John F. Thorton and Susan B. Varenne (New York, HarperCollins Ebooks, 2008), p. 230.
[13]Benedict XVI, *The Essential Pope Benedict*, p. 334.
[14]John Polkinghorne, *Quantum Theory and Theology: An Unexpected Kinship* (New Haven: Yale University Press, 2008), p. xii.

entirely different perspective from which to evaluate reality. In spite of its structural closeness to the sciences, faith in an overall sense is never inductive. Rather, as Aristotle suggests in the opening sentence of this chapter, faith works '*from* the first principles'. That is, the starting point of faith is *the fact* of divine revelation. Revelation can be seen in two ways: as the fact itself (*revelatio qua*) and as its contents (*revelatio quae*). While the contents of revelation have been the same throughout the centuries, the question 'what is revelation?' may receive a better answer. Revelation is not merely propositional or historical, it is not only about certain doctrines formulated in a language nobody speaks today and it is not about a description of mythological figures in clumsy historical texts. Revelation is first of all about God's infinite love disclosed in the act of self-donation in the person of his Son for the salvation of human beings. Revelation is better understood today as *radical revelation*, the utmost act of love by God to save us from our mistakes, failures and sins. Radical revelation *calls for* radical faith, a faith which involves entire human persons and opens them to the infinite and self-giving love of God.[15]

This understanding of faith defines our attitude to the sciences in our contemporary culture. Theologically, we need the sciences so that we may better understand what faith means in our culture today. This attitude, however, not only outlines the structure of reciprocity in which faith and the sciences react to one another in fruitful ways but also enacts an approach which does not understand faith in term of a function. Faith is not merely the functional faith of Polanyi's personal knowledge. Its structures do not merely parallel the structures of scientific thinking. Faith is about something more important, namely our salvation. Faith, ultimately, may be compared to love, this unique human phenomenon in which everything becomes secondary with respect to the only purpose we perceive in love: to be united with the beloved one. Faith is about total self-donation for the realization of the unity of the loving soul with the loving God. Faith is an irreplaceable relationship which does not tolerate anything in-between; its only thought, will and desire, its only reality is embodied in the beloved one. If we lose sight of this ultimate nature of faith, we become unable to understand its fundamentally non-functional character. Faith can be fruitful for the sciences, and it also can be purified by them in many ways, but ultimately faith is something absolute coming from, and groping for, the Absolute.

Study questions

1. What are the two kinds of reasoning characteristic of faith and science?
2. Which are the models of relationship between faith and science?
3. What role has faith played in the development of the sciences?
4. What role has science played in the development of faith?
5. Why cannot faith be merely functional in science?

---

[15]See Balazs Mezei, 'Faith and Reason', in Lewis Ayres (ed.), *The Oxford Handbook of Catholicism* (Oxford: Oxford University Press, forthcoming 2015).

Further reading

Barr, Stephen M., *Modern Physics and Ancient Faith* (Notre Dame: University of Notre Dame Press, 2003).

Dixon, Thomas, *Science and Religion: A Very Short Introduction* (Oxford: Oxford University Press, 2008).

Jaki, Stanley, *The Savior of Science* (Grand Rapids, Mich.: Eerdmans, 2000).

Polkinghorne, John, *Belief in God in the Age of Science* (New Haven: Yale University Press, 2003).

22
Faith and Liberation

A wandering Aramean was my ancestor; he went down into Egypt
and lived there as an alien, few in number, and there he became a great
nation, mighty and populous. When the Egyptians treated us harshly
and afflicted us, by imposing hard labor on us, we cried to the Lord,
the God of our ancestors; the Lord heard our voice and saw our affliction,
our toil, and our oppression. The Lord brought us out of Egypt with a
mighty hand and an out-stretched arm, with a terrifying display of power,
and with signs and wonder; and he brought us to this land, a land flowing
with milk and honey. (Deuteronomy 26.5–9)

Along with the above summary of the Exodus, Scripture is full of passages which
many have found to be genuine words of life, consolation and encouragement.
Among many others we could look to Mary's Magnificat (Lk. 1.46–55), Jesus'
quoting of Isa. 61 at the outset of his public ministry in Lk. 4 and Paul's declaration
that in Christ there is neither male nor female, Jew nor Greek (Gal. 3.28).

The preaching and reception of the good news of the gospel always take place
in particular contexts. Within the twentieth century in particular, there has been
a flowering of theologies which developed from groups of people who have been
subjected to systematic exclusion, oppression and humiliation. There is a long list
of theologies and theologians who have interpreted and preached the liberating
and consoling words of Scripture from the perspectives of the struggles of different
groups within specific contexts. There have been liberation theologies in Latin
America, the United States, South Africa and Asia which have developed in response
to the plight of the poor and those subjected to systemic racism. There have also been
feminist, womanist and mujerista theologies which have pointed out the specific
denigrations of women in past and present social situations and theologies. Not all
of these theologies say the same thing, and there can be sharp disagreements among
their practitioners themselves. In this chapter, we can only touch on some of the
themes raised regarding faith, and none of the viewpoints offered can be taken as
characteristic for the rest of those working from these frameworks and commitments.

The preferential option for the poor

For Gustavo Gutiérrez (1928–), a Pervuian Dominican priest, one of the basic
characteristics of the God of Scripture is God's solidarity with and concern for the
poor and downtrodden. This solidarity and concern can be seen in God's acts within

history as narrated by Scripture. It is shown in the liberation of the Israelites from Egypt, an event and memory which affected how some of the authors and editors of the Old Testament described creation in Genesis and Isaiah. It is also shown in the New Testament through the new creation effected by Jesus Christ. The work of Jesus Christ liberates in two related ways, redeeming human beings from sin as well as from the consequences of sin, such as destitution, oppression and hatred. There are also the eschatological promises of God, for the healing of creation, the pouring out of the Spirit upon flesh and the lifting up of the lowly. As God works within history, so too are these promises fulfilled in history. These promises are, however, only partially fulfilled at any given moment and so we must await their final realization. Yet by their very presence they throw into question the sentiment that the current state of affairs, especially that of the poor, is necessary, inevitable or natural. As Gutiérrez notes, 'Biblical faith is, above all, faith in a God who reveals himself through historical events, a God who saves in history'.[1]

A simple way of summarizing this view of Scripture's portrayal of God is the line 'preferential option for the poor'. This statement does not mean that God is only concerned about the poor and oblivious to everyone else. The point is that the God of Scripture is *particularly* concerned with the well-being and treatment of the poor. As a summary for how the God of Scripture acts in history, the preferential option for the poor names a guideline for reading Scripture (a 'hermeneutical rule') as well as a guideline for preaching, the Christian life and political action. A similar phrase and concern (although not identical!) can be seen in the 1971 apostolic letter *Octogesima adveniens*, penned on the occasion of the eightieth anniversary of the encyclical *Rerum novarum*. In this letter, Pope Paul VI lamented that legislation is often far behind in recognizing human rights. Furthermore, legislation is insufficient in itself for promoting justice and equality. 'In teaching us charity, the Gospel instructs us in the preferential respect due to the poor and the special situation they have in society', even offering the recommendation that 'the more fortunate should renounce some of their rights so as to place their goods more generously at the service of others'. Without love, then, even legislation on behalf of the good goal of equality might be abused and become a means of further discrimination and contempt for others. Gutiérrez is also aware of the importance of love for the life of faith and for the improvement of the social condition of others. Faith is, he says, 'the vital acceptance of the gift of the word, heard in the community of the church as encounter with the Lord and love for one's fellow human beings. Faith pervades Christian existence in its entirety'.[2]

God is black

James Cone (b. 1938), one of the founders of Black theology within the United States, has said that the God of Scripture 'is known and worshipped as the Lord

---

[1]Gustavo Gutiérrez, *Theology of Liberation: History, Politics and Salvation*, ed. and trans. Sister Caridad Inda and John Eagelson Maryknoll (New York: Orbis Books, 1973), p. 154.
[2]Gustavo Gutiérrez, *The Truth Shall Make You Free: Confrontations*, trans. Matthew J. O'Connell (Maryknoll, NY: Orbis Books, 1991), p. 6.

who brought Israel out of Egypt, and who raised Jesus Christ from the dead. He is the political God, the Protector of the poor and the Establisher of the right for those who are oppressed'.[3] In electing Israel, the oppressed, instead of Pharaoh, the oppressor, the God of Scripture reveals himself to be on the side of the weak, vulnerable and helpless. Having been liberated by God from Egypt, the covenant at Sinai shows that Israel has been liberated to be for God. The prophets of the Old Testament deliver the message of the liberating God to Israel as Israel herself begins to forget the poor and destitute (Am. 4.2; Hos. 13.5–6). This same God is revealed in the New Testament. The Incarnation itself means that 'God in Christ comes to the weak and the helpless and becomes one with them, taking their conditions of oppression as his own and thus transforming their slave-existence into a liberated existence'.[4] Here Cone points to Jesus' reading of Isa. 61 at the beginning of his public ministry in the Gospel of Luke, Jesus' continual identification with the poor and the destitute and the Kingdom's message of good news to the poor and the downcast. The crucifixion and resurrection of Jesus Christ is confirmation that in Jesus' ministry and teaching we are dealing with God himself and that in Jesus Christ God was working to liberate the oppressed. In Jesus Christ is found the freedom to struggle.

For Cone, the stories of the Exodus and Jesus Christ are a revelation of who God is and what God has done. These stories are interpreted from the experience of those who have been and are oppressed within the United States. Given the historic and systemic racism of the dominant white society towards blacks, that God identifies and works among the oppressed means that we can say that 'God is black', and that 'Jesus Christ is black'. Cone thinks that such statements are salutary and necessary at this particular historical moment and place inasmuch as the Exodus and the Incarnation reveal to us the extent and nature of God's identification with the oppressed and the history of blacks within the United States. Yet the stories of the Exodus and the Incarnation in turn illuminate and transform the experience of blacks. Regarding the nature of faith, Cone states

> to believe is to receive the gift and utterly to reorient one's existence on the basis of the gift. The gift is so unlike what humans expect that when it is offered and accepted, we become completely new creatures. This is what the Wholly Otherness of God means. God comes to us in God's blackness, which is wholly unlike whiteness. To receive God's revelation is to become black with God by joining God in the work of liberation.[5]

Faith, then, means freedom from oppressive structures and groups, the 'trust and conviction' that one is in God and beloved by God, and the freedom to work for the liberation of others.[6]

---

[3]James Cone, *The God of the Oppressed* (New York: Seabury Press, 1975), p. 62.
[4]Cone, *The God of the Oppressed*, p. 76.
[5]James Cone, *A Black Theology of Liberation* (Maryknoll, NY: Orbis Books, 1986), p. 66.
[6]Cone, *A Black Theology of Liberation*, p. 141.

Faith, sin and the self

The British feminist theologian Daphne Hampson (1944–) raises some questions regarding Luther's account of the dynamic of faith.[7] She palpably senses the allure and power of Luther's portrayal of faith as fundamentally a matter of trust in another, as trust in God. When placing my trust, the whole centre of my being and living in God, my very self is redefined. One's relationship to God is not seen as something external or accidental, but as a fundamental aspect of who one is. Within such a perspective, sin names the continual attempts to define oneself apart from God, as one who has my being and source within myself. The irony for Hampson is that in the self's isolation, a deep anxiety is also present. This anxiety of being alone is then expressed through attempts to dominate and control others. Sin is the state of being *incurvatus in se* and the refusal to live in another and to have another live within me. As the desire for self-isolation and reliance, as the desire to demonstrate my own abilities, as the desire to control my relationship to God and to others, sin is pride.

Faith is the reception of my being, living and self as something which comes from God, and not from myself. It is trust in who God is, which means living as God's creature, not as my own self-creation. Faith in God takes the form of love of one's neighbour, for I am no longer worried about myself but am now concerned with caring for and loving others. Instead of seeking to dominate others, the self seeks to love them. Faith, then, is a breaking of the prideful self, a reorientation from oneself to others by being placed in God.

Hampson's question is simple. Who is described in this dynamic of pride, sin and faith? Does this description apply equally well to men as to women? Hampson's sense is that the historical situation and temptation of women have not been to view themselves as fundamentally isolated, as controlling others in turn, and thus in need of being related to God and to others. It seems that the problem of women, historically and socially, has not been having 'too much self', or thinking of oneself as isolated. In Hampson's words, 'Women are not typically self-enclosed and in need of finding connectedness. Their problem has rather been a lack of centeredness in self; their need, to come to themselves. The whole dynamic of being a self is very different from what Lutheranism has proposed. Thus its prescription must appear irrelevant, indeed counter-productive'.[8] As an analysis of temptations historically common to men, Luther's account of faith seems helpful. As a description of women, however it appears 'counter-productive'. Luther's understanding of the 'problem' of pride and its 'solution' of faith does not seem to fit women. Hampson goes on to say that feminists may be able to appropriate Luther's (and Schleiermacher's) account of God as the very source and centre of one's self. What is important, however, is that religion, Christian or otherwise, promote the empowerment of women.

---

[7]Daphne Hampson, 'Luther on the Self: A Feminist Critique', *Word and World* 8:4 (1988), pp. 334–342.
[8]Hampson, 'Luther on the Self', p. 339.

Study questions

1. What do you find convincing or unconvincing about Gutiérrez's account of the God of Scripture?
2. What do you think Cone is trying to express by saying that 'God is Black' and that 'Jesus Christ is Black'?
3. What is Hampson's understanding of Luther? Is she right regarding the argument that Luther's account of faith better describes the historical and social situation of men rather than of women?

Further readings

Cone, James, *A Black Theology of Liberation* (Maryknoll, NY: Orbis Books, 1986), pp. 21–39.

Gutiérrez, Gustavo, *The Truth Shall Make You Free: Confrontations*, trans. Matthew J. O'Connell (Maryknoll, NY: Orbis Books, 1991), pp. 1–17.

Hampson, Daphne, 'Luther on the Self: A Feminist Critique', *Word and World* 8:4 (1988), pp. 334–342.

23

Basic Beliefs:
Reformed Epistemology

Foundationalism and philosophy of religion

Reformed Epistemology was, in 1983, an uncharacteristically *religious* standpoint within philosophy of religion. Since the Enlightenment, most philosophies of religion have not been religious philosophies. As we saw in Chapter 10, at that time, Anglicans such as John Locke led the way in affirming that faith ought to be *beyond* reason but should not contradict reason. Many philosophers then and since have sought literally to underwrite the rationality of faith by first proving that God exists, and then proceeding, *on this basis*, to articulate God's revelation in Scripture and in history. A standard procedure in the eighteenth-century Scholasticisms of Catholicism *and* Protestantism has been to think of revealed truths as resting upon and gaining their rational credibility from a supporting structure of proofs of the existence of God. This procedure somehow survived into the late twentieth century.

Going back a long way historically, the procedure and the assumptions behind it probably derive from René Descartes' efforts to give rational foundations to all human knowledge. This idea that all human knowledge has rational and indeed *certain* foundations is called 'foundationalism'. It originates with the Continental Rationalists, like Descartes, but is also present in empiricists, like John Locke. A foundationalist maintains that knowledge is knowledge if it rests on secure and certain foundations. Its counterpart in religion is *evidentialism*, the idea that religious beliefs require evidence and argument in order to be rationally or well founded.

Foundationalism lies behind the efforts of Locke and his contemporaries in England, and of their Continental counterparts, to justify faith in God's revelation on the grounds of prior evidence and argumentation that God exists. The assumption that evidentialism is true was normative in the teaching of philosophy of religion in the twentieth century right down to the end of the 1970s. Then, at the end of the 1970s, foundationalism was subjected to highly serious philosophical criticisms, for instance, by Richard Rorty, in *Philosophy and the Mirror of Nature* (1979). At the same time, the 'Enlightenment' ceased to function as an incontestable token of cultural advance.

With foundationalism shaken, some Anglicans and Calvinists took the opportunity to mount a counter-attack against evidentialism. The effort to reclaim philosophy of religion for *religious belief* was the start of Reformed Epistemology.

Calvinism: three reformers

The original proponents of Reformed Epistemology were Nicholas Wolterstorff (b. 1932), Alvin Plantinga (b. 1932) and William Alston (1921–2009). Plantinga notes in his obituary of Alston the singular importance of 'a powerful religious experience at evensong in Christchurch Cathedral, Oxford'.[1] This 'powerful religious experience' greatly deepened Alston's commitment as an Episcopalian. Wolterstorff and Plantinga were both Calvinists: 'Reformed' Christians are members of the various churches which owe their origins to the catechesis of John Calvin. 'Reformed Epistemology' and 'Calvinist Epistemology' are effectively synonymous.

Reformed Epistemology sees its rejection of Lockean evidentialism as a return to basic, original Reformed attitudes. Its proponents would say that it is integral to the Reformed, Calvinist tradition to be averse to evidentialism and to hold as a matter of religious principle that belief in God should not be founded on argumentative evidence. In an essay which launched the new movement in philosophy of religion, Plantinga notes that the two most outstanding Reformed churchmen of the past hundred years, Hermann Bavinck and Karl Barth, were both staunch foes of founding faith in God upon rational argumentation or evidence. Plantinga points out that according to the Dutch Bavinck, proofs from nature to God are not needed before we can *trust* in God. More importantly as evidence of anti-evidentialism, Bavinck also claims that rational argument to God's existence is not needed in order for belief in God to be *rationally justified*.[2]

John Calvin himself was no foundationalist, according to Plantinga. Plantinga cites Calvin as maintaining that 'there is within the human mind, and indeed by natural instinct, an awareness of divinity'.[3] 'Calvin's claim', Plantinga says, 'is that God has created us in such a way that we have a strong tendency or inclination toward belief in him'.[4] On the Calvinist account, as Plantinga would have it, it is *unnatural*, as it were, perverse to *prove* by rational argument that God exists. Plantinga compares it to proving that one's wife is not a robot or that other people exist. As odd as it sounds, these are both commonplace exercises within foundationalism (Descartes asks in the *Meditations*, for instance, whether the people outside his window might not be robots). It is only as a result of *sin* that people even think of *demonstrating* that God exists or imagining that our trust in him is reliant upon such a demonstration. The knowledge itself should be inborn or immediate, because God put it in us, in our original state. So, according to the founder of Calvinism, we ought not to wish to demonstrate that God exists, as a foundation for believing in him, and, conversely, we ought to maintain that 'belief in God is properly basic'.[5]

---

[1] Alvin Plantinga, 'In Memoriam: William P. Alston, 1921–2009', *Faith and Philosophy* 26:4 (2009), pp. 359–360 (359).

[2] Alvin Plantinga, 'Reason and Belief in God', in Alvin Plantinga and Nicholas Wolterstorff (eds), *Faith and Rationality: Reason and Belief in God* (Notre Dame: Notre Dame University Press, 1983), pp. 16–93 (64–65).

[3] Calvin, *Institutes*, I.III.1, p. 43.

[4] Plantinga, 'Reason and Belief in God', pp. 65–66.

[5] Plantinga, 'Reason and Belief in God', p. 72.

Plantinga would not be making a very interesting claim if he were just contending that believers should not strive for evidence and should, instead, repose on faith in God. Rather, he means to say that belief in God without evidence is not 'just belief' or private opinion or whatever secular moderns usually mean by unevidenced faith. He means that it is perfectly *rational* and cogent for belief in God to dispense with evidential argument. Plantina argues that, for Calvin and the Reformed tradition, 'one who takes belief in God as basic can *know* that God exists. Calvin holds that one can *rationally accept* belief in God as basic ... one can *know* that God exists even if he has no argument, even if he does not believe on the basis of other propositions'.[6] To the average evidentialist, this seems rather a paradoxical contention. It made sense for professional philosophers like Plantinga to argue in this way because they thought classical 'foundationalism' was untenable.

Collapse of classical foundationalism

Classical foundationalism could be thought of as picturing human rationality like a house. Cemented into the foundations and upholding the structure are 'basic beliefs', that is, beliefs which *nothing* could overthrow, such as evidence from the senses, or self-evident truths or truths about how consciousness appears to me which are simply incorrigible because *it is undeniable that my consciousness appears to me the way it appears to me*. Basic truths are the undeniables, like 'I know I am thinking'. If one doubted that one were thinking, that itself would be an act of thought. The basic beliefs provide structural support (foundations) for all the rest of our (nonbasic) beliefs: that is what, according to classical foundation, makes the 'house' of our thought stand up tall and rational.

Classical foundationalists set up various conditions for beliefs being given rational permission to count as basic. Sometimes such beliefs are said to come from the evidence of the senses, and other times such beliefs are said to be 'self-evident' (like those about one's own consciousness). It is difficult to see what exactly makes a belief sufficiently rational or evidential to count as basic.

It is an oddity of empiricist foundationalism, like that of Locke, that on the one hand it treats sensation as 'basic', but on the other, it wants us to make rational argument our support structure, for a sensation is not a rational argument, it is just a sensation. We recall that Locke was tied to the representative theory of perception, according to which the *immediate* object of our perception is not an object, but rather, the sensed image of that object. We must infer from the 'representation' of the object in our consciousness *to* the real object outside ourselves. He treated sensations, those so-called interior 'representations' of outward things, as if they were silent 'rational arguments', clues to something beyond themselves. As dumb 'representatives' of a world beyond themselves, sensations became the starting point of chains of inferences. Sceptical critics of foundationalism like Rorty saw that this

---

[6]Plantinga, 'Reason and Belief in God', p. 73.

depiction of knowledge left us knowing very little. David Hume had seen that long before! Hume pointed out that imagination could add a lot to what we 'infer' about the objects which we believe 'cause' our sensations.

Do we really *infer* from our (basic) sensations to objects outside of ourselves? Or do we not, rather, *immediately grasp objects*? Reformed Epistemology drew an analogy: if we do not actually infer from (basic) sensations to objects, but rather, immediately 'sense' objects, so likewise, we do not infer from worldly evidence to God, but rather, immediately 'know' or perceive God. Wolterstorff wrote that 'basic beliefs' could also be called 'immediate beliefs, on the ground that they are not formed by the "mediation" of inference'.[7] Perhaps God is not tucked away beyond a chain of inferences, but rather 'hiding in plain sight', present immediately to our experience or perception.

The conditions foundationalists set for counting as a basic belief are questionable. Reformed Epistemologists challenge these conditions, and ask, why cannot belief in God count as a basic belief, one which lies beyond or beneath doubt, question or argument, and which supports all the rest of our beliefs. So Reformed Epistemology does not accept without question the overthrow of foundationalism. Instead, it accepts that some beliefs must be foundational, and asks why not belief in God?

The evidentialist challenge

Ever since the Enlightenment, religion had been wrong-footed by rationalism. For, Plantinga claimed, religion allowed itself to be told by Enlightenment thinkers that it is wrong to accept theism unless theism is rational, and that theism is not rational unless religious conviction is based on *other* evidence than itself. In accepting this challenge, and with it the principle that religion cannot be its *own* evidence, theism allowed itself always to be governed by higher criteria than itself. Plantinga and other Reformed Epistemologists reject the demand that religion give 'warrants' for its beliefs from *outside of religious belief* itself. It is like being asked to pay in a foreign currency.

Against the 'Evidentialist challenge' that all beliefs must be warranted by rational evidence, Reformed Epistemologists argue that it is not irrational to believe things that cannot be proven with rational evidence. Plantinga rhetorically asks, 'Why is it not permissible to believe in God without any evidence – proof or argument – at all?'[8] He claims that many things such as, to give a favourite example, belief in other minds are held, and held perfectly rationally, without demonstrative, logical evidence. As Wolterstorff puts it, 'religious belief does not have to be rationally grounded to be rational'.[9]

---

[7]Nicholas Wolterstorff, 'Religious Epistemology', in William J. Wainwright (ed.), *The Oxford Handbook of Philosophy of Religion* (Oxford: Oxford University Press, 2005), pp. 244–271 (261).
[8]Plantinga, 'Reason and Belief in God', p. 39.
[9]Wolterstorff, 'Religious Epistemology', p. 247.

What does believing without evidence mean in this context?

Reformed Epistemology's claims about believing 'without evidence' or without rational argument occur in the context of its disputing certain foundationalist and evidentialist claims. The broader context is its contending against the Enlightenment claim to test religion against the bar of human reason. When Reformed Epistemology states that religious belief does not need evidence, this has to be understood in context. It does not mean that Reformed Epistemologists think there is no evidence that God exists. Far from it. What it means is that 'evidence', such as rational argument and especially a chain of inference from various clues to something beyond them and wholly different from them, is not the *basis* of religious beliefs. In the context of foundationalism, 'evidence' means that which supports other beliefs. So to say that belief in God is without evidence means that it is not taken to reside on the back of *other and different* beliefs and arguments. Belief in God is directed immediately at God, and no higher criteria than itself mediates it to the believer.

Thus, Reformed Epistemologists can argue simultaneously, and, so it says, without contradiction, that there is no 'evidence' for religious belief and that evidence for religious belief lies all around us. The evidence for religious belief is twofold: on the one hand, God is exhibited in and through the universe he has designed, and on the other, as noted earlier, God has created in us a tendency to believe that the world was created by him. We are surrounded by 'evidence' that God exists. And yet, our belief in God is 'basic': it is what makes us construe the evidence as evidence. The 'warrant' or justification which a Reformed Epistemologist gives for belief in God is an epistemological one: that the human mind is built to organize its knowledge on the basis of belief in God.

Study questions

1. Is it possible to prove that Reformed Epistemology is true? Is it possible to disprove it?

2. Is Reformed Epistemology biblical?

3. Do you think we see God 'immediately' or 'mediately', through the universe?

4. Compare Plantinga's view of 'belief' with Karl Barth's idea of 'faith'.

5. Is there an analogy between knowing other people exist and knowing God exists?

Further reading

Plantinga, Alvin, 'Reason and Belief in God', in edited by Alvin Plantinga and Nicholas Wolterstorff, *Faith and Rationality: Reason and Belief in God* (Notre Dame: Notre Dame University Press, 1983), 16–93.

24
The Phenomenology of Faith:
Fides et ratio

The journey

In 1998 Pope John Paul II issued the encyclical *Fides et ratio*, *Faith and Reason*. The encyclical begins with the image of the 'human spirit' flying like a bird on 'two wings', faith and reason. The 'two wings' of faith and reason enable the 'human spirit' to 'ris[e] to the contemplation of truth'.[1] Beginning from this image of the human spirit as a 'bird', the encyclical frequently uses the metaphor of the *journey* in search of truth. It says, 'human knowledge is a journey which knows no rest'.[2] Old Testament believers were strengthened on their 'way to truth' by their certainty that God created them 'explorers'.[3] *Fides et ratio* speaks of *Journeying in Search of Truth* along a 'a path which the human being may choose to take, a path which begins with reason's capacity to rise beyond what is contingent and set out towards the infinite'.[4] The basic metaphor is of the human person as a *seeker*, flying through the heavens in pursuit of truth. It does not undermine this metaphor when John Paul claims that people only explore because they figure that one day they will find what they are looking for: 'Only the sense that they can arrive at an answer leads them to take the first step.'[5] Human life is a search driven by desire for someone to whom to confide our need for meaning. Human beings are wayfarers travelling through infinite realms, but their journey has a goal and terminus:

> men and women men and women are on a journey of discovery which is humanly unstoppable – a search for the truth and a search for a person to whom they might entrust themselves…In Jesus Christ, who is the Truth, faith recognizes the ultimate appeal to humanity, an appeal made in order than what we experience as desire and nostalgia may come to its fulfillment.[6]

Human beings have a homing device by which they navigate towards the object of their quest. This is the infinite desire for God.

---

[1]John Paul II, *Fides et ratio* (1998), § Introduction.
[2]*Fides et ratio*, §18.
[3]*Fides et ratio*, §21.
[4]*Fides et ratio*, §24. Italics in the original.
[5]*Fides et ratio*, §29.
[6]*Fides et ratio*, §33.

Comparison with earlier doctrine

Fides et ratio travels in the wake of magisterial statements on faith and reason over the previous century and a half. Following numerous papal Briefs and encyclicals about these topics, in 1870 Vatican I devoted a whole constitution, *Dei Filius*, to faith and reason.[7] In 1879, Pope Leo XIII issued *Aeterni Patris: On the Restoration of Christian Philosophy*, which exhorted Christians to learn how to harmonize faith and reason from Thomas Aquinas. *Fides et ratio* is similar to *Dei Filius* and *Aeterni Patris* in many ways. Like *Dei Filius*, it claims we can know God from nature.[8] Following its predecessors, its stresses the 'unity of truth', that is, that the 'two modes of knowledge' of faith and reason balance each other and cannot contradict one another.[9] In line with its precedent, *Fides et ratio* foregrounds the importance of *metaphysics*.

There are also new emphases, perhaps amounting to a development of doctrine. The earlier magisterial teachings had observed the negative features of modern philosophies. *Fides et ratio* does that too, but it also notes, 'Modern philosophy clearly has the great merit of focusing attention upon man'.[10] For this encyclical, *the* basic human question is 'Who am I?' Here it mentions the Delphic Oracle with its injunction 'Know Thyself'.

The personalist or existential understanding of human reason and philosophy in this encyclical builds on the Second Vatican Council (1962–1965). The Vatican II Constitution *Gaudium et spes* is the link between the earlier magisterial teaching and *Fides et ratio*. As the young bishop of Kraków, John Paul II (then Karol Wojtyla) was one of the authors of *Gaudium et spes*. This Constitution states that 'only in the mystery of the incarnate Word does the mystery of man take on light ... Christ, the final Adam, by the revelation of the mystery of the Father and His love, fully reveals man to man himself and makes his supreme calling clear'.[11] This principle, that Christ 'fully reveals' humanity to itself, is at the heart of *Fides et ratio*. *Gaudium et spes* talks about human beings in their concrete historical relationship to the final end of their desires and hopes, Jesus Christ. Like *Gaudium et spes*, *Fides et ratio* observes how sin darkens what should be the translucent appearance of God in the cosmos: that is, it takes the historicity of reason (its historical, post-lapsarian situation) seriously.[12]

Fides et ratio develops the core principles of *Gaudium et spes* and earlier magisterial teaching towards a *phenomenological* understanding of the goal of human knowledge. Both faith and reason, as it understands them, are keyed towards understanding *human experiences*. *Fides et ratio* commends non-Catholic thinkers such as Jean Paul Sartre for his 'penetrating analyses of perception and experience,

---

[7]See the chapter on Vatican I.

[8]*Fides et ratio*, §19.

[9]*Fides et ratio*, §34.

[10]*Fides et ratio*, §5.

[11]Documents of Vatican II, *Pastoral Constitution on the Church in the Modern World: Gaudium et spes* (1965) §22.

[12]*Fides et ratio*, §22, *Gaudium et spes*, §§10, 13, 14, 15, 17.

of the imaginary and the unconscious'. It doffs its tiara to the Catholic existentialist philosopher Martin Heidegger when it notes that the 'theme of death … can become for all thinkers an incisive appeal to seek within themselves the true meaning of their own life'.[13] The deepest truth we seek is the truth about who we are.

In keeping with this personalist orientation, the encyclical claims that St. Thomas Aquinas should be emulated 'not only because of what he taught but also because of the dialogue which he undertook with the Arab and Jewish thought of his time'.[14] The Dominican Saint exercised his reason in *dialogue with diverse religions and philosophies*. The idea that human beings are *relational* is important in the encyclical. It states that *belief* (the human equivalent of faith) is valuable just because, unlike 'mere evidence … it involves an interpersonal relationship'. In *belief* we trust and lean on other people, something which is 'humanly richer' than autonomously ascertaining the validity of evidence.[15] Since, on the one hand, every man and woman is a 'philosopher', a seeker after truth, and on the other, most of what we 'know' is gained by trusting the reports of other people, 'the human being – the one who seeks the truth – is also *the one who lives by belief*'. If reason rests ultimately on human beliefs, can reason and supernatural *faith* be at odds?

Wisdom

The biblical Wisdom literature recognizes no zero-sum game between faith and reason. The Wisdom literature, like Proverbs, is convinced that 'there is a profound and indissoluble unity between the knowledge of reason and the knowledge of faith'. 'Faith sharpens the inner eye' of the human person as philosopher.[16] It does not stunt or replace it. In line with contemporary biblical scholarship, which has unearthed 'wisdom' literatures in several ancient Near Eastern Civilizations, John Paul mentions that 'these biblical texts … embody not only the faith of Israel, but also the treasury of cultures and civilizations which have long vanished. As if by special design, the voices of Egypt and Mesopotamia sound again … in these pages which are so singularly rich in deep intuition'.[17] For *Fides et ratio*, it is not just 'reason' in the abstract which is in tune with faith, but the human culture of all nations, in their striving for meaning.

Freedom

The other Vatican II document which Bishop Wojtyla was involved in writing was the Declaration on Religion Freedom, *Dignitatis humanae*. *Dignitatis humanae* taught, magisterially, that religious freedom is a positive human good, and not just

---

[13]*Fides et ratio*, §48.
[14]*Fides et ratio*, §43.
[15]*Fides et ratio*, §32.
[16]*Fides et ratio*, §15.
[17]*Fides et ratio*, §16.

something Christians are compelled to tolerate because they no longer have the power to suppress non-Christians (or other kinds of Christians). Religious freedom is good because human beings need to explore, discuss, debate with opposing positions and even make mistakes in order to find the truth.[18] Freedom is positively oriented towards the discovery of truth. *Fides et ratio* stays with this insight, observing that 'faith liberates reason'[19] to set out in search of its deepest goals. No new Christian teaching ever quite *overturns* the tradition, and *Dignitatis humanae* finds a precedent for its defence of religious freedom in the fact that coercion of faith and enforced baptism were always forbidden by the Church. *Fides et ratio* has high praise for the inalienable *freedom* of the personal act of faith:

> By faith, men and women give their *assent* to this divine testimony … This is why the Church has always considered the act of entrusting oneself to God to be a moment of fundamental decision which engages the whole person. In that act, the intellect and the will display their spiritual nature, enabling the subject to act in a way which realizes personal freedom to the full … freedom is part of the act of faith: it is absolutely required … it is faith that allows individuals to give consummate expression to their own freedom. Put differently, freedom is not realized in decisions made against God.[20]

People who lack faith also lack the liberation it brings from the intellectually restricting consequences of harmful habits, negative reasoning and a human nature wounded by sin. 'The coming of Christ … redeemed reason … from the shackles in which it had imprisoned itself.'[21]

Light from the cross

With its focus on existential and personal meaning, *Fides et ratio* often implies that the most significant place where faith and reason stand together is in the face of death. The 'first absolutely certain truth of our life, beyond the fact that we exist', John Paul says, 'is the inevitability of our death'. This truth makes 'the search for a full answer … inescapable'. Human beings need to know if anything lies beyond death. The fearless way Socrates faced death, refusing to stop asking questions even when it made people condemn him, was a personal testimony that death cannot defeat the human spirit. 'It is not insignificant that the death of Socrates gave philosophy one of its decisive orientations'[22] towards asking about immortality and transcendence. Philosophy questions death and immortality, and revealed faith gives its answer in the face of the crucified and risen Christ. The teaching of the death and resurrection of Christ is, paradoxically, both where faith most conflicts with reason

---

[18]*Dignitatis humanae: Declaration on Religious Freedom*, §3.
[19]*Fides et ratio*, §19.
[20]*Fides et ratio*, §13.
[21]*Fides et ratio*, §22.
[22]*Fides et ratio*, §26.

and where it corresponds most profoundly with our human quest for meaning. *Fides et ratio* claims that

> [t]he preaching of Christ crucified and risen is the reef upon which the link between faith and philosophy can break up, but it is also the reef beyond which the two can set forth upon the boundless ocean of truth. Here we see not only the border between reason and faith, but also the space where the two may meet.[23]

Just as the widest and greatest aim of philosophy is to grasp the meaning of death, so the ultimate aim of theology is to articulate what it means for God to 'empty himself' (Phil. 2) and take the form of a servant, upon the Cross: 'the prime commitment of theology is … the understanding of God's *kenosis*, a grand and mysterious truth for the human mind, which finds it inconceivable that suffering and death can express a love which gives itself and seeks nothing in return.'[24] Socrates' quest to 'know himself' is answered by the 'folly' of the Cross.

Theology and philosophy

Philosophy has learned from revelation many things which it now takes for granted, and whose origin it forgets: that the human person has his 'being in relation' to others,[25] the idea of a 'free and personal God' and the correlative idea that the 'person' is a 'spiritual being' of absolute value.[26] No culture without biblical revelation has had a firm grip on these truths.

Like *Aeterni Patris*, *Fides et ratio* tells the story of the relation between philosophy and theology in the West. It notes the origins of this story with Justin Martyr and Clement of Alexandria, speaking of Christianity as 'the true philosophy'.[27] With Origen comes the recognition that 'theology' has now changed its meaning. For Aristotle, 'theology' meant the highest part of philosophy, but now, with the early Christian Fathers, it means '*the true doctrine* about God'. The 'new Christian thought' used philosophy but also 'tended to distinguish itself clearly from philosophy'.[28]

Augustine is perhaps the hero of this story, as Thomas was in *Aeterni Patris*. Augustine realizes that philosophies, based on reason, can only pretend to answer all human questions. The 'modest' claim of the Church *not* to be able to 'demonstrate' its teaching, but only to receive it from God, impressed him and led to his conversion.[29] Augustine was among the first Christians to synthesize philosophy and theology. 'Reinforced by his personal story', he was able to lend his own 'experience' to 'future developments' in philosophy.[30]

---

[23] *Fides et ratio*, §23.
[24] *Fides et ratio*, §93.
[25] *Fides et ratio*, §21.
[26] *Fides et ratio*, §76.
[27] *Fides et ratio*, §38.
[28] *Fides et ratio*, §39.
[29] *Fides et ratio*, §40.
[30] *Fides et ratio*, §40.

Fides et ratio speaks of Thomas' greatest achievement as his ability to describe 'the primacy of the wisdom of the Holy Spirit … which opens the way to a knowledge of the divine realities'.[31] Albert the Great and St. Thomas 'were the first to realize the autonomy' required by philosophy. This realization unwittingly and unintentionally led from a 'legitimate distinction' to a 'fateful separation' in later mediaeval authors.[32] The separation turned rapidly from rationalism, or excess confidence in reason, to an abandonment of trust in reason, or 'nihilism'.[33] Philosophy is no longer a driving force in modern culture: restricted to a 'marginal role', it plays second fiddle to 'instrumental reason'.[34] The separation has not benefitted faith either, for without philosophy, faith often shrivels into 'myth or superstition'.[35]

So although reason relies on faith, faith also needs reason to be fully itself. The encyclical claims that 'the relation between theology and philosophy is best construed as a circle. Theology's source and starting point must always be the word of God revealed in history … Yet, since God's word is Truth … the human search for truth – philosophy, pursued in keeping with its own rules – can only help to understand God's word better'.[36] *Fides et ratio* concludes with the injunction to '*philosophari in Maria*', philosophize in Mary, the Mother of God and Seat of Wisdom.[37]

Study questions

1. Review the chapters on Augustine and on St. Thomas Aquinas and say which is more important in *Fides et ratio*.

2. Why cannot faith be externally coerced?

3. Why would someone argue that faith deprives us of freedom? On what grounds does *Fides et ratio* disagree?

4. Why does *Fides et ratio* draw on human experience in order to argue that faith and reason do not conflict?

Further reading

John Paul II, *Fides et ratio* (1998).
Leo XIII, *Aeterni Patris* (1879).

---

[31] *Fides et ratio*, §44.
[32] *Fides et ratio*, §45.
[33] *Fides et ratio*, §46.
[34] *Fides et ratio*, §47.
[35] *Fides et ratio*, §48.
[36] *Fides et ratio*, §73.
[37] *Fides et ratio*, §108.

EPILOGUE:
THE FUTURE OF FAITH

Faith has been one of the most important notions in the history of ideas. It has also shown a spectacular trajectory of development beginning with the biblical sources up to the twentieth century. From elemental firmness of a physical nature, it has come to express an existential stance, a transcendental aspiration and the discovery of the realm of a naturally basic belief in God. At the same time, the contexts of faith have changed immensely. There is no Roman Empire, medieval Christendom nor even a unified Protestantism or an imperial Catholic Church in our contemporary world. Christianity, the natural home of the notion of faith, has changed and it faces today the immense tide of secularization. On the other hand, religious forms like Hinduism, Buddhism or Islam retrieved their traditions and seek their own answers to modern technological society. After the collapse of Soviet communism, many people in Central and Eastern Europe hoped for a new beginning of faith, a hope stimulated by the charismatic personality of John Paul II.

Today, nevertheless, faith is in a delicate situation. The reason is the apparently unquenchable global thirst for material and technological satisfaction. The sciences have achieved unprecedented results and offer ever more coherent models of reality. The quest for the infinite, the supernatural, the spiritual is much less apparent; and the very meaning of such words as 'God' and 'divine' is in constant erosion. In this context, how can we outline the possible further development of faith? Which options seem to be the most probable with respect to the future?

The first possibility is that faith dies out in our culture and God sinks into forgetfulness. The world continues its march towards ever greater scientific and technological discoveries and it remains satisfied with the possibilities the new universal culture proposes. We term this *the futuristic option*.

The second possibility is a definitive renewal of traditional faith: faith in God as declared by the Christian churches. Both as *fides qua* and *fides quae*, faith simply returns to its earlier position in the minds of human persons and their societies at least in the Western world. We term it *the fundamentalist option*.

The third possibility is the opening of faith fully to contemporary culture, the sciences and technology and to religious forms and philosophies of various sorts, and then trusting God and His providence that a new form of faith – or something substituting faith – will eventually emerge. We may name this *the liberal option*.

The fourth possibility is also about the renewal of faith. This renewal takes into consideration the rich legacy of faith – as is demonstrated in the present volume – and aspires to reach a new understanding and practice not in contradistinction to the old ones but as their organic development. This approach takes a serious look at the crisis of faith in history and makes sincere efforts to receive the strength necessary for a renewal. We may term this *the Franciscan option*.

The authors of this book lend their voices to the fourth option. The futuristic possibility is a sheer impossibility and contradicts the structure of cultural development. The fundamentalist option is not plausible either, for the nature of history does not allow a return to earlier positions as they exist in historical memory. History is about a development, in most cases an organic and sound development of organic and sound traditions. The liberal option may be found unnatural, because the price of big gestures has to be paid in hard currency. By giving up consistency, faith would not be able to maintain itself and offer solutions for the contemporary world; there would be hardly any difference between faith and unbelief.

Thus we can keep the fourth option as reasonable and faithful at the same time. This option takes the history of faith seriously both in its continuity and change. It takes seriously the tragic experiences of the history of faith as described in Chapter 20 of this book. But it also takes seriously the rich heritage of faith as is shown in all chapters here. As Michael Polanyi among others argued, the fundamental act of human persons has become faith, and faith involves the whole of the person in his or her absolute openness to the Absolute. As Hegel already saw, the logic of history is prefigured in the story of the Gospels, and the great and transforming experience of humanity has remained the experience of resurrection in the aftermath of a dramatic death.

As Pope Francis writes:

There is an urgent need, then, to see once again that faith is a light, for once the flame of faith dies out, all other lights begin to dim. The light of faith is unique, since it is capable of illuminating *every aspect* of human existence. A light this powerful cannot come from ourselves but from a more primordial source: in a word, it must come from God. Faith is born of an encounter with the living God who calls us and reveals his love, a love which precedes us and upon which we can lean for security and for building our lives. Transformed by this love, we gain fresh vision, new eyes to see; we realize that it contains a great promise of fulfillment, and that a vision of the future opens up before us. Faith, received from God as a supernatural gift, becomes a light for our way, guiding our journey through time. On the one hand, it is a light coming from the past, the light of the foundational memory of the life of Jesus which revealed his perfectly trustworthy love, a love capable of triumphing over death. Yet since Christ has risen and draws us beyond death, faith is also a light coming from the future and opening before us vast horizons which guide us beyond our isolated selves towards the breadth of communion.[1]

(Easter 2014, Notre Dame, Indiana)

[1]Encyclical Letter *Lumen fidei* of the Supreme Pontiff Francis: http://www.vatican.va/holy_father/ francesco/encyclicals/documents/papa-francesco_20130629_enciclica-lumen-fidei_en.html. Accessed 15 March 2014.

GLOSSARY

Agnosticism is not knowing whether there is a god or not (from the Greek *agnoeo*, 'I do not perceive', 'am ignorant').

Anthropology the scientific study of human nature (from Greek, *anthropos*, 'human', and *logos*, 'a science').

Apocalyptic a term that means 'to lift the veil' in Greek. Apocalyptic is lifting the veil on the end times and judgement, heaven and hell. It became important within Judaism between the second century BC and the second century AD. There is apocalyptic material in both the Old and New Testaments, such as the Books of Daniel and Revelation.

Aristotle (384–322 BC) a student of the Greek philosopher Plato, and as important as his teacher. He wrote highly influential works such as *Ethics*, *Metaphysics*, *Politics* and *The Soul*.

Atheism (from the Greek *theos*) a belief that there is no God.

Bible the Christian Scripture, comprising the Old Testament, the original scriptures of the Jewish people, and the New Testament, the Scriptures written by the early Christians including the Gospels and Paul's letters.

John Calvin (1509–1564) a Protestant Reformer. He wrote the *Institutes of the Christian Faith* and developed an interpretation of Protestantism which influences Presbyterians, Baptists, New Reconstructionists, Evangelicals and many other 'Reformed' Protestant communities.

Christ, Jesus *Christos* is Greek for 'anointed one' and is the Greek translation of the Hebrew *masiah*. An anointed one is a king. Calling Christ 'anointed' means he is God's anointed *masiah*, who had been foretold by the Jewish prophets and described in the apocalyptic literature.

Deism a term that comes from the Latin word *deus*, God. Deists argue that we can reason from nature to the existence of one God, but we must stop there, because this God does not perform miracles or reveal himself to prophets or other authors of sacred literature. There can be no evidence for the Triunity of God on deist assumptions, as God does not reveal himself, and deists think God is unitary all the way down.

Dominican the Dominican Order was founded by St. Dominic in the thirteenth century to preach the gospel in an intelligent way and to practice poverty. Well-known Dominicans include Albert the Great, Thomas Aquinas, Savonarola, Saint Martin de Porres, Catherine of Siena, Aidan Nichols, Gilles Emery, Olivier-Thomas Venard, Charles Morerod and Serge-Thomas Bonino. They wear white tunics, black capes and a belt from which hangs a rosary.

Empiricism a philosophy which claims that all our knowledge comes from empirical, sensed or physical facts.

Epicureanism the philosophy (attributed to the Greek philosopher Epicurus, 341–270 BC) that claims that the core of reality is a meaningless dance of atomic particles. Epicureans are materialists, thinking matter is the only reality.

Epistemology the scientific study of knowledge. The word comes from the Greek *episteme*, knowledge, and *logos*, science. Historically, it is one of the three branches of philosophy: metaphysics, ethics and epistemology.

Eschatology a study of the end times that is aligned with apocalyptic. There is eschatology in the Old Testament prophets, in Revelation and in some of Jesus' own sayings.

Established Church the Church established by law in a country. After the Reformation, many countries or regions had 'established churches' with the head of State as the leader of the Church, in Protestant countries, and with a 'Concordat' (treaty) with the Vatican as to the selection of bishops in Catholic countries.

Evidentialism an idea in Christianity that religious beliefs and doctrines must be justified by evidence or rational argument.

Existentialism a philosophy which analyzes the joys, anxieties and other modes of human existence. Famous existentialists include Kierkegaard, Jean-Paul Sartre, Martin Heidgger and Gabriel Marcel.

Fathers of the Church the theologians of the first five centuries, such as Justin Martyr, Clement of Alexandria, Tertullian, Origen, Jerome and Augustine.

Feuerbach, **Ludwig** (1804–1872) a nineteenth-century thinker who invented the idea that 'God' is a projection of humanity. He claimed that humans project themselves into a 'God' and worship that imaginary projection, instead of exercising benevolence towards other human beings.

Fideism a term meaning 'faith-ism'. It is most often a derogatory term to denote those who believe without the accompaniment of evidence or rational justification. The term seems to have been invented in the 1850s.

Fides qua short for *fides qua creditur*, the faith which believes. It refers to the believer and his or her personal faith.

Fides quae short for *fides quae creditur*, the faith *which is* believed. It refers to the *contents* of the faith, such as the historical biblical narratives or the creeds or catechisms.

Foundationalism a view that goes back to Descartes' quest for a certain foundation on which to stack his knowledge. Foundationalists think that our knowledge is grounded on certain truths.

Fundamentalists a term used originally to refer to a group of early twentieth-century Protestants who announced that they believed in 'the fundamentals', such as biblical inerrancy and substitutionary atonement. Today it is applied to any set of hardcore believers, such as Wahabi Muslims, and especially to religious groups which take their sacred texts very literally. Fixation with only the literal truth of sacred texts is a modern phenomenon.

Gnosticism a movement that claims *to know* secret information about God (from the Greek *gnosis*, knowledge). The gnostics were dualists who claimed Jesus as one of their own, composing 'Gnostic Gospels', in which Jesus is a protagonist. Their claims to inside knowledge about God and Jesus were exaggerated.

Historico-critical biblical scholarship it originates with printed books, and the consequent effort to determine 'critical' editions of ancient texts. Editorial skills allied with some historical knowledge applied by scholars to the Bible give us 'historical-critical Biblical scholarship'. Like Fundamentalism, it is a modern phenomenon.

Jesuit a member of the Society of Jesus, a religious body created by St. Ignatius Loyola in the sixteenth century. Like Luther, Ignatius Loyola was critical of the Church. Loyola created the Jesuits as an instrument of Church reform and for missionary work. Famous Jesuits include Joseph Kleutgen, Erich Przywara, Karl Rahner and Pope Francis.

Justification God's declaring that a human being is 'just' in God's sight. In the case of sinful human beings, justification requires that God *makes them just in his sight.*

Kenosis (from the Greek *kenos*, empty) means emptying. Philippians 2 states that God 'emptied himself, taking the form of a servant' in the Incarnation.

LXX see **Septuagint.**

Magisterial Reformation (non-magisterial) the Protestant groups like the Lutherans who got the nation-state on their side and formed Established Churches. The opposite are non-Magisterial Protestants, who were hostile to political involvement for Christians, and also, at the time of the Reformation, often hostile to the State, such as Anabaptists and Mennonites.

Magisterium the teaching office of the Roman Catholic Church. *Magister* is Latin for teacher. 'Magisterial teaching' is not tautologous as it means the 'official teaching' of the Catholic Church.

Miracle an event that occurs when God alters the course of nature for some providential end. The raising of Lazarus and the Crossing of the Red Sea were miracles. The resurrection of Jesus from the dead is *the* most important miracle of all.

Myth (from the Greek *muthos*, word, tale) in religious terminology, a story which is not literally true but has some illustrative or conceptual truth in it. Although some, such as C. S. Lewis, speak of Christianity as 'true myth', the term 'myth' is nearly always used in a derogatory way.

Neo-Orthodoxy the revival of traditional beliefs about the centrality of Scripture and the primacy of God's action within Protestantism. Neo-Orthodox Protestants are not usually liberals.

New Testament see **Bible.**

Nicene Creed/Niceno-Constantinopolitan Creed the Nicene Creed was composed at the Council of Nicaea in 325 and states that Jesus Christ, the Son of God, is *homoousios* with God the Father, that is, 'of one substance'. The Constantinople Creed of 381 repeats all of the Nicene Creed and adds that the Holy Spirit is 'worshipped together with Father and Son'.

Old Testament see **Bible.**

Pantheism a belief that god is everything. The word comes from *pan*, Greek for 'all', and 'theism', such that god is all and all is god. A pantheist does not believe in a supernatural God, but rather that all nature is divine.

Patristics see **Fathers.**

Pentateuch the first five books of the Old Testament: Genesis, Exodus, Deuteronomy, Leviticus and Numbers. Jews call the Pentateuch 'the law', the Torah. It is a bit dry after Exodus, consisting of extensive legal codes.

Pentecost (from the Greek 'fifty', i.e., the fiftieth day after Easter) is the feast of the descent of the Holy Spirit on the Apostles and Mary and the start of Christianity. It is described in Acts 2, where the Spirit descends on the Apostles, and enables them to preach in many languages.

Philo of Alexandria a Jew living in Alexandria in roughly 50 BC–AD 50. He wrote about Judaism in Greek, trying to explain the Torah to Greek thinkers by describing Yahweh as the Greek (Stoic) *Logos* (mind).

Platonism the philosophy of Plato, which holds that there are universal truths (Forms) and that the goal of the philosophical life is to know universal truth.

Polytheism the belief in many gods.

Protestant Christian 'Protestant' groups who originally in the sixteenth century left the Catholic Church in disgust over many serious abuses, and never returned, forming their own communities. They include Anglicans, 'Reformed', Lutherans, Evangelicals and others.

Protestant Reformation a formation of Protestant Christianity, outside the Catholic Church and in protest against it, in the sixteenth century.

Rationalism the belief that reason dictates reality.

Restoration the restoration of the English Monarchy. Oliver Cromwell murdered King Charles I and established a Puritan dictatorship (1649–1660) called the

'Commonwealth'. Charles II was restored to his rightful throne in 1660.

Roman Catholic the Church that claims apostolic succession from the original twelve apostles among whom it regards 'Peter' as the one gifted with leadership. It views Peter as the first pope. Peter went to live in Rome, where he was killed by the Romans. The pope is the bishop of Rome where he lives in the Vatican. There are 1.2 billion Catholics today, 40 percent of whom live in South America. 'Catholic' means universal.

Romanticism a secular movement which treats nature, geniuses, poetry, art, music, creativity and love with quasi-religious reverence. It began in the nineteenth century and continues today. Romantics place more value on emotion than reason: they have more sensibility than sense.

Rule of faith the commonly held rule by which Scripture is interpreted.

Sanctification an imparting to Christians of the godliness and holiness by the holy God. It is the means by which Christians improve and become saintly. The mission of sanctification is traditionally appropriated to the Holy Spirit.

Septuagint Greek translation of the Hebrew Bible. It was made in the third and second centuries BC, traditionally by seventy inspired sages in seventy days. Septuagint comes from the Latin *septuaginta*, seventy.

Socinianism an adherence to the teachings of Faustus Socinus, which include a non-Trinitarian god and a sacred text which is thought not to refer metaphorically, symbolically or prophetically to Christ, and therefore is to be read literally. The group was invented in the seventeenth century.

Theism a term that means belief in God.

Theocentric a term that means God-centred. It comes from *theos*, Greek for 'God'.

Theology the study of God. It comes from *theos* (Greek for god) and *logos* (Greek for talk, description, science).

Transcendent metaphysically it means transcending or going beyond all the natural categories, and epistemologically it means transcending the categories of our understanding.

Trinity a term that refers to the God who is three persons in one being: Father, Son and the Holy Spirit.

Unitarianism the denial of the Triune personhood of God. Unitarians are not Christians.

Wisdom literature biblical books such as Proverbs, Job, Ecclesiastics and the Wisdom of Solomon, in the Old Testament are classified as wisdom literature. It makes comparisons among natural events (proverbs) and sees God at work in nature, through creation and providence.

BIBLIOGRAPHY

Adam, Robert Merrihew, 'Faith and Religious Knowledge', in Jacqueline Mariña (ed.), *The Cambridge Companion to Schleiermacher* (Cambridge: Cambridge University Press, 2005), pp. 35–51.

Aristotle, *Nicomachean Ethics*, ed. and trans. Roger Crisp (Cambridge: Cambridge University Press, 2000).

Aquinas, Thomas, *Summa Theologica*.

———, *Commentary on II Corinthians*.

Arminius, James, *The Works of James Arminius*, ed. James Nichols, vol. 2 (London: Longman, Bees, Orme, Brown and Green, 1828).

Augustine, 'On the Holy Trinity', in Philip Schaff (ed.), *Nicene and Post-Nicene Fathers*, trans. Arthur West Haddan; First Series, vol. III (Grand Rapids, Mich.: Christian Classics Ethereal Library), pp. 6–475.

———, *The City of God*, trans. Henry Bettenson (New York: Penguin Books, 1984), XIV, 9, p. 563.

———, 'Two Books of Soliloquies', in Philip Schaff (ed.), *Nicene and Post-Nicene Fathers*, trans. C. C. Starbuck; First Series, vol. VII (New York: Cosimo, 2007), pp. 537–560.

Balthasar, Hans Urs von, *The Glory of the Lord: A Theological Aesthetics, Vol. 1, Seeing the Form*, trans. Erasmo Leiva-Merikakis (Edinburgh: T&T Clark, 1982, 1989).

———, *Theo-Logic: Theological Logical Theory, Vol. 1, The Truth of the World*, trans. Adrian J. Walker (San Francisco: Ignatius Press, 2000).

———, *Cosmic Liturgy: The Universe according to Maximus the Confessor*, trans. Brain E. Daley, S. J. (San Francisco: Ignatius Press, 2003).

Barth, Karl, *Church Dogmatics IV/1, The Doctrine of Reconciliation*, ed. G. W. Bromiliey and T. F. Torrance, trans. G. W. Bromiley (Edinburgh: T. & T. Clark, 1961).

———, *Der Römerbrief (Erste Fassung) 1919*, ed. Hermann Schmidt (Zürich: Theologischer Verlag Zürich, 1985).

———, *Der Römerbrief (Zweite Fassung) 1922*, ed. Cornelius van der Kooi and Katja Tolstaja (Zürich: Theologische Verlag, 2010).

Bauckham, Richard, *Jesus and the Eyewitnesses: The Gospels as Eyewitness Testimony* (Grand Rapids, Mich: Eerdmans, 2006).

Bavinck, Herman, *Reformed Dogmatics, vol. 4, Holy Spirit, Church, New Creation*, ed. John Bolt, trans. John Vriend (Grand Rapids, Mich.: Baker Academic, 2008).

Benedict XVI, *The Essential Pope Benedict XVI: His Central Writings and Speeches*, ed. John F. Thorton and Susan B. Varenne (London: HarperCollins Ebooks, 2008).

Blackwell, Richard J, *Behind the Scenes of Galileo's Trial* (Notre Dame: University of Notre Dame Press, 2006).

Buren, Paul M. van, *The Secular Meaning of the Gospel* (New York: Macmillan, 1963).

Butler, Joseph, *The Analogy of Religion: Natural and Revealed to the Constitution and Course of Nature*, part II, chap. 3. Available on Christian Classics Ethereal Library, http://www.ccel.org/ccel/butler/analogy.html. Accessed 25 March 2014.

Calvin, John, *Institutes of the Christian Religion*, ed. John T. McNeill, trans. Ford Lewis Battles; vol. 1 (Louisville: Westminster John Knox Press, 1960).

——, *The First Epistle of Paul the Apostle to the Corinthians*, trans. John W. Fraser (Grand Rapids, Mich.: Eerdmans, 1960).

Carroll, Thomas D, 'The Traditions of Fideism', *Religious Studies* 44:1 (2008), 1–22.

Chemnitz, Martin, *Loci Theologici*, trans. J. A. O. Preus, vol. 2 (St. Louis: Concordia Publishing House, 1989).

Clement of Alexandria, *Stromata 1–3*, trans. John Ferguson (Washington, D.C: Catholic University of American Press, 1991).

Cone, James, *The God of the Oppressed* (New York: Seabury Press, 1975).

——, *A Black Theology of Liberation* (Maryknoll, NY: Orbis Books, 1986).

Craig, William Lane and Sinnott-Armstrong, W. *God?* (Oxford: Oxford University Press, 2008).

Dennett, Daniel, *Breaking the Spell: Religion as a Natural Phenomenon* (New York: Viking, 2006).

Dixon, Philip, '*Nice and Hot Disputes': The Doctrine of the Trinity in the Seventeenth Century* (London: T&T Clark, 2003).

Donovan, Daniel, 'Faith and Revelation', in Declan and Hines (eds), *The Cambridge Companion to Karl Rahner* (Cambridge: Cambridge University Press, 2005), pp. 83–97.

Duffy, Stephen J, 'Experience and Grace', in Declan Marmion and Mary E. Hines (eds), *The Cambridge Companion to Karl Rahner* (Cambridge: Cambridge University Press, 2005), pp. 43–62.

Dulles, Avery, *The Assurance of Things Hoped For: A Theology of Christian Faith* (Oxford: Oxford University Press, 1994).

Garrigou-Lagrange, Réginald, 'La nouvelle théologie où va-t-elle?', *Angelicum* 23 (1946), pp. 126–145.

Gondos-Grünhut, László, *Die Liebe und das Sein* (Bonn: Bouvier, 1990).

Gutiérrez, Gustavo, *Theology of Liberation: History, Politics and Salvation*, ed. and trans. Sister Caridad Inda and John Eagelson Maryknoll (New York: Orbis Books, 1973).

——, *The Truth Shall Make You Free: Confrontations*, trans. Matthew J. O'Connell (Maryknoll, NY: Orbis Books, 1991).

Hampson, Daphne, 'Luther on the Self: A Feminist Critique', *Word and World* 8:4 (1988), 334–342.

Harris, Sam, *Letter to a Christian Nation* (New York: Random House, 2006).

Hegel, G. W. F., *On Christianity: Early Theological Writings*, trans. T. M. Knox and Richard Kroner (New York: Harper, 1948).

——, *Philosophy of Mind, Part 3 of the Encyclopaedia of the Philosophical Sciences 1830* (Oxford: Clarendon, 1971).

——, *Faith and Knowledge*, ed. and trans. H. S. Harris and Walter Cerf (Albany: SUNY Press, 1977).

——, Lectures on the Philosophy of Religion, ed. Peter C. Hodgson, trans. R. F. Brown, P. C. Hodgson and J. M. Stewart (Los Angeles: University of California Press, 1984).

Heidegger, Martin, 'Nietzsche's Word: "God Is dead', in *Off the Beaten Track*, ed. and trans. Julian Young and Kenneth Haynes (Cambridge: Cambridge University Press, 2002), pp. 157–199.

Heisenberg, Werner, *Physics and Beyond: Encounters and Conversations* (New York: Harper & Row, 1971).

Hitchens, Christopher, *God Is Not Great: How Religion Poisons Everything* (Crows Nest: Allen & Unwin, 2007).

Hodge, Charles, *Systematic Theology, Vol. 3* (New York: Scribner and Sons, 1873).

Hume, David, 'Of Miracles', in *Enquiries Concerning Human Understanding and Concerning the Principles of Morals*, 3rd ed., ed. L. A. Selby-Bigge; rev. P. H. Nidditch (Oxford: Oxford University Press, 1975), pp. 109–131.

——, *A Treatise of Human Nature: Being an Attempt to Introduce the Experimental Method of Reasoning into Moral Subjects, Vol. 1, Of the Understanding*, 2nd ed., ed. L.A. Selby-Bigge; rev. P. H. Nidditch (Oxford: Oxford University Press, 1978).

——, 'Dialogues Concerning Natural Religion', in J. C. A. Gaskin (ed.), *Principle Writings on Religion Including Dialogues Concerning Natural Religion and the Natural History of Religion* (Oxford: Oxford University Press, 1993), pp. 29–130.

Kant, Immanuel, *Grounding for the Metaphysics of Morals* (Indianapolis: Hackett, 1993).

——, *Critique of Pure Reason*, ed. Paul Guyer, trans. Allen Wood (Cambridge: Cambridge University Press, 1998).

——, *Religion within the Boundaries of Mere Reason*, ed. and trans. Allen Wood and George di Giovanni (Cambridge: Cambridge University Press, 1998).

Katz, Steven T., Shlomo Biderman, and Gershon Greenberg (eds), *Wrestling with God: Jewish Theological Responses during and after the Holocaust* (Oxford: Oxford University Press, 2007).

Kierkegaard, Søren, *Journals and Papers*, ed. and trans. Howard V. Hong and Edna H. Hong; vol. 1 (Bloomington: Indiana University Press, 1967).

—— (Johannes Climacus), *Concluding Unscientific Postscript*, trans. David F. Swenson and Walter Lowrie (Princeton: Princeton University Press, 1968).

——(Johannes de Silentio), *Fear and Trembling*, ed. C. Stephen Evans and Sylvia Walsh, trans. Sylvia Walsh (Cambridge: Cambridge University Press, 2006).

——(Anti-Climacus), *Training in Christianity and the Edifying Discourse which 'Accompanied' It*, trans. Walter Lowrie (Oxford: Oxford University Press, 1941).

Kilby, Karen, *Karl Rahner: Theology and Philosophy* (London: Routledge, 2004).

Knox, Zoe, *Russian Society and the Orthodox Church: Religion in Russia after Communism* (London: RoutledgeCurzon, 2005).

Kolakowski, Leszek, *Main Currents of Marxism, Vol. 2, The Golden Age*, trans. P. S. Falla (Oxford: Oxford University Press, 1978).

Lafont, Ghislain, *Histoire théologique de l'Église catholique* (Paris: Du Cerf, 1994).

Lamm, Julia A, *The Living God: Schleiermacher's Theological Appropriation of Spinoza* (University Park, Penn: Pennsylvania State University Press, 1996).

Locke, John, *An Essay Concerning Human Understanding*, ed. Roger Woolhouse (London: Penguin Books, 1997).

Luther, Martin, *Commentary on the First Twenty-Two Psalms*, trans. Henry Cole; vol. 1 (London: Simpkin and Marshall, 1826).

——, 'Die Zirkulardisputation *de veste nuptiale*', in *Luthers Werke*, Weimar Ausgabe, vol. 39/1 (Weimar: Hermann Böhlaus Nachfolger, 1926), pp. 264–333.

——, *Luthers Werke* (Weimar: Hermann Böhlaus Nachfolger, 1927), p. 98, quoted in Bernd Wannenwetsch, 'Luther's Moral Theology', in Donald H. McKim (ed.), Cambridge: Cambridge University Press, 2003, pp. 120–135. Weimar Ausgabe, vol. 17/II.

——, *A Compend of Luther's Theology*, ed. Hugh Thompson Kerr (Philadelphia: Westminster Press, 1943).

——, *Commentary on Romans*, trans. J. Theodore Mueller (Grand Rapids, Mich.: Zondervan, 1954).

——, 'Against the Heavenly Prophets in the Matter of Images and the Sacraments', in ed. Conrad Bergendoff, trans. Berhard Erling and Conrad Bergendoff, vol. 40, *Luther Works* (Philadelphia: Muhlenberg Press, 1958), pp. 79–223.

——, 'Disputation on Humanity', in *Luther's Works*, ed. Lewis W. Spitz, vol. 34 (Philadelphia: Muhlenberg Press, 1960), pp. 135–144.

————, 'Bondage of the Will', in John Dillenberger (ed.), *Martin Luther: Selections from His Writings* (New York: Anchor Books, 1962), pp. 166–203.

————, 'On the Papacy in Rome, against the Most Celebrated Romanist in Leipzig', in ed. Eric W. Gritsch, trans. Eric W. and Ruth C. Gritsch, vol. 39, *Luther's Works* (Philadelphia: Fortress Press, 1970), pp. 49–104.

————, 'Against the Sabbatarians: Letter to a Good Friend', in ed. F. Sherman; trans. Martin H. Bertram; vol. 47, *Luther's Works* (Philadelphia: Fortress Press, 1971), pp. 59–98.

————, *The Table Talk of Martin Luther*, ed. and trans. William Hazlitt (London: Bell & Daldy, 1972).

————, 'Babylonian Captivity of the Church', in Timothy F. Lull (ed.), *Martin Luther's Basic Theological Writings* (Minneapolis: Fortress Press, 1989), pp. 267–313.

————, 'Disputation against Scholastic Theology', in Timothy F. Lull (ed.), *Martin Luther's Basic Theological Writings* (Minneapolis: Fortress Press, 1989), pp. 13–20.

————, 'Commentary on Galatians', in John Dillenberger (ed.), *Martin Luther: Selections from His Writings* (New York: Anchor Books, 1962), pp. 99–165.

————, 'Freedom of a Christian', in Timothy F. Lull (ed.), *Martin Luther's Basic Theological Writings* (Minneapolis: Fortress Press, 1989), pp. 585–629.

————, 'Large Catechism', in *The Book of Concord: The Confessions of the Evangelical Lutheran Church*, ed. by Robert Kolb and Timothy J. Wengert, trans. Charles Arand, Robert Kolb, Timothy Wengert, Eric Gritsch, William Russell, Jane Strohl, James Schaaf (Minneapolis: Fortress Press, 2000), pp. 377–480.

————, 'Preface to the Epistle of St. Paul to the Romans', in John Dillenberger (ed.), *Martin Luther: Selections from His Writings* (New York: Anchor Books, 1962), pp. 19–34.

————, 'Preface to the New Testament', in Timothy F. Lull (ed.), *Martin Luther's Basic Theological Writings* (Minneapolis: Fortress Press, 1989), pp. 112–117.

Matthias, Markus, 'Bekehrung und Wiedergeburt', in Hartmut Lehmann (ed.), *Geschichte des Pietismus, vol. 4, Glaubenswelt und Lebenswelt* (Göttingen: Vandenhoeck & Ruprecht, 2004), pp. 49–79.

McKinnon, Alastair, 'Kierkegaard and the Leap of Faith', *Kierkegaardiana* 16 (1993), pp. 107–125.

Meister, Chad, *Introducing Philosophy of Religion* (London, New York: Routledge, 2009).

Melanchthon, Philip, 'Apology of the Augsburg Confession', in *The Book of Concord: The Confessions of the Evangelical Lutheran Church*, ed. by Robert Kolb and Timothy J. Wengert, trans. Charles Arand, Robert Kolb, Timothy Wengert, Eric Gritsch, William Russell, Jane Strohl, James Schaaf (Minneapolis: Fortress Press, 2000), pp. 107–294.

————, *Loci communes (1521): Lateinisch-Deutsch*, trans. Horst Georg Pöhlmann (Gütersloh: Mohn, 1993).

Metz, Johann Baptist, *Memoria passionis* (Freiburg: Herder, 2006).

Mezei, Balazs, *Religion and Revelation after Auschwitz* (New York: Bloomsbury, 2013).

————, 'Faith and Reason', in Lewis Ayres (ed.), *The Oxford Handbook of Catholicism* (Oxford: Oxford University Press, forthcoming 2015).

Milbank, John, *Theology and Social Theory: Beyond Secular Reason* (London: Blackwell, 1993).

Moriarty, Michael, 'Grace and religious belief in Pascal', in Nicholas Hammond (ed.), *The Cambridge Companion to Pascal* (Cambridge: Cambridge University Press, 2006), pp. 144–164.

Muller, Richard A, *The Unaccomodated Calvin: Studies in the Foundation of a Theological Tradition* (Oxford: Oxford University Press, 2000).

Nietzsche, Friedrich, *Thus Spoke Zarathustra: A Book for All and None*, ed. Adrian Del Caro and Robert Pippin, trans. Adrian Del Caro (Cambridge: Cambridge University Press, 2006).

Pascal, Blaise, *Pensées*, trans. Roger Ariew (Indianapolis: Hackett, 2004).

Payne, Harry C, 'Elite versus Popular Mentality in the Eighteenth Century', *Historical Reflections/Réflexions Historiques* 2:2 (1976), pp. 183–208.

Plantinga, Alvin, 'Reason and Belief in God', in Alvin Plantinga and Nicholas Wolterstorff (eds), *Faith and Rationality: Reason and Belief in God* (Notre Dame: Notre Dame University Press, 1983), pp. 16–93.

———, 'In Memoriam: William P. Alston, 1921–2009', *Faith and Philosophy* 26:4 (2009), pp. 359–360.

———, *Where the Conflict Really Lies: Science, Religion, and Naturalism* (Oxford: Oxford University Press, 2011).

Polanyi, Michael, *Personal Knowledge: Towards a Post-Critical Philosophy* (London: Routledge, 1962).

Polkinghorne, John, *Science and Theology* (London: SPCK/Fortress Press, 1998).

———, *Quantum Theory and Theology: An Unexpected Kinship* (New Haven: Yale University Press, 2008).

Przywara, Erich, *An Augustine Synthesis* (New York: Sheed & Ward, 1936).

Rahner, Karl, 'On the Theology of the Incarnation', in *Theological Investigations IV* (London: Darton, Longman & Todd, 1974), pp. 105–120, 116.

———, 'Atheism and Implicit Christianity', *Theological Investigations IX*, trans. Graham Harrison (London: Darton, Longman and Todd, 1979), pp. 145–164.

———, 'Religious Enthusiasm and the Experience of Grace', in *Theological Investigations XVI* (London: Darton, Longman and Todd, 1979), pp. 35–51, 41.

———, *Hearers of the Word*, trans. J. Doncell (New York: Continuum, 1994), p. 33.

———, 'Nature and Grace', *Theological Investigations IV* (London: Darton, Longman & Todd, 1974), pp. 165–188, 177.

——— and Joseph Ratzinger, *Revelation and Tradition*, trans. W. J. O'Hara (Montreal: Palm, 1965).

Ratzinger, Joseph, *Principles of Catholic Theology: Building Stones for a Fundamental Theology*, trans. Sister Mary Frances McCarthy, S.N.D (San Francisco: Ignatius Press, 1987).

Rubenstein, Richard, *After Auschwitz: History, Theology, and Contemporary Judaism* (Baltimore and London: John Hopkins University Press, 1992).

Schleiermacher, Friedrich, *On Religion: Speeches to Its Cultured Despisers*, trans. John Oman (New York: Harper & Row, 1958).

———, *The Christian Faith* (Berkeley: Apocryphile Press, 2011).

Schmid, Heinrich, *The Doctrinal Theology of the Evangelical Lutheran Church*, 3rd ed. (Philadelphia: United Lutheran Publication House, 1899) reprint, Minneapolis: Augsburg Publishing House, 1961, trans. Charles A. Hay and Henry E. Jacobs.

Schweitzer, Albert, *The Quest of the Historical Jesus: A Critical Study of Its Progress from Reimarus to Wrede*, trans. W. Montgomery (London: Adam and Charles Black, 1910).

Spener, Philipp Jacob, *Pia desideria*, ed. and trans. Theodore G. Tappert (Philadelphia: Fortress Press, 1964).

Stewart, Jon, ''Kierkegaard and Hegel on Faith and Knowledge', in Stephen Houlgate and Michael Baur (eds), *A Companion to Hegel* (Oxford: Blackwell, 2011), pp. 501–519.

Stock, Brian, *Augustine's Inner Dialogue: The Philosophical Soliloquy in Late Antiquity* (Cambridge: Cambridge University Press, 2010).

Swift, Jonathan, 'An Argument against Abolishing Christianity', in Claude Rawson and Ian Higgins (eds), *The Essential Writings of Jonathan Swift* (New York: W. W. Norton, 2010), pp. 135–145.

Swinburne, Richard, *Was Jesus God?* (Oxford: Oxford University Press, 2008).

Taylor, Charles, *A Secular Age* (Cambridge, Mass: Harvard University Press, 2007).

Tertullian, *Treatise on the Incarnation*, ed. and trans. Ernest Evans (London: SPCK, 1956).
Tillich, Paul, *The Courage to Be* (New Haven: Yale University Press, 1952).
———, *Systematic Theology*, vol. 2 (Chicago: University of Chicago Press, 1957).
———, *The Dynamics of Faith* (New York: Harper, 1957).
———, *Systematic Theology*, vol. 3 (Chicago: University of Chicago Press, 1963).
Tindal, Matthew, *Christianity as Old as Creation* (London: Routledge, 1995).
Toland, John, *Christianity not Mysterious* (London: Routledge, 1995).
Turretin, Francis, *Institutes of Elenctic Theology*, ed. James T. Dennison Jr.; trans. George
    Musgrave Giger (New Jersey: Presbyterian and Reformed Publishing, 1994).
Vickers, Jason E, *Invocation and Assent: The Making and Remaking of Trinitarian Theology*
    (Grand Rapids, Mich.: Eerdmans, 2008).
Voderholzer, Rudolf and Michael J. Miller, *Meet Henri de Lubac* (San Francisco: Ignatius
    Press, 2007).
Voegelin, Eric, *In Search of Order* (Columbia: University of Missouri Press, 1999).
Waldstein, Michael, 'The Trinitarian, Spousal, and Ecclesial Logic of Justification', in
    Matthew Levering and Michael Dauphinais (eds), *Reading Romans with St. Thomas
    Aquinas* (Washington: Catholic University of America Press, 2012), pp. 274–287.
Walsh, David, *The Modern Philosophical Revolution* (Cambridge: Cambridge University
    Press, 2008).
Wang, Hao, *Reflections on Kurt Gödel* (Cambridge, Mass: MIT Press, 1995).
Wesley, John, 'On Zeal', in John Emory (ed.), *The Works of the Reverend John Wesley*, vol. 2
    (New York: Emory and Waugh, 1831), pp. 287–294.
———, *Christian Perfection as Believed and Taught by John Wesley*, ed. Thomas S. Kepler
    (New York: Cleveland, 1954).
Wiesel, Elie, *Night*, trans. Marion Wiesel (New York: Hill and Wang, 2006).
Winthrop, John, 'A Model of Christian Charity', in Wayne Franklin, Philip F.Gura, and
    Arnold Krupat (eds), *The Norton Anthology of American Literature, vol. A, Beginnings
    to 1820* (New York: Norton, 2007), pp. 165–185.
Witsius, Herman, *The Oeconomy of the Covenants between God and Man*, trans. William
    Crookshank; vol. 1 (Edinburgh: Turnbull, 1803).
Wollebius, Johannes, 'Compendium Theologiae Cristianae', in *Reformed Dogmatics:
    J. Wollebius, G. Voetius, F. Turretin*, ed. and trans. John W. Beardslee III (New York:
    Oxford University Press, 1965), pp. 26–262.
Wolterstorff, Nicholas, 'Religious Epistemology', in William J. Wainwright (ed.), *The
    Oxford Handbook of Philosophy of Religion* (Oxford: Oxford University Press, 2005),
    pp. 244–271.
Zizendorf, Count Nicolaus, 'Brotherly Union and Agreement at Herrnhut', in Peter C. Erb
    (ed.), *The Pietists: Selected Writings* (New York: Paulist Press, 1983), pp. 325–330.
———, 'Concerning Saving Faith', in Peter C. Erb (ed.), *The Pietists: Selected Writings*
    (New York: Paulist Press, 1983), pp. 304–310.

INDEX